D0885322

SOUTHWEST BIRDS OF SACRIFICE

Charmion R. McKusick

Southwest Bird Laboratory
9025 South Kellner Canyon Road
Globe, Arizona 85501

July 2001

THE ARIZONA ARCHAEOLOGIST

JULY 2001   NUMBER 31

PURPOSE OF THE SOCIETY

The Arizona Archaeological Society is an independent non-profit organization formed for the purpose of investigation, study, and interpretation of prehistoric and historic cultures, particularly of Arizona and adjacent areas. It is further a purpose of the Society to encourage a constructive public attitude toward archaeology and to promote compliance by its members and by the public with the state and federal antiquities laws governing archaeological activity. The preservation of archaeological sites is of primary concern.

The Society welcomes inquiries for affiliation or organization of Chapters, and for membership, either active or associate, in existing or new Chapters. Details may be obtained from the Secretary, Post Office Box 9665, Phoenix, Arizona 85068.

The cover art shows a Maya sacrifice: a severed turkey head atop an altar. From the Nuttall Codex. Redrawn by Ron Beckwith from Alice Wesche's drawing in Di Peso 1974 (Vol. 2:568).

This is the publication for Arizona Archaeological Society Member Year 1998. Publication was significantly aided by a generous contribution from the Salado Chapter of AAS, Globe, Arizona.

ISBN 0-939071-35-5

COPYRIGHT
ARIZONA ARCHAEOLOGICAL SOCIETY
2001
ALL RIGHTS RESERVED

TABLE OF CONTENTS

PART II: TAXONOMY AND COMPARATIVE OSTEOLOGY

LIST OF FIGURES

LIST OF TABLES

ACKNOWLEDGEMENTS

Since 1963, when this project began, many people have contributed to its progress. Those who assisted by loaning specimens include:

Lyndon L. Hargrave, Prescott College.

Chester A. Thomas, Thomas W. Mathews, and Gloria J. Fenner of the U. S. National Park Service.

Donald Heiser and Todd Bostwick of the Pueblo Grande Museum.

Alexander Wetmore of the Smithsonian Institution.

Richard L. Zusi of the U. S. National Museum.

Hildegarde Howard of the Los Angeles County Museum of Natural History.

Edward B. Danson, Steve Emslie, Terrence J. Merckel, Mike Morales, and Scott Cutler of the Museum of Northern Arizona.

Emil W. Haury, Raymond H. Thompson, William A. Longacre, Alexander J. Lindsay, Jr., Stanley J. Olsen, and Mike Jacobs of the Department of Anthropology, University of Arizona, and the Arizona State Museum.

Sean Coughlin, Department of Anthropology, University of Tennessee, Knoxville.

Another group contributed much to the content:

Arlie W. Schorger, who, though his sight had failed, had someone read the Southwest Indian Turkey manuscript to him shortly before his death. He confirmed my findings, and made helpful comments on the introduction of turkeys into the Southwest Culture Area.

Hildegarde Howard read the comparative eagle osteology section, and made many helpful suggestions on eagles of the Pleistocene and Early Recent and on the captions for the illustrations.

Lyndon L. Hargrave demonstrated the importance of separating specimens by age stage, which is largely responsible for our present view of the macaw trade.

Gary Nabhan discovered that the early Basketmaker turkey mummy was a corn fetish as well as a bird of sacrifice.

Christy G. Turner, II, devised guidelines for the statistical analysis of the occurrence of turkeys with plumage of aberrant coloration.

Amadeo M. Rea kept me on the "strait and narrow" regarding taxonomy.

Carroll L. Riley provided encouragement and information on the proto-historic period.

Noel Parsons, editor, and the readers of the Texas A and M Press were not only encouraging, but provided many useful comments and suggestions.

Kathleen McKusick Condit, my daughter, prepared many of the comparative specimens.

Thierry M. Condit, my grandson, has kept the computer running in spite of brownouts.

Robert T. McKusick, my husband, has served as a sounding board for over fifty years, and with Maureen Davidheiser did the final proofreading.

Dale Stewart King said "Be temperate."

Thomas W. Mathews said "Tell it like it is."

Alden C. Hayes said "Pull an even strain."

Most recently, the completion of this manuscript has been assisted by Gloria Fenner, an unfailing source of instant information; Jonathan Reyman, whose suggestions are responsible for the present organization of the manuscript; Alan Ferg, old friend and patient editor; the Salado Chapter of the Arizona Archaeological Society, which has supported this publiction financially, and especially George F. Carter who has primed the pump with a steady stream of reprints, facilitated the loan of bones, and has browbeaten me into stopping hunting long enough to write it all down.

This summary of the Birds of Sacrifice started out about twice as long as it is now. If I had followed all the good suggestions that I have received over these many years, it would be at least three times as long as it is now. These are the bare bones as I see them today. The rest will have to wait for another chapter, in another book, on another day.

ABSTRACT

Bones of Birds of Sacrifice have been recovered from excavations of archaeological sites dating as early as 300 B.C. to the present. A four-part model is presented which relates the occurrences of these specimens to socio-politico-religio-economic stages in the development of the prehistory of the American Southwest. These include Paleo-Indian Big Game Hunting, Dry Farming, Canal Irrigated Farming, and Population Aggregation phenomena as illustrated by archaeological excavation, osteological remains, and iconography in Southwestern and Mesoamerican sites. The Protohistoric period is characterized by the presence of three systems: the persistence of Archetypal Deity Cults to which various avian species were sacrificed, the development of the Pueblo Katsina Cult which required vast numbers of feathers for prayer sticks, and the Societies which used birds in still other ways.

RESUMEN

Huesos de aves sacrificadas han sido recuperados de excavaciones arqueológicas de sitios que van desde 300 a.C. hasta el presente. Un modelo, compuesto de cuatro partes, es presentado para relacionar las ocurrencias de esto especímenes con diferentes estados socio-politico-economico-religios en el desarrollo de la prehistoria del Suroeste Americano. Éstos incluyen los fenómenos de las grandes cacerías del periodo Paleoindio, Agricultura de Temporal, Agricultura con Canales de Irrigación, y la Agregación Poblacional, ilustrada por excavaciones arqueológicas, restos osteologicos e iconografía en sitios del Suroeste Americano y de Mesoamerica. El periodo Protohistórico es caracterizado por la presencia de tres sistemas: la persistencia de cultos a deidades arqueotipicas a las cuales se sacrificaban varias especies avícolas; el desarrollo del culto a las Katsinas en el área Pueblo que requería un gran número de plumas para las varas de oración; y por ultimo, las diferentes organizaciones sociales o sociedades que usaban pájaros de varias maneras.

PART I

SOCIAL, RELIGIOUS, AND POLITICAL ASPECTS

CHAPTER 1

BIRDS OF CEREMONY, RITUAL, AND SACRIFICE

During the late 1960s my work at the U. S. National Park Service's Southwest Archeological Center, Gila Pueblo, Globe, Arizona, included the identification of avian remains from Paquimé, also known as Casas Grandes, Chihuahua, and from the Point of Pines Area, Arizona. During these identification studies, it became apparent that Scarlet Macaws from Paquimé were being traded to Point of Pines, and that very large turkeys from Point of Pines were being traded to Paquimé. Another identification study involved the birds and mammals from Mound 7, Gran Quivira, Salinas National Monument, New Mexico. Among the specimens of worked mammal bone was a disc made from a human parietal bone similar to one which Kidder (1932:199) had recovered from Pecos, that was incised with a four-pointed star. According to Alden C. Hayes, the excavator, the design on this human bone artifact was associated with the Twin War Gods of the pueblos on the one hand, and with the Mesoamerican Quetzalcoatl on the other. These evidences of Mesoamerican-type ceremonial activity in the North American Southwest led to a study of birds of ceremony, ritual, and sacrifice which has extended into the present.

SOURCES OF BIRDS FOR CEREMONIAL AND RITUAL USE

Birds intended for ceremonial and ritual use may be distinguished from birds of sacrifice by the way they are obtained and treated. Birds whose feathers, wings, beaks, or feet are desired for ceremonial and ritual use may be taken from the wild by various methods of hunting and trapping. My first attempt to make sense of the vast avian collections I was studying was to turn to ethnology in search of parallel patterns of usage. In 1963, Ladd (1963:10-11) reported that older, traditional Zuni tribal members were taking birds for ceremonial and ritual use with a variety of specialized snares intended for birds of the fields, ground feeding birds, brush feeding birds, and water birds. In contrast, younger tribal members were taking these birds with small arms and sling shots. Since young boys usually kept the feather boxes filled, most birds of ritual were taken with sling shots, particularly during the summer months when small, colorful, migratory birds were available. Adult men used .22 calibre rifles to obtain large birds such as hawks, eagles, ravens, crows, and owls, while they were herding sheep. Small steel traps baited with a dead rabbit were occasionally employed to take these species. Road kills found along the highways were also being plucked for ceremonial and ritual use. Ladd further reported that birds other than road kills were brought to the house, where a female member laid the birds out in the center of the room. She placed them in a row with their heads to the east. The female family members who were present then faced east, recited a short prayer, and sprinkled the birds with white cornmeal. After they had rested thus for several hours, the hunter, or the senior male of the household, plucked the birds, wrapped most of the feathers in bundles, and placed them in a feather box for storage. The feathers of birds which could only be used by special priests or other functionaries were carried to the house of the appropriate priest or society member, and presented as a gift. The recipient then blessed the hunter with "long life, abundance of material wealth, and good crops" (Ladd 1963:12).

No special treatment was given to the carcass, which generally ended up in the trash dump. Birds treated in this manner undoubtedly account for the vast majority of specimens which constitute avian collections from Southwestern archaeological sites, both as relatively complete skeletons or, scattered by scavengers, as random bones. If the birds were taken far from the pueblo, while on long hunting expeditions, they were skinned in the field, and the carcass discarded there. When the hunter returned home, the ritual was the same, except the skins were not plucked. They were draped over the beams of the house, to which they adhered as they dried, until needed.

Since the bodies of birds of ceremonial and ritual use were of no importance, it is reasonable to suppose that, once they were plucked, other body parts could have been utilized. The bones from wings and legs could have been saved as raw materials for tube manufacture. If prehistoric bird use was similar to that at Zuni Pueblo in the early 1960s, the prehistoric inhabitants of the northern and eastern peripheries of the Southwest, where great numbers of tubes were manufactured for trade to Plains Indians, may have been using birds taken for ceremonial and ritual use for commercial purposes as well. One argument against this possible generalization is the fact that the late Herbert Dick, who excavated Picuris Pueblo in the 1960s for Adams State College, Alamosa, Colorado, found that modern Picuris Pueblo tribal members made no use at all of feathers in ceremonies or rituals, nor did they have any traditions of such use. To the best of their knowledge, the harvesting of wild birds, especially eagles, was a commercial enterprise carried on at their pueblo from early to late, specifically to provide feathers and tubes for trade to Plains tribes (Dick, personal communication).

BIRDS OF CEREMONY

The differentiation between birds of ceremony and birds of ritual was apparently dictated by the attitude of the culture toward each species. Ladd designates birds of ceremonial use as those which are employed in the decoration of dance masks and dance costumes. Feathers of ravens, crows, owls, and Turkey Vultures are not used by Zunis for ritual purposes such as prayer sticks, because "they eat dead things." According to Ladd, the feathers of 15 to 20 ravens or crows, sometimes mixed with the feathers of Turkey Vultures and owls, are used in the large ruffs which decorate the bases of dance masks. He believes that this usage may account for the large numbers of raven, crow, owl, and vulture bones recovered from the trash dumps of many Southwestern archaeological sites (Ladd 1963:13-14).

BIRDS OF RITUAL

Ladd (1963:15-16) lists species which are used only by certain persons or groups such as Zuni

Rain Priests, Bow Priests, Curing Society, Clown Society, and Beast Society. Certain feathers of these species are worn as insignia of a particular priestly office, or are employed in making their prayer offerings.

CAPTIVE BIRDS KEPT AS PETS

An intermediate category of birds is that of birds kept as a living source of feathers and/or pets. Among the Zuni, this included eagles and a Military Macaw which was the gift of Neil Judd (1954:Plate 75). The Military Macaw is green, not red, yellow, and blue like the Scarlet Macaw usually found in archaeological sites in the Southwest. Ladd (1963:16-17) notes the ceremonial use of parrot feathers, but states that they were not used ritually in prayer sticks. Whether this is due to traditional constraints, or is because the feathers were green rather than red, is not known. When captive birds died, they were usually buried in a field outside the village or under a room floor. Seldom were they buried in the trash dump. In any case, they were buried, not just thrown out. This is an important point in evaluating the archaeological proveniences in which avian remains are found.

Wild birds generally do not live long enough to get old. When they start to slow down, something catches and eats them. Captive birds kept as sources of feathers or as pets would have been fully adult, if not old, when they finally died and were buried. Aged birds of this type are found in archaeological sites in small numbers. An example of this is the skeleton of a very old, very arthritic Canada Goose recovered from Paquimé.

BIRDS OF SACRIFICE

Native birds of sacrifice are taken from the nest very young and are raised by hand. These include hawks, eagles, macaws, parrots, owls, and ravens. Specific breeds of domestic turkeys, and chickens (at least in Mexico), were and still are raised with the intent of sacrifice. For example, Antelope House in northern Arizona had turkey pens where two breeds of turkeys were kept separate for hundreds of years, as were three different aberrant turkey colorations. At Paquimé, whole plazas fitted with nest boxes were devoted to breeding and to raising both turkeys and macaws. Birds of ceremony and ritual are acquired rather opportunistically, wherever and whenever available, even as road kills. In contrast, everything about birds of sacrifice is deliberate. For example, modern Hopis make special trips to obtain eaglets from areas to which a family, and only that family, has the right to harvest young from Golden Eagle nests. Special baskets or miniature cradleboards are used to transport the eaglets. Boys are assigned to hunt for them, to grind their meat, and to feed them. Special miniature blankets are woven and artifacts made for their burial in a separate eagle cemetery. Everything about individual birds of sacrifice is sacred.

When domestic turkeys were raised for sacrificial purposes, the aboriginal inhabitants of the Southwest took pains to keep them genetically pure. Small Indian Domestic Turkeys were kept separate from Large Indian Domestic Turkeys in Arizona and New Mexico for about twelve hundred years. Individuals of both breeds were traded into areas where they were not kept, but where they appear as sacrificial deposits. A breed set aside for sacrifice by a given group was not normally eaten by the members of that group.

Birds of sacrifice may be distinguished in archaeological avian collections by condition and age. Barring post-burial disturbance of the deposit, the skeleton will most often be intact, since most birds are now, and presumably were in the past, smothered or strangled before they are blessed, plucked, and buried. If the skeleton is not intact, it may be missing specific parts, which were offered to particular supernaturals. Examples would be the head in the case of a Small Indian Domestic Turkey sacrificed to Tlaloc, or the unfeathered leg and foot of a Large Indian Domestic Turkey sacrificed to Tezcatlipoca. Another example of a missing part is the lack of the whole breast of a female Small Indian Domestic Turkey which accompanied a male dog heart-sacrifice placed beneath the floor of a kiva at Gran Quivira (McKusick 1981:61; Judd 1954: Plate 76a).

In addition to being more or less intact, the bird of sacrifice is, over and over, of a specific age. One reason for this is the fact that they were most often sacrificed at a specific ceremony which occurs on the same date year after year. Another reason is that the birds of sacrifice are killed in their prime plumage. For example, Scarlet Macaws are usually hatched during the month of March. They were normally sacrificed in Pre-columbian times at about the Spring Equinox of the following year when their first full plumage including the long central tail feathers was mature. Thus, almost all Scarlet Macaw bird of sacrifice specimens recovered from Southwestern sites were about a year old at their death. Birds of sacrifice are often buried in or adjacent to places where ceremonies are conducted, and also depicted in ceremonial spaces (see Smith 1952, Dutton 1963, and Hibben 1975).

To summarize, birds of sacrifice are generally killed at an age of one year or less, whereas pets often live to be very old and arthritic, or may even be crippled. Both are buried rather than just being thrown on the trash dump.

CHAPTER 2

ARCHAEOLOGICAL AVIAN REMAINS

There are about 75 avian species which occur regularly in collections from Southwestern archaeological sites. An average site will include a selection of about 35 of these species, depending upon such factors as location, altitude, proximity to water, time level, and position of the site along prehistoric trade routes.

Table 1, originally prepared in 1968, summarized avian remains identified from Southwestern archaeological sites at the Southwest Archeological Center. These sites included many of large size which were ceremonial centers with extensive trade connections. The large avian collections recovered from these sites provided a solid base of prehistoric avian usage. Subsequently, additional collections identified at the Southwest Bird Lab, and by other reputable investigators have been checked against the original list. No species have been added. The reason for this is no doubt that much recent excavation has been related to salvage projects, many involving small sites, which did not produce the large numbers and variety of avian specimens that were found in the extensive excavations of the past. Pima avian usage has been added to serve as a comparison with Hohokam avian usage.

The time span represented in Table 1 covers the past 2000 years. Hohokam listings include only pre-Classic Hohokam. Avian usage in Classic Hohokam and late Salado sites shows a growing similarity to Western Pueblo usage and is included with those sites for the sake of brevity. Western Pueblo as here used includes materials from post-1000 sites from Paquimé, on the south, up the Mogollon Rim, to Grasshopper Pueblo on the north. The Mimbres sites, which have very early time levels, are included with Mogollon. Other major areas covered are self-explanatory. Antelope House was a cultural crossroads. The avian collection shares 25 species with Western Pueblo, 24 species with Rio Grande Pueblo, and 15 each with Chaco Canyon and Mesa Verde. Avian remains have been identified from many isolated areas, but the samples are so small they have been deleted from the table.

Some species, such as ducks, geese, quail, and doves, which are tender and still form part of our diets, are fairly universally utilized for food and feathers through both time and space. Turkeys were introduced in already domesticated forms. The Small Indian Domestic which was in the Four Corners Area by about 300 B.C., became a specialty of the Tompiro Pueblos between about 1250 and 1672, and was not eaten often, if at all. The Large Indian Domestic Breed, introduced in the A.D. 500s, was eaten in the Mesa Verde Area from about 960. In other areas where they were not so numerous, domestic turkeys were kept mainly for their feathers which were fashioned into light, but warm, twined robes. Merriam's Wild Turkey, the feral form of the Large Indian Domestic, was hunted and apparently eaten in the areas where it became naturalized from the 600s on.

Many other species were hunted for their feathers. The Sparrow Hawk, really a tiny falcon, is found at most sites in early to late deposits. Beginning between A. D. 900-1100 in northwestern New Mexico, ravens and crows were heavily utilized for feathers, bird skins, fetishes, and raven-bill scratchers. With time these special usages spread into the Rio Grande, the Galisteo Basin, and the Tompiro Pueblos.

Buteonine hawks became prominent in the Western Pueblo Area during the late 1200s. Many occur as wing and foot elements, but others are found as burials in trash, in great kivas, and under room floors. Scarlet Macaws, the only parrots traded into the Southwest in economically important numbers, were brought from the humid tropical lowlands below Mexico City. The first peak in the macaw trade centers around ca. 1100. A secondary peak of macaw usage occurs in the 1300s, and is often found in conjunction with heavy buteonine hawk usage. Like hawks, macaws usually occur as burials in areas where humans are buried or in connection with ceremonial structures such as kivas or dance platforms. Burials of macaws, buteonine hawks, and eagles are characteristic of Western Pueblo sites during the late 1200s and 1300s.

Another shift in avian usage is apparent on the Eastern Periphery. By 1500, great numbers of eagles and the larger buteonine hawks were taken for the manufacture of bird bone tubes, many of which seem to have been traded out into the Plains Culture Area.

While many birds occur in a variety of sites at different time levels, it is possible to distinguish typical assemblages of species and usages which characterize certain cultural groupings at various times in their development. A collection of adequate size to provide a valid sample can usually be placed fairly accurately in time and space without knowing the site from which it comes. One reason for this is that avian collections reflect intangible aspects of culture not otherwise obvious in data commonly preserved in archaeological sites. Socio-politico-religious considerations determined birds to be used, not the area in which a group lived at a given point in their wanderings. Repeatedly, prehistoric Indians made long journeys to obtain birds of an area in which we know they formerly lived rather than using local forms. In addition to possible former homes and trade connections, avian remains give clues to such political units as moieties which are distinguished by the use of certain birds, or by periods of influence by Mesoamerican ceremonial complexes such as the Quetzalcoatl Cult, which is connected with the macaw trade.

Avifaunal assemblages are useful in testing uncertain dates. For example, the Snaketown avian collection had an early assemblage which was originally dated at ca. 300 B.C. This assemblage was one which was characteristic of the remainder of the Southwest at ca. A.D. 400, a difference of 700 years. This discrepancy in time was noted in the Snaketown avian report (McKusick 1976:377). Present dating of the early phases at Snaketown agrees with the A.D. 400 date indicated by the avian assemblage (Dean 1991:91).

TABLE 1. ARCHAEOLOGICAL AND ETHNOLOGICAL AVIAN REMAINS FROM THE SOUTHWEST

PIMA AVIAN USAGE (Rea, 1983)

AVIAN REMAINS FROM ARCHAEOLOGICAL SITES (McKusick) See bottom of table for key.

FEATHER USAGE AMONG THE ZUNI COMPARED TO OTHER PUEBLOS (Ladd) See bottom of table for key.

	PIMA	HOHOKAM	MOGOLLON	WEST PUEBLO	SINAGUA	KAYENTA	MESA VERDE	CHACO CANYON	RIO GRANDE	E. PERIPHERY	ZUNI	TIWA	TEWA	TOWA	EAST KERES SAN	WEST KERAS SAN	HOPI
Common Loon				X					X	X							
Eared Grebe					X	X			X								
Pied-billed Grebe				X	X	X			X	X							
White Pelican			X	X													
Brown Pelican		X															
Double-crested cormorant				X													
Great Blue Heron		X		*	X				X		C					X	
Green Heron				X	X												
Common Egret				X					X								
Snowy Egret									X								
American Bittern				X													
Wood Ibis					X				X								
White-Faced Ibis				X													
Whistling Swan					*		*		*	*							
Canada Goose		X		x*	X		*	X	X	X	X						
White-fronted Goose		X		x*	X				X	X							
Snow Goose		X		X	X				X	X							
Mallard/Mexican Duck				X		X	X		x*	x*	X	?	X	X	?	X	
Gadwall				X	X												
Pintail		X		X	X		X	X	X	X							
Green-winged Teal		X		X						X							
Blue-winged Teal									X								
Cinnamon Teal				X	X				X	X							
American Widgeon				X	X			X	X	X							
Shoveler							X		X								
Canvasback				X	X				X								
Redhead					X		X		X	X							
Ring-necked Duck		X					X		X	X							
Common Goldeneye				X					X	X							
Bufflehead									X								
Ruddy Duck		X		X	X				X								
Common Merganser				X	X				X								
Red-breasted Merganser				X	X												
Turkey Vulture	P	X		x*	X		x*		X	x*	A					X	

7

Species	PIMA	HOHOKAM	MOGOLLON	WEST PUEBLO	SINAGUA	KAYENTA	MESA VERDE	CHACO CANYON	RIO GRANDE	E. PERIPHERY	ZUNI	TIWA	TEWA	TOWA	EAST KERESAN	WEST KERESAN	HOPI
Goshawk				X			*	X	x*	X							
Sharp-skinned Hawk		X		X				X	X		C					X	
Cooper's Hawk		X	X	X	X		X	X	X		C					X	
Red-tailed Hawk	P		X	x*	X		x*	X	X	x*	X					X	
Swainson's Hawk		X		x*			X	X	X	x*							
Rough-legged Hawk				X			X	X	X	x*							
Ferruginous Hawk				x*	X		x*	X	x*	x*							
Gray Hawk				X													
Zone-tailed Hawk				X													
Harris Hawk				X					X								
Black Hawk				X													
Bald Eagle								X	X		X	X	?	X	X	X	X
Golden Eagle	P		X	x*	x*		x*	x*	x*	x*	X	X	?	X	X	X	X
Marsh Hawk		X		X				X	X	X	X						
Osprey										*							
Prairie Falcon				X	X		X	X	X	x*							
Peregrine Falcon					X			X	X								
Pigeon Hawk								X	X								
Sparrow Hawk	P	X	X	X	X		X	X	X	X	X					X	X
Caracara				X													
Blue Grouse							X										
Sharp-tailed Grouse							X										
Sage Grouse							X		X								
Prairie Chicken							X		X								
Scaled Quail	P				X	X	X	X	X	X	B						
Gambel's Quail	P	X	X	X	X				X								
Harlequin Quail				X													
Chicken		X							X								
Merriam's Wild Turkey			X	x*	X												
Lg. Indian Domestic Turkey				x*		x*	x*	x*	x*		X	?	X	X	X	X	X
Sm. Indian Domestic Turkey		X		X			X			x*							
Sandhill Crane		X		x*	X		x*	x*	x*	x*	C						
Sora				X					X								
American Coot				X	X				X	X	C						
Killdeer				X						X	C						
Long-billed Curlew				X					X								
Willet					X												
Short-billed Dowitcher				X													
American Avocet		X															
Least Sandpiper								X	X								
Red-billed Pigeon				X													
Band-tailed Pigeon			X	x*					X								
Mourning Dove	P	X	X	X	X		X	X	X	X	A						
Military Macaw			X	X													

8

	PIMA	HOHOKAM	MOGOLLON	WEST PUEBLO	SINAGUA	KAYENTA	MESA VERDE	CHACO CANYON	RIO GRANDE	E. PERIPHERY	ZUNI	TIWA	TEWA	TOWA	EAST KERESAN	WEST KERESAN	HOPI
Scarlet Macaw	P	X	X	x*	X	x*		x*	X	X							
Thick-billed Parrot		X	X	X	X			X									
White-fronted Parrot				X													
Lilac-fronted Parrot				X													
Roadrunner		X	X	X				X			C						
Lesser Roadrunner				X													
Barn Owl		X		X				X									
Screech Owl				X	X		X	X	X								
Great-horned Owl			X	X	X	X	x*	x*	x*	x*	A						
Pygmy Owl				X													
Burrowing Owl				X	X			X			A						
Spotted Owl				X			X										
Long-eared Owl				X	X		X	X	X								
Short-eared Owl				X	X		X										
Boreal Owl								X									
Saw-whet Owl							X	X									
Poor-will				X			X										
Common Nighthawk			X					X	X		X						
White-throated Swift							X				C						
Broad-tailed Hummingbird						*					C	X					
Red-shafted Flicker				X			X	X	X		X				X	X	
Gilded Flicker		X															
Acorn Woodpecker				X					X								
Lewis' Woodpecker									X		X						
Hairy Woodpecker											X						
Downy Woodpecker											X						
Cassin's Kingbird											X						
Ash-throated Flycatcher											X						
Say's Phoebe											X						
Horned Lark				X				X	X	X	D						
Violet-green Swallow											C						
Rough-winged Swallow											C						
Cliff Swallow											C						
Purple Martin									X	X	C						
Gray Jay							X										
Steller's Jay		X	X						X		X						
Scrub Jay	X			X	X	X	X		X	X	X						
Magpie							X	X	X	x*	C						
American Raven	X	X		x*	X	X	X	X	x*	X	A						
White-necked Raven		X	X				X		X	X							
Crow				X			X		X	X	A						
Pinyon Jay				X			X	X	X								
Clark's Nutcracker				X					X								
White-breasted Nuthatch											C						
Cactus Wren				X				X									
Canyon Wren				X							X						

	PIMA	HOHOKAM	MOGOLLON	WEST PUEBLO	SINAGUA	KAYENTA	MESA VERDE	CHACO CANYON	RIO GRANDE	E. PERIPHERY	ZUNI	EAST KERES TIWA	WEST KERAS TEWA	TOWAN	HOPI
Rock Wren											B				
Mockingbird	P	X									X				
Sage Thrasher							X				X				
Robin							X	X	X		X		X	X	X
Western Bluebird				X		X					X				
Mt. Bluebird											X				
Townsend's Solitaire											X				
Western Gnatcatcher											B				
Loggerhead Shrike				X	X			X		X	X				
Yellow Warbler											X	X	X	X	
Western Meadowlark		X		X					X	X	C				
Yellow-headed Blackbird		X		X					X		X				
Red-winged Blackbird				X		X	X		X		X				
Bullock's Oriole											X				
Brewer's Blackbird				X					X		X				
Brownheaded Cowbird											D				
Tanagers											X				
Hooded Oriole		X													
Blackheaded Grosbeak											X				
Lazuli Bunting											X				
House Sparrow											D				
House Finch										X	D			X	
Arkansas Goldfinch											X				
Green-tailed Towhee											X				
Spotted-tailed Towhee											X				
Canyon Towhee											X				
Abert's Towhee	P										X				
Lark Bunting	P														
Grasshopper Sparrow											X				
Lark Sparrow											X				
Vesper Sparrow				X											
Junco	P	X		X						X	D				
White-crowned Sparrow	P														

KEY:
X=Refuse bone
*= Artifact bone and feather artifacts
x*=both

P=Pima avian usage

KEY:
X=general use by tribe (Zuni column also means ritual use)
ZUNI COLUMN ONLY
A = used ceremonially but not ritually--not used on prayersticks
B = Taboo
C = special use-reserved
D = Not taboo but not used

CHAPTER 3

AVIFAUNAL USAGE AMONG THE ZUNI

Edmund J. Ladd

Written in 1972

As reflected in the archeological data (Table 1), avian materials were used by various groups throughout the Southwest, from aboriginal times to, as discussed below, the present period. The following materials from the Pueblo of Zuni covering a period from circa 1900 to the present, is based on the personal knowledge of the author as a tribal member.

The Zuni reservation is located in west-central New Mexico, in what is typically the Upper Sonoran and Transitional life zones. In these life zones are a number of resident bird species and many that migrate annually through the region. These birds are taken with small arms and shotguns. A variety of snares were used before the introduction of fire arms.

Capturing winged creatures prior to the introduction of small arms required special skills and an intimate knowledge of the habitat and feeding habits of each bird. Large birds such as hawks and eagles were taken as nestlings and raised in cages for their plumage. For small birds, special snares were designed; there were snares for perching and open field feeding birds; for brush living and feeding birds; for water feeding birds, and for ground feeding birds. All snares used the same principle of a sliding horsehair noose anchored to a weight. Human hair was probably used in prehistoric times. Snares and snare parts having no ceremonial or ritual significance were abandoned in the field. They would be rarely, if ever, found in archeological sites.

Captive birds were kept for their feathers and as pets. Eagles were taken from their nests and kept for several years in wooden cages. Upon the death of a bird it was buried in the fields, under the floor, and sometimes in the rubbish dump. Formerly, it was never just thrown on the trash pile. The Red-tailed Hawk, *pippi-k/at//ajjon/ona*, was also kept. To my knowledge owls were never kept. With the introduction of firearms for taking birds, the need of captive birds has been reduced to zero. In 1962 there were only two captive eagles in the village, and by 1972 there were no captive eagles or hawks (Jonathan Reyman reports one captive eagle still held in 1996, personal communication).

Smaller birds were and are generally kept as pets. The mockingbird, *k/ya cho/wa*, is a very popular bird. These are sometimes live-trapped by snare, and sometimes taken as nestlings. They are kept in small screened wooden cages. The Zuni believe that a child, if fed the tongue from an adult mockingbird, would be gifted with many languages. When the bird died it was simply discarded on the trash pile. The Sparrow Hawk, Steller's Jay, and White-crowned Sparrow are also popular as pets (Reyman reports plumage of mockingbird and Steller's jay used in 1996).

11

Macaws, traded up from Mexico from prehistoric to modern times, were kept for their plumage. In 1940, there were four macaws in Zuni including one given to the Sun Priest (*pequinne)* by Neil Judd in 1924. A raven was kept as a pet by a family living outside the village in the late 1930s; it spoke Zuni, as did the Judd macaw.

Plumage is the principle reason birds are taken by the Zuni. A variety of feathers are used in the annual seasonal public and special ceremonies performed by the masked gods and in the ritual making and offering of prayer sticks involving the entire tribe. Depending on individual religious position, each Zuni must "plant" from 16 to 80 prayer sticks annually, using from 80 to 400 feathers of various kinds.

The Zuni recognize and classify 72 birds found in their region (see Table 1). Some of these, especially the smaller birds, are specifically identified and classified, while others tend to be lumped. There are, for example, a number of duck species common to the region including Mallard, Pintail, Cinnamon Teal, Canvasback, etc.; all are called by the common name of */eya.* Two ducks are specifically named but unidentified as to species: these are *na/na/lhi* and *je/palo/chapik/ya.* Geese are called */owa;* turkeys, domestic or wild, are called *tona.* Large buteonine hawks are called *pippi;* the Red-tailed Hawk, *pippi-k/at//ajon/ona,* and the Marsh Hawk, *shok/apiso,* are specifically identified. Feathers from geese, ducks, turkeys and hawks, regardless of species, are used ceremonially and ritually in the same manner.

Feathers from raven, crow, turkey vulture, and owls are used only for making ceremonial mask decorations. Feathers from 15 to 20 ravens, crows and turkey vultures, and feathers from two to three owls or large buteonine hawks are required for each mask decoration. Exotic or introduced species such as macaw, peacock, pheasant, guinea hen, and domestic chickens are used for ceremonial mask decoration but not in ritual use, as in making prayer sticks.

Generally speaking, birds were never an important part of Zuni diet, although in recent times small birds taken for plumage were eaten, not as a "main course" but as a delicacy. The Horned Lark, *Eremophila alpestris,* was taken in large numbers as late as 1970 and eaten after roasting over an open fire. Other birds which were eaten include Robin, sparrow, and Steller's or Scrub Jay. Only in recent times have turkey, duck, and dove become a part of Zuni diet. Quail is still a taboo bird. Of the 72 identified and classified birds, not including those which are lumped, found in the region, 16 are not used because of various taboos, 16 have limited or special usage, leaving 40 which are commonly used.

Zuni ceremonial uses of avian material, as compared to other Southwestern Pueblos, for which there is inadequate information, are as follows (see Table 1):

    18 species are used in common with the Western Keresan
    5 species, one questionable, are used in common with Eastern Keresan
    4 species, two questionable, are used in common with Tiwa
    4 species, two questionable, are used in common with Tewa
    6 species are used in common with Towa
    8 species are used in common with Hopi

The most widely used birds are duck, turkey and eagle; and as might be suspected, Acoma-Laguna and Hopi Pueblos have the most in common with Zuni. Very clearly the Pueblo People made distinctions in bird usages for ritual and for feathers for ceremonial use. Macaw and chicken feathers are used in ceremonial masks, but not in making prayer sticks. There was a huge demand for feathers for ceremonial use, so that birds of many sorts found roles in ceremonies demanding feathers.

Figure 1. Left, masked face of man in bat costume pictured on a Mimbres Polychrome bowl after Brody *et al.* (1983:Figure 6). See Figure 44 for complete figure. Center and right, masked faces depicted on Mimbres Black/white bowl sherds, after Cosgrove and Cosgrove (1932:Plate 226).

CHAPTER 4

AVIFAUNAL USAGE AMONG THE PIMAS

In southern Arizona, bird usage was much different from that in the pueblos. I have come to regard the vast quantity of a wide variety of bird remains recovered from many pueblos as evidence of the operation of the Katsina Cult, which appeared in a full blown form along the middle Little Colorado ca. A.D. 1275 (Adams 1991:91-121) and in what appears to be developmental form in Mimbres pottery designs ca. A.D. 1100 (Figure 1), and in Jornada Mogollon rock art as early as A.D. 1150 (Schaafsma 1999:164-192). Schaafsma presents a convincing model which connects the transformation of departed ancestors into bringers of rain with the Tlaloc Cult both in Mesoamerica and in the Southwest. I find evidence of the Tlaloc Cult in the Southwest even earlier than these dates. Apparently the beginning of accelerated use of birds was not an integral part of the Katsina Cult in its developmental period. Present evidence suggests that accelerated bird use is a function of the beginning of the manufacture of prayer sticks. Prior to that development, non-commercial avian remains from archaeological sites in the Southwest were less numerous, and, I believe, represent usages connected with a pan-Southwestern socio-politico-religious complex which echoes that found in Mesoamerica. Pre-classsic Hohokam collections are representative of this usage pattern, and have been kept separate in Table 1 from Classic Hohokam and Salado Collections which are included with Western Pueblo Collections.

Ethnographic parallels for Hohokam collections are drawn from Amadeo M. Rea's 15-year study of Pima ethno-ornithology which culminated in the volume *Once a River* (Rea 1983). This is appropriate because the Pima now inhabit the same area as did the Hohokam, and also because the Pima have not adopted the Katsina Cult. Of the 240 birds Rea indicates are now or were formerly in the area, the Pimas have names for 82. Of these, only 14 were actually used by the Pimas.

Whereas the inhabitants of the pueblos kill many birds as a source of feathers, the Pima kill relatively few. They tend to gather the dropped feathers of wild birds, or to pluck the feathers of captive birds which are later released. If the early residents of the Southwest followed this same pattern of feather harvest, it may account for the pre-Katsina Cult dearth of avian remains which is so evident among the Hohokam. It was not that feathers were not used, it is rather that the avian producers of these feathers generally lived out their lives and died away from human habitation, rather than being killed and tossed on the local trash dump for archaeologists to find.

Turkey Vulture is probably the most important bird among the modern Pima. Turkey Vulture is prominent in legend and song. One of the moieties of the Pima and Tohono O'odham is named after the Turkey Vulture. Turkey Vulture feathers found beneath a roost

15

were used for fletching arrows. Other than this use, the species was tabooed (Rea 1983:127).

Tail feathers of young Red-tailed Hawks were the most prized for arrow fletching, and were also used as hair decoration. The young birds were lifted down from their nests in saguaros with a saguaro rib, the tail feathers were plucked, and the young were replaced in the nest. Up until the early 1900s juvenile Red-tailed Hawks were raised in cages. Young boys who hunted small rodents, lizards and fish to feed the birds expected to receive some of the feathers in return. The feathers were harvested at the time the birds normally molted. If a bird died in captivity, it was considered a very ill omen. Therefore, each May, new nestlings were obtained, and the captive birds were released (Rea 1983:132).

Golden Eagle nestlings were obtained by descending the cliffs from above by means of ropes. All the young were taken from the nests. Golden Eagles were kept in stout cages of mesquite limbs equipped with a small house. Eagle feathers were used to fletch arrows intended for shooting Apaches. A pair of matched eagle primaries was used by the shaman to brush away disease during curing ceremonies (Rea 1983:136).

Both the meat and the eggs of Gambel's Quail were eaten. The quail were taken with traps constructed of arrow weed bound with willow bark. The head was removed and discarded, a measure taken to prevent the handler from becoming blind. The Scaled Quail was hunted where available (Rea 1983:139). White-winged Doves were trapped for food, or like the Mourning Dove, were shot with arrows by boys (Rea 1983:159, 160).

Parrots figure in Pima legend, and there are indications that in the past Pimas were familiar with wild Thick-billed Parrots. Scarlet Macaws were kept in the Pima villages to supply the lucrative feather trade at least as late as 1716 (Rea 1983:162-163).

The Mockingbird is an important figure in Pima legend and song. Its meat, either roasted or boiled, was fed to a child who was slow to talk (Rea 1983:208). This is an interesting parallel to Zuni usage of the species.

Abert's Towhee was regularly trapped for food. Alternatively, it was taken during nocturnal torch-lighted hunts following rains. The Lark Bunting was trapped in the winter, when it was an important food source, as were the Dark-eyed Junco and the White-crowned Sparrow (Rea 1983:234, 235, 238-239).

Pima avian usage appears next to Hohokam in Table 1 for easy comparison.

CHAPTER 5

A PROPOSED MODEL OF BIRDS OF SACRIFICE

Mankind, according to Jung (1968:58), is possessed of a variety of archetypal concepts. These concepts may be symbolized in some cases by supernaturals. Di Peso saw evidences of Mesoamerican supernaturals such as Quetzalcoatl, Xiuhtecutli, Xipe Totec, Tlaloc and an unnamed female deity at Paquimé (Di Peso 1974:Vol. 2, 546-569; Vol. 3, 770). The sacrifice of large numbers of macaws and turkeys, and even children, at Paquimé, in manners identical to those of the high cultures of Mesoamerica, interested Di Peso in tracing Mesoamerican supernaturals in the Southwest Culture Area. Unfortunately he died before the project could be carried out.

It is difficult in many cases to associate supernaturals depicted in Mesoamerican art with supernaturals depicted in stylistically different Southwest Pre-columbian art, but the birds sacrificed to these supernaturals are the same, regardless of location either north or south of the international border. The occurrences of these birds of sacrifice in time and space has led me to formulate a four-part model to attempt to make order out of the chaos of these specimens. Aztec names are used for the supernaturals since they are widely published and generally familiar to Southwesternists. In brief these four categories are:

1. Paleo-Indian Period -- Black God as Raven, the primal flux which existed before creation, the Lord of Beasts. This supernatural is holarctic in distribution, found in the arctic regions of both the eastern and western hemispheres, beginning with the Upper Paleolithic in Europe and Siberia. Black God and Wife are believed to have entered the New World with the Paleo-Indians (Luckert 1975). Clovis Tradition Paleo-Indians were present in southern Arizona by about 9300 B.C. (Haury 1975:v, 179-180), presumably carrying Black God and Wife with them as part of their non-material culture. Luckert (1975) believes that the Paleo-Indian religion has survived in the Southwest in the historic Hunter Tradition as well as in their Mesoamerican counterparts. The appropriate sacrifice to these supernaturals is the Common Raven, *Corvus corax*.

2. Archaic/Formative Transition -- This period begins about 300 B.C. with the acceptance of serious dry farming dependant upon adequate water and the warmth of a suitable growing season. Tlaloc was the patron of gentle rain on the fields. The appropriate sacrifice to Tlaloc in Mesoamerica was the head and blood of the South Mexican Turkey, *Meleagris gallopavo gallopavo*. The Dresden Codex pictures the Ocellated Turkey, *Agriocharis ocellata*, as a sacrificial bird among the Maya. The Small Indian Domestic Turkey, *Meleagris gallopavo silvestris* (formerly *"tularosa"*), was introduced into the Southwest at least as early as the Lolomai Phase, A.D. 100 to 300 on Black Mesa (Whitecotton and Lebo 1980:168; Lebo and Warburton 1982:82; Leonard *et al.* 1984:371, 387; Leonard 1989:10-11), but may date to as early as 200 B.C (Powell *et al.*, 1980:167:168). The Small Indian Domestic Turkey occurs earliest as a headless mummy in a Basketmaker II deposit (McKusick 1986c:3-4, Figures 16, 17), an apparent sacrifice to Tlaloc which parallels Mesoamerican usage depicted in the Dresden Codex.

The Sun, which provides the light and warmth necessary to make plants grow, is represented by the high-flying Golden Eagle, *Aquila chrysaetos,* which is holarctic in distribution. The sun was known to the Aztecs as Tonatiuh. Evidence of the use of Golden Eagles begins contemporaneously with the introduction and sacrifice of the Small Indian Domestic Turkey, and eagle sacrifice continues among the Hopi to this day.

3. Introduction of Water Control Devices such as canals, ditches, and reservoirs. Quetzalcoatl is an early patron of artificially flowing water (Di Peso 1972:15). In Mesoamerica the appropriate sacrifice to Quetzalcoatl is the Scarlet Macaw, *Ara macao.* At Paquimé, and throughout the remainder of the Southwest, Scarlet Macaws were sacrificed at the spring equinox. Water control devices, along with Scarlet Macaws, appear in the Southwest at different times in different areas:

> Hohokam Area -- beginning possibly 500s, definitely 600s
> Mimbres, Chaco Canyon, Sinagua -- 1060 (or earlier at Chaco Canyon) - 1150
> Eastern Arizona, Southwestern New Mexico, Northern Chihuahua -- 1250-1400
> Rio Grande, Salado -- post 1400

Chalchihuitlique, a prominent Mesoamerican manifestation of the Great Mother, is the spouse of Tlaloc and patroness of lakes and rivers. She is associated with green stones such as jade and turquoise. It is probable that the appropriate avian sacrifice is the Military Macaw, *Ara militaris,* at the spring equinox, or possibly the Thick-billed Parrot, *Rhynchopsitta pachyrhyncha,* as a substitute. Avian indications of her presence parallel those of Quetzalcoatl:

> Hohokam Area -- beginning 600s
> Mimbres, Chaco Canyon, Sinagua -- ca. 1060-1150
> Southeastern Arizona -- 1275-1300
> Northern Chihuahua -- 1350-1450

4. Introduction of the Tezcatlipoca Cult. This Warrior Cult is quite late over much of the Southwest. In Mesoamerica, the appropriate sacrifice is the unfeathered shank and foot of the South Mexican Turkey. In the Southwest, the unfeathered shank and foot of the Large Indian Domestic Turkey, *Meleagris gallopavo merriami,* is secreted in a dark crevice or cave.

> Chaco Canyon -- 1000
> Tularosa Cave -- 1100s
> Eastern Periphery and Salado -- post-1400

The appropriate sacrifice in areas where turkeys were not raised was the owl.
> Sinagua, Nalakihu --1130-1200

According to Vaillant (1950:170-171), Aztec belief was based on a concept of five earth eras presided over by Tezcatlipoca, Quetzalcoatl, Tlaloc, Chalchihuitlicue, and Tonatiuh, in that order.

18

Although Aztec cosmology is too late for all but the Salado and the Eastern Periphery, these important Mesoamerican deities represent basic archetypal supernaturals present in Mesoamerica much earlier. It is not surprising that they are the same five deities which appear in art and in bird-of-sacrifice bone collections from the Formative Period in the North American Southwest. The Paleo-Indian Raven and Wife, and the Mesoamerican supernaturals are considered below in detail in the order in which they arrived in the Southwest Culture Area.

Figure 2 locates the most important dated sites considered in these chapters. Figures 3 through 9 indicate locations of indications of supernaturals represented by avian remains from early agricultural through historic time periods.

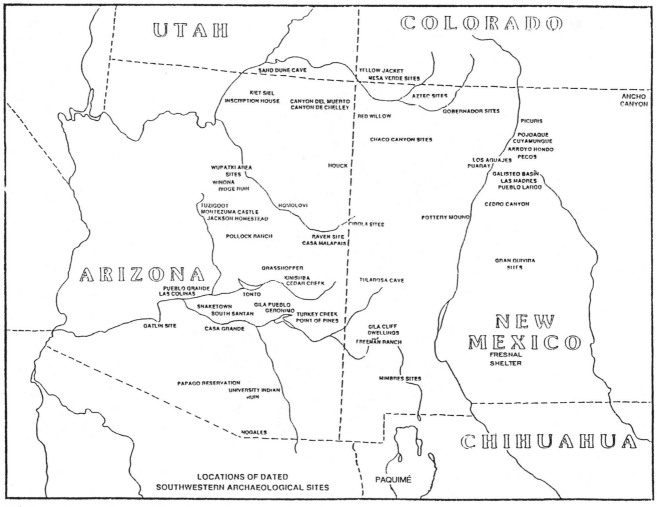

Figure 2. Locations of dated Southwest archaeological sites relevant to text.

19

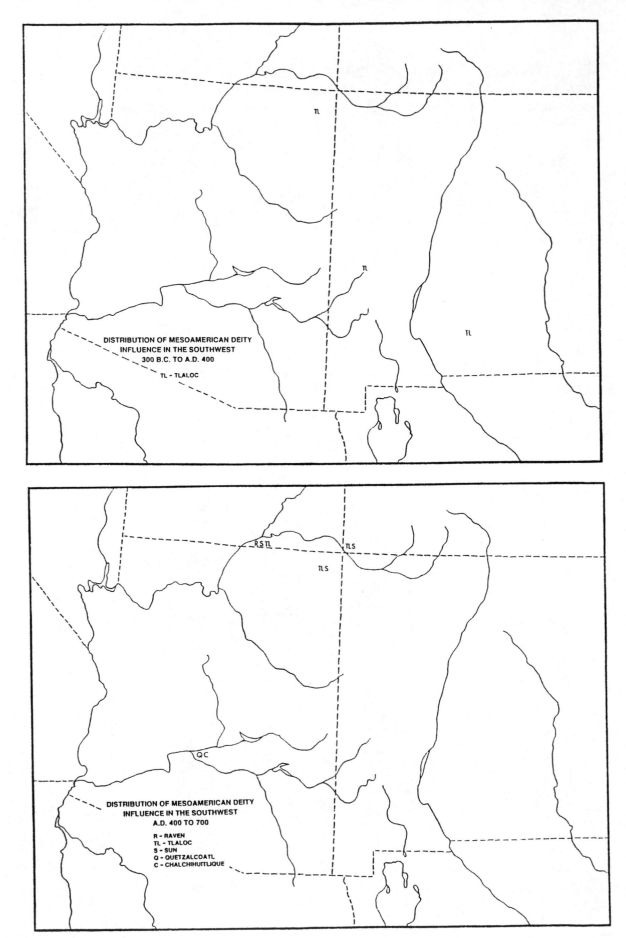

Figure 3, top and Figure 4, bottom.

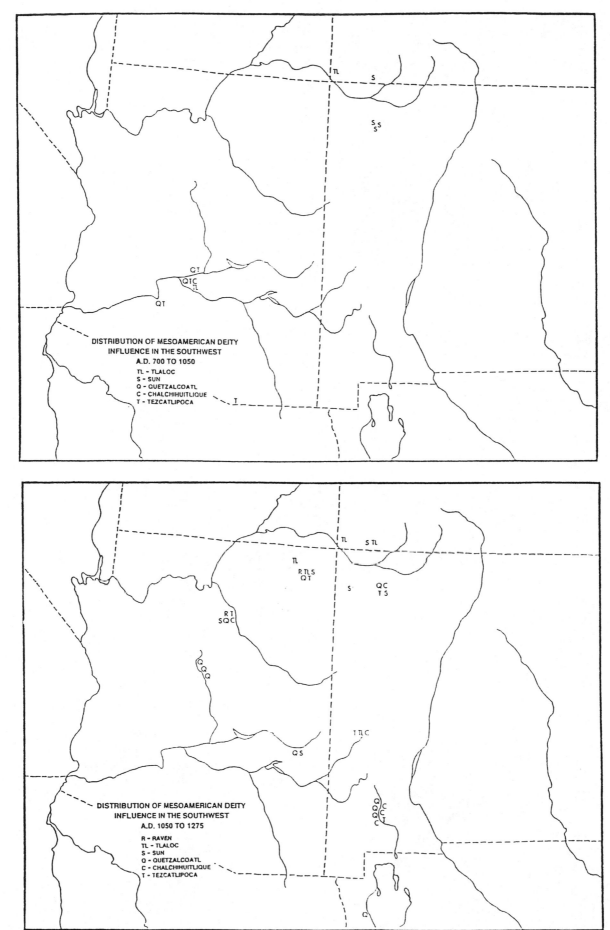

Figure 5, top and Figure 6, bottom.

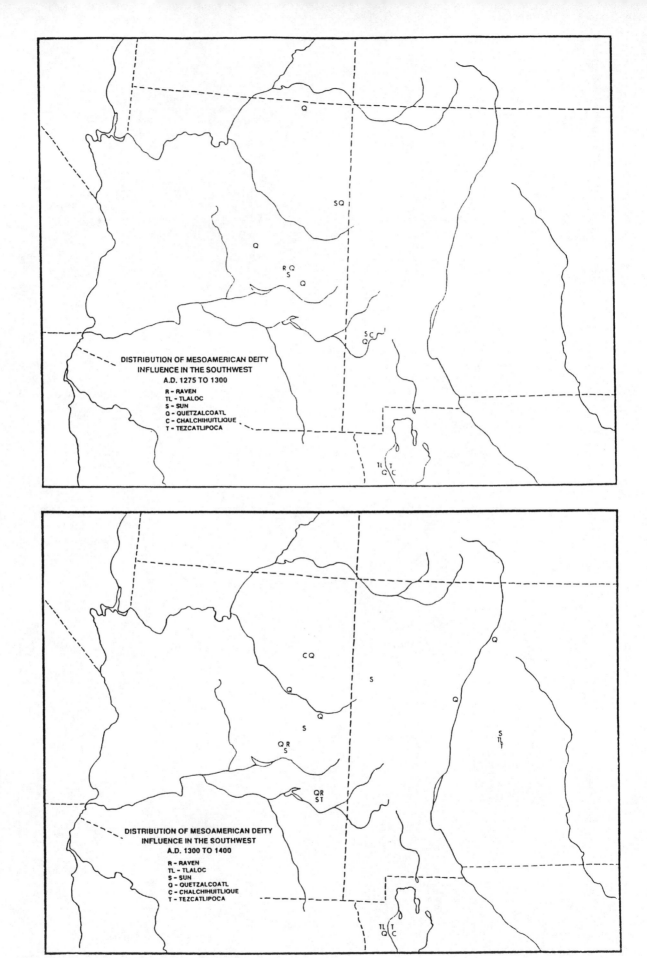

**DISTRIBUTION OF MESOAMERICAN DEITY
INFLUENCE IN THE SOUTHWEST
A.D. 1275 TO 1300**

R – RAVEN
TL – TLALOC
S – SUN
Q – QUETZALCOATL
C – CHALCHIHUITLIQUE
T – TEZCATLIPOCA

**DISTRIBUTION OF MESOAMERICAN DEITY
INFLUENCE IN THE SOUTHWEST
A.D. 1300 TO 1400**

R – RAVEN
TL – TLALOC
S – SUN
Q – QUETZALCOATL
C – CHALCHIHUITLIQUE
T – TEZCATLIPOCA

Figure 7, top and Figure 8, bottom.

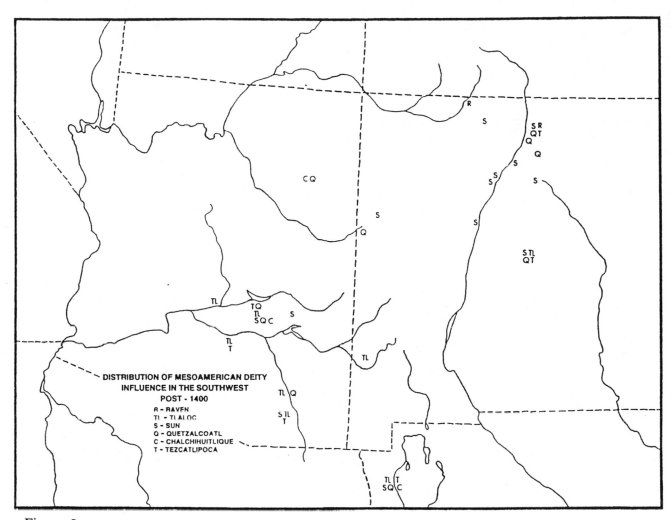

Figure 9.

CHAPTER 6

RAVEN, XIUHTECUTLI, AND MASSAU

Raven is the chaos which existed before creation was organized. And when, finally, creation ceases to exist, that entropy will be Raven. The archetypal concept of a "primal flux" or "prehuman flux" is holarctic (Luckert 1975; Bancroft 1987:18-19). In this concept there is no firm differentiation between different types of beings. Humans, animals, trees, rocks, may all change their forms as necessity indicates. It is only at the moment of creation that they are trapped in a given form. Even then, some are able to transcend the limitations of the constraints of this universe or of this everyday state of consciousness. The shaman can travel in both worlds (Harner 1982:1-7).

The Upper Paleolithic wall painting of a shaman in the great cave of Les Trois Freres, France, is considered to be the earliest surviving realistic portrayal of a human being (Figure 10). He wears a stag headdress with antlers, bear paws over his hands, and a horse's tail hanging from his waist. One leg is lifted in the steps of a dance. He looks straight at the viewer, exposing what hunters call "the predator face". This is a frontal view of a flat face with eyes, nose, and mouth shared by such predators as the great cats and man, which acts as a trigger to send herbivores into instinctive flight. Other paintings in the same cave show only stick figures with flutes and animal headdresses. This beautifully executed figure was at first called "The Sorcerer". Now it is interpreted not as just a shaman, but as The Shaman, the earliest known depiction of a supernatural (Bancroft 1987:12-15). Bancroft suggests that the black outlining of the facial features and the figure may indicate that this personage was already known, at least part of the time, as Black God. His animal garb is indicative not only of his role as Lord of Beasts, but also of his nature as a shape-changer and "great Magician, the supreme shaman, through whose power the masked dancers moved to the sound of pipes, flutes, and drums" (Bancroft 1987:19).

The Black God concept was most likely spread across northern Europe by the rapid expansion of the Magdalenian hunters, and across the Bering Strait by the Paleo-Indians. The Maritime Archaic was probably important in reinforcing the tradition, and perhaps in carrying it to new areas of habitation. Black God appears in the Celtic Mysteries as Bran, an enormous dark man. He was so large that on one military expedition he led his army, carried in ships, by wading across the Irish Sea with his musicians riding on his shoulders. Bran is equated with Chronos, the Lord of Time and Transmutation. He is "the titan who stands at the Strong Door keeping the destructive enchantments of earlier times at bay"(Matthews 1987:54). Bran still guards the holy places of Britain. When Bran was finally killed, his head was enshrined in the White Tower of London. His ravens are still there today as emblems of his guardianship of the nation.

Another 10,000 year-old depiction of a musical, phallic shaman, masked and garbed as a European bovid from a cave drawing of Dordogne, is considered an attempt to increase the fertility of game animals (van Renterghem 1995:62-65). It is so similar in appearance to the large-phallused,

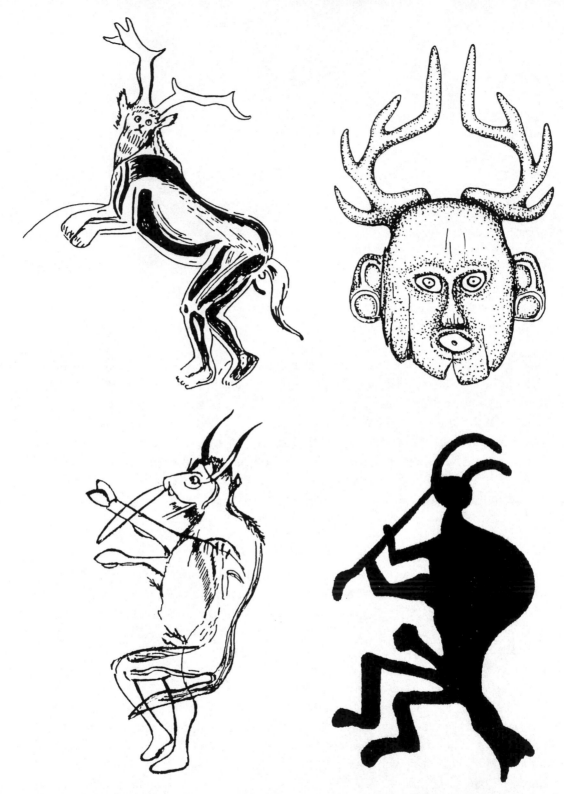

Figure 10. Upper left, Black God, Lord of Beasts, Upper Paleolithic, Le Trois Freres, Ariege, France. After Prideaux 1973:126. Upper right, cedar mask with shell eyes and mouth from Spiro, Oklahoma, a Post-A.D. 800 Caddoan Mississippian Site. After Time-Life, Mound Builders and Cliff Dwellers, 1992:56. Lower left, European Bison Shaman, cave carving, 10,000 B.C., Dordogne, France. After van Renterghem 1995:63, 64. Lower right, Kokopelli, petroglyph, La Cieneguilla area. After Cunkle 1993:Figure 71. The similarity of the two lower figures suggests that Kokopelli may continue the long history of the musical shaman.

hump-backed flute player Kokopelli, that I am led to wonder if some examples of this common Southwestern motif did not originally represent a flute-playing bison shaman (Figure 10).

The bison shaman apparently existed among the Paleo-Indian inhabitants of North America at the same time as Old World examples. Archaeological evidence from the Jones-Miller site near Wray, Colorado, is interpreted by Dr. Dennis J. Stanford of the Smithsonian Institution as representing the remains of the gear of a pole-riding hunt shaman. These 10,000 year old items include the socket in the ground for the pole, a miniature stone spear point, the broken fragments of an antler flute, and the remains of a sacrificial animal with which he sought to secure the success of bison drives on several occasions at different seasons. Stanford's illustration depicts the sacrifice as a raven. This technique of hunting bison with the aid of a pole-riding shaman was perpetuated by the Cree and Assiniboin who hunted bison on foot in historic times (de la Haba 1976:40-46).

It is an archaeological rule of thumb that most culture traits flow through the Southwest from north to south from the coming of the Paleo-Indian big game hunters until about 1500 B.C. At this point the flow of most culture traits reverses, passing from south to north until the American Revolution. Then, it reverses once more, again flowing from north to south. The development in the New World of the supernatural we know as Raven, or Black God, follows this pattern of ebb and flow. Raven has three advents in the North American Southwest. First, Raven apparently accompanied the Paleo-Indian hunters into Southern Arizona by 9300 B.C. Second, he is present in Mesoamerica earliest in the guise of Huehueteotl, the Old, Old God, later as Xiuhtecutli, the Old Fire God, and in Yucatan as Ek Chuah the black merchant god, then in the Southwest as Massau. Third, Southern Athapaskans, the Navajos and Apaches, come with their hunter tradition.

The Raven Complex, as it arrived with the Paleo-Indians, is apparently similar to its roots in the Old World. Raven is a culture hero on the other side of the Bering Strait. He is a bringer of light and of culture; he is a shape-changer; and he is a trickster (Hultkrantz 1979:36). Among the Koryak of eastern Siberia, Raven, and Wolf as well, are considered as shaman/culture heroes. Further, Raven and Wolf are in some sense considered twins (Hultkrantz 1979:40). Perhaps this is an extension of the more familiar companions of Odin, the Norse All-Father. At his feet sat a pair of wolves, and on his shoulders perched a pair of ravens named Hugin and Munin, Thought and Memory. These birds flew over the whole world each day, and brought back reports of all that was happening (Herzberg 1945:362; Feher-Elston 1991:4, 186).

Although Black God/Raven and Wife are a product of the Old World, the later supernaturals, who partake of fragments of Black God's essence, developed in the New World. It appears that the big game hunters of the Paleo-Indian Culture Stage swept through Mesoamerica with great speed. There is little concrete evidence in Mesoamerica of Paleo-Indian religious beliefs. However, parallels with very early Old World religious beliefs include such elements as a many-layered heaven and earth, the importance of world directions, and directional trees, the "rabbit in the moon" (Figure 11), male/female polarity, and traditions of shamanic transformation (Miller and Taube 1993:26-27).

The Archaic Culture Stage was also relatively brief. A large population backed up by the Panama bottleneck was forced into horticultural experimentation quite early in comparison to the Southwest. Excavations of Archaic burials in the Tehuacan Valley of Puebla revealed two groups of

Figure 11. Rabbit in the Moon motifs. Left, Florentine Codex, 16th c. Aztec. After Miller and Taube 1993:143. Right, Mimbres Black-on-white bowl design, Cameron Creek Village. After Bradfield 1931:Plate LXXIV, 105.

mutilated and partially burned humans. The bodies were wrapped in blankets and nets and accompanied by baskets. Whatever the intent of the mutilation, a concern with an afterlife is indicated. A later site, dating from 5000 to 4000 B.C., was found in the uplands of Oaxaca. It consists of lines of parallel rocks that may have outlined a dance ground or a ball court, and suggest that ritualized games may have been a part of the Archaic ceremonial complex (Miller and Taube 1993:26-27).

The early Mesoamerican Formative saw the development of farming villages, production of pottery, and population growth. The Ocos Culture of the southern coastal region of Chiapas displays characteristics which develop in various directions as they spread in time and space. Ocos burials contained mica mirrors; obsidian, pyrite, and other reflective stones were made into mirrors through the historic period. Ocos pottery figurines included full-bodied women, curious combinations of human and animal forms, and enthroned figures of shamanic functionaries wearing the costumes of their animal counterparts (Miller and Taube 1993:28).

The Olmecs provide the earliest concrete representations of Mesoamerican supernaturals. Their Formative Period development culminated in small cities. Although we do not know how these cities functioned, autonomously or under a larger confederation, several concepts appear which persisted into the historic period. Shortly after 1200 B.C., these included personifications of supernaturals in the form of the large felines, harpy eagles, sharks, caiman lizards, and snakes. Like man, all of these are meat-eaters at the top of the food chain. Places of conjunction of sky, water, and the underworld were considered especially sacred. These included the tops of mountains and the mouths of caves. Mountains which contained both caves and springs appear to have been the most awe-inspiring of all. Like later New World farmers, the Olmecs were preoccupied with earth, water, and maize. Religious practices which persisted throughout Mesoamerican development include pilgrimages, animal and bird sacrifice, bloodletting, human sacrifice (Figure 12), a four-part division of the world, rituals held in caves, offerings of ritual objects in caches, and the use of mirrors. Physical facilities which persisted into the historic period in both Mesoamerica and the Southwest

Figure 12. Left, Aztec depiction of human heart sacrifice, Codex Laud, Late Postclassic. After Miller and Taube 1993:97. Heart sacrifice of turkeys and dogs was practiced at Gran Quivira. The Mimbres Black-on-white bowl motif showing a man with a hole in his torso may indicate knowledge of this type of sacrifice, if not its practice. Eby site, after Brody 1977:198, Figure 161.

include dual division of the community along a central axis which had begun by 1500 B.C., and ceremonial platforms. In Mexico pyramids may actually represent volcanos (Miller and Taube 1993:28).

The earliest surviving Mesoamerican manifestation of Raven was Huehueteotl, the most ancient of gods who was most often depicted in pottery, a diagnostic of the Formative Culture Stage, as a thin, bearded, wrinkled, old man who is seated hunched over to support a censer. Huehueteotl was the father/mother of all the gods, another expression of the "primal flux", and thereby the ultimate source of their divinity (Brundage 1979:22).

Raven next appears as Xiuhtecutli, who like the Old World Bran, was equated with Chronus; he was the Lord of Time. At the end of each Aztec epoch, the derived gods died and were born anew in the new age. Xiuhtecutli alone survived from one epoch to the next. Xiuhtecutli was not only the ancestor of all beings, he was also the god of fire, and master of the hearth. His place of abode was the volcanic underworld.

A Gila Polychrome Bowl design from Besh-Ba-Gowah, Globe, Arizona, expresses the essence of Xiuhtecutli (Figure 13). It consists of four offset quarters centered with a stylized butterfly somewhat similar to the one illustrated in Figure 15 which could only be worn by Xiuhtecutli. In this design his personal symbol is coupled with his centrality in the space-time continuum.

In the Mesoamerican world view, Xiuhtecutli was the focus of all things. The four cardinal directions spread out from him. He was the center, the fifth direction. The north-south axis was based on the annual apparent north-south movement of the sun. The east-west axis was established by the diurnal path of the sun across the sky. The north-south axis was associated with the solstices, the east-west with the equinoxes. The Mesoamerican world was oriented to correspond

Figure 13. Xiuhtecutli wore a turquoise butterfly on his breast. Upper left, Gila Polychrome bowl with butterfly motif as the center of the four directional quarters. Besh-Ba-Gowah Pueblo, Globe, pre-1440. Lower left, Sikyatki Polychrome design, 1375-1625. After Pilles and Danson 1974:22. Upper right, Kechipawan Polychrome bowl, ca. 1345-1385. After Smith *et al.*, 1966:Figure 48. Middle right, Tularosa Black-on-white jar design, 1200-1300. After Cunkle 1993:Photo 46. Lower right, Kwakina Polychrome bowl design, 1325-1400. After Cunkle 1993: 75.

with the path of the sun, so "right" was north, and "left" was south. Each of the five directions had a special name, symbol, color, bird, animal, plant, and patron deity.

As Lord of Time, Xiuhtecutli established both the solar year and the sacred year (Brundage 1979:1-5, 15). The month was composed of 20 days, four sets of five, or a "full count", the normal number of fingers and toes. In their world view the score constituted totality, a special number which should not be exceeded. Perhaps the practice of killing infants with six fingers reported by missionaries to the San Carlos Apaches was based upon a taboo against exceeding this sacred number. The solar year was divided into 18 months of 20 days each, with five or six uncountable and unnamed days which were considered unlucky and purposeless because they lacked patron deities. The yearly round of the ceremonial calendar was based on the solar year. The great feast of Xiuhtecutli took place in January, ending the 18 month year. The sacred year was composed of four solar years. Each four years special ceremonies and sacrifices were conducted to mark the event.

Time was further broken up into 52-year sets. At the end of each such cycle, all fires were extinguished, even the 52 year-old fire in the temple. A New Fire Ceremony was held in which the priests ascended an extinct volcano, and when the Pleiades, symbol of Black God, or the star Aldebaran reached the zenith, a fire was kindled with a bow drill in the chest cavity of a sacrificial victim. Torchbearers dashed through the night, lighting the fires of all the temples throughout the countryside. From these fires the people carried the new fire to their own hearths. The sun rose the next morning on a new 52-year cycle, and the populace rejoiced that the world had not yet come to an end (Vaillant 1950:199, 200).

RAVEN MYTHS

According to Athapaskan myth, Raven was originally a white bird (see Figure 14), but his feathers were blackened when he stole the sun and escaped with it through the smoke hole of the lodge of its former owner. This deed precipitated the moment of creation. Raven was caught with his sooty feathers, and has remained black ever since. All animals were tame in the state of primal flux. They were like the talking animals which appear in the shamanic state of consciousness. When, at the moment of creation, they were fixed in animal form, they needed protection. Black God was forced to hide the animals, because man had not yet learned the proper rules of hunting (Luckert 1975:178). He told his wife to give the animals the sense of smell to protect them from the hunters. She accomplished this feat by thrusting their snouts into her crotch, giving them a symbolic rebirth (Luckert 1975:135-6). Black God's wife will be considered in detail under Chalchihuitlique.

Raven's original condition as a white bird seems peculiar until one considers the extremely reflective nature of raven feathers. In 1997, my husband and I were driving from Payson to Roosevelt, Arizona. The road led along a ridge top above Slate Creek. The sun was high in the sky when suddenly our attention was attracted by two flashing mirror-like objects in the valley below. The flashes continued, moving rapidly toward us. As they drew closer, the sources of the flashing lights became apparent as two large, white, mirror-like birds winging their way up out of the valley. As they passed overhead, and their feathers ceased reflecting the bright sunlight, their true identity as a pair of ravens was revealed (cf. Feher-Elston 1991:13-18).

31

Procreation is another aspect of the prehuman primal flux. It partakes of the state before the solidification of creation, when the individual is "not yet". Similarly, myths of marriage with animals signify union with the gods in the state of prehuman flux (Luckert 1975:146). According to Navajo tradition, Black God/Fire God created all the stars. His own symbol is the Pleiades, which mark his face (Coe 1975:24).

The history of Raven is complex. In a Jicarilla Apache myth, Raven's trickster aspect earns him the name of "Gambler". In this story, Gambler, along with his pet turkey, floated down the river inside a hollow log. The turkey shook corn from his wings so that man could start a farm (Luckert 1975:220). This myth, outlining the introduction of improved seed stock as part of a Mesoamerican complex, will be considered below under Tlaloc.

Finally, Black God achieved his historic status among the Navajos as god of the north who is the patron of all the wild animals who raise their own young. The historic status of Black God has been greatly affected by Pueblo myth. Raven from the north becomes fused with the dark-skinned god of fire, death, and the underworld. Instead of the vigorous titan, Black God has become the Massau of the pueblos under the guise of the Navajo black keeper of the game, *Haashch'eeshini* (Luckert 1975:178-9).

ARCHAEOLOGICAL RAVEN SPECIMENS

Where the Raven artifacts and sacrifices known from Southwest archaeological sites belong in all this confusion, is not always clear. Some pertain to the original introduction of Raven/Black God. Some pertain to the Mesoamerican Old Fire God/Guardian of the Hearth derivation of Raven/Black God. Some pertain to the Southern Athapaskan reintroduction of Black God as Lord of Beasts. Considering that most archaeological material comes from the excavation of Formative Stage sites, it is reasonable to expect that the context of their occurrence is that of a community raising Mesoamerican crops and practicing rituals necessary to assure the fruitfulness of those crops.

In modern times, Raven has sometimes become an element of dread. When I mentioned archaeological finds of ravens to an elderly Hopi informant, he shuddered, saying "Raven, the Destroyer!" He didn't want to talk about ravens. They didn't use them. " Perhaps down in [another village]" where he intimated there were reputed to be "bad people", someone might know about ravens.

In March 1993 I asked Michael Lacapa, Hopi/Tewa/Apache story-teller, about ravens and crows. He indicated that modern Hopis tend to associate Raven with deliberate, malicious, mental mal-practice which they classify as witchcraft, but Crow-Mother is often referred to as the mother of all the katsinas. Although this is the stated Hopi position today, it does not reflect the specimens recovered from archaeological sites. The earliest Raven remains I have seen are feathers which came from Sand Dune Cave near Navajo Mountain in the western Basketmaker area which is dated ca. A.D. 300-700. Common Raven bones are numerous in Southwest archaeological sites from Basketmaker to the historic period, but White-necked Raven and Crow bones are comparatively rare. A man depicted on a Mimbres B/W bowl appears to personify Raven (Brody *et al.* 1983:89). This representation is startlingly similar to an Upper Paleolithic cave painting of an entranced shaman

Figure 14. Left, entranced shaman with bird mask and bird staff from the bottom of a 23 foot shaft at Lascaux, France, Upper Paleolithic. After Prideaux 1973:130. Center, Mimbres Black-on-white bowl motif. After Brody 1983:89. Right, Mimbres Black-on-white bowl man-bird motif, which may depict Raven in both his human form and original white coloration. After Brody 1983:112.

with a bird mask and bird staff found at the bottom of a 23 foot shaft in the cave at Lascaux (Prideaux et al 1973:131). Modern Siberian shamans still use the stick or spear thrower topped by a bird as an emblem (Figure 14).

By the late 1200s, extending into the 1300s, Common Ravens are particularly conspicuous at Point of Pines and at Grasshopper Pueblo. At Grasshopper Pueblo, Common Ravens are clustered in one section of the pueblo, while Scarlet Macaws are clustered in another portion of the site, suggesting the presence of a social system marked by special usage of different birds of sacrifice by various segments of the community. In addition, these birds were deposited under and near the great kiva, suggesting that this structure was used for integrative activities pertaining to the whole community (McKusick 1982:91-92). The same situation is found at AZ W:10:50 at Point of Pines with clusterings of Scarlet Macaws, Ravens, and other birds of sacrifice and ritual usage in two separate parts of the dual community and a few specimens of each species in or adjacent to the great kiva, again suggesting integrative activities on behalf of the whole community (Avian files, Southwest Bird Laboratory).

Another contemporaneous site, which was occupied even longer, Mound 7 at Gran Quivira in New Mexico, had many Common Ravens, White-necked Ravens, and Common Crows. One find of interest from that site suggesting interchangability of species was a set of three left wing fans in graduated size from large to small: Common Raven, White-necked Raven, and Common Crow (McKusick 1981:53).

RAVEN SACRIFICES

In the late 1960s, Lyndon L. Hargrave had at Gila Pueblo a box about 2' x 2' x 3' tall completely filled with desiccated ravens. There were about two dozen birds. All but one had been sacrificed by a chop with a sharp-edged instrument through the bulbous rear of the skull (cf. Feher-Elston 1991:16-17). The other individual had been shot through the body with an aboriginal arrow which was still in place. Hargrave was unwilling to discuss the find, but indicated that it had been recovered from a volcanic tube, apparently in the badlands southwest of Albuquerque, probably near Grants, New Mexico. In addition to the ravens, the tube had contained the desiccated remains of a rattlesnake and an old woman. Who dropped the sacrificed ravens down this shaft year after year, or when they did it is unknown. Jon Young, who was also at Gila Pueblo during that time period suggested that the ravens might have been deposited one by one, every 52 years, as a reflection of the Mesoamerican New Fire Ceremony. If they can ever be located, it would be helpful to have them carbon dated. It seems most likely that they may be pueblo period sacrifices to Massau, since a volcanic tube is associated with both fire and the black underworld. Similarly, it would be interesting to know what may have been dropped into the subterranean blow hole at Wupatki during the years of the prehistoric visitation and occupation of that site.

RAVEN FETISHES

Hester (1962:114,118) illustrated three raven skin fetishes which had been cached in caves in the Gobernador district of New Mexico. Hester tended to associate them with early Navajos, but the fact that they were found in Pueblo jars is equally suggestive of their being Pueblo artifacts. These fetishes (McKusick 1981:45) seem, from probing with a fine needle, to be composed of the feathered skin, the anterior portion of the cranium, and the intact wings of the ravens. The skins are stuffed with wood and other vegetable material, and tightly wrapped around the sides with cordage.

Similar specimens consisting of the bones of the raven beaks and anterior crania have been found. One from Atsinna in the Cibola Area is dated A.D.1200-1400, one from Los Aguajes near Santa Fe is dated A.D. 1400-1500, and twelve Common Raven specimens and one Common Crow specimen recovered from Mound 7 at Gran Quivira, Salinas National Monument, in central New Mexico date between A.D. 1300 and 1540.

Placing the fetishes in caves may have been for safe storage, or it may have been ritually meaningful in that they were placed in a dark cave as a permanent offering. In any case, this usage predates the most recent movement of Athapaskans into northern and central New Mexico.

RAVEN SCRATCHERS

Another special Common Raven usage is the "Scratcher". Hester (1962:119) and the Franciscan Fathers (1929:372) describe the use of raven or crow beaks as scratchers in the "Enemy Way", a sing that Laura Gilpin (1968:235) described in detail in *The Enduring Navajo*. This ritual is concluded when the patient who is being cleansed from enemy contamination emerges from the ceremonial hogan on the last night of the sing with the scratcher in his hand. He jabs repeatedly at a pile of ashes representing the fallen foe. The scavenger bird symbolically devours the slain enemy, freeing the patient from the effects of the contamination of conflict. Premaxillae with wear on the beaks associated with use as a scratcher have been found in several archaeological sites. One from

BC 51 at Chaco Canyon dates ca. 1000-1100; two from Puaray date ca.1400-1500; and three from Mound 7, Gran Quivira, span the entire occupation, between 1300 and 1672 (McKusick 1981:45).

Stephen mentioned the Hopi custom of impaling a raven on the point of a lance "to feed on the enemies to be slain", which may antedate the Navajo use of the raven in the Enemy Way (Parsons1936:95).

RAVENS IN LATE MESOAMERICAN COSMOLOGY

Whether these artifacts were made from birds which had been deliberately raised for sacrifice, or were just from those which had been taken in the wild, cannot be determined. They do demonstrate a continuing regard for the raven as the destroyer, but not always as a harmful destroyer. Perhaps the term "unmaker" is more meaningful. Sometimes things have to be unmade so that they can be made again. All of this harks back to the state of flux symbolized by Raven before creation.

This concept also has a connection with Xolotl, a sinister aspect of Quetzalcoatl. As Quetzalcoatl, in the form of Venus as the Morning Star, called Tlahuizcalpantechutli, brings the sun up, Xolotl, in the form of Venus as the Evening Star, brings the sun down. Xolotl is depicted as frightful and sinister in appearance; but he is still a necessary part of the scheme of things. Raven is an early giver of good things from the north; Quetzalcoatl is a later giver of good things from the south. Luckert's suggestion of the blending of Raven with the dark side of Quetzalcoatl is a reasonable explanation but only partly accounts for a complicated chain of events.

On one hand, Di Peso (1974:Vol.2, 556-559) found evidence at Paquimé of the Xiuhtecutli Complex. Xiuhtecutli, Lord of Fire, has many guises. One is Xiuhcoatl, the fire Serpent, a sectioned blue serpent wearing a helmet or crest, which remains in modern pueblo religion as *Pa'lululona*. Still another appears to be, as Luckert suggests, the Western Pueblo Massau.

On the other hand, Di Peso had ample evidence at Paquimé of the cult of Xipe Totec, Our Lord the Flayed One, an aspect of Tezcatlipoca. Di Peso equates the observance of this deity which included scalping, the taking of trophy heads, cannibalism, and ceremonial intoxication, with modern Hopi activities of the Agave Society and Massau Katsinas (Di Peso 1974:Vol.2, 560-561).

Since the Quetzalcoatl Cult and the Tezcatlipoca Cult are complementary in the late years of the northern Southwest, aspects of both could have been combined in rituals which have come to honor Massau. From the Quetzalcoatl Cult comes the aspect of the Old Fire God. From the Tezcatlipoca Cult come the paraphernalia of Xipe Totec. Tezcatlipoca is above all the patron of the surface of the earth, so his survival as the Hopi earth god is reasonable. Luckert's view that the modern Navajo Raven partakes of the nature of the Hopi Massau moves the process of acculturation one step further.

On the surface, this sounds indescribably complex, but in the context of Mesoamerican world view, it is perfectly rational. The principal of personation is basic to any consideration of Mesoamerican supernaturals. Each supernatural had identifying masks, costumes, insignia of office,

Figure 15. Xiuhtecutli, wearing a paper fire serpent as a backpiece, and a stylized turquoise butterfly on his breast. The bird is a brilliant blue Cotinga. Codex Borbonicus. After Brundage 1979:23.

and face paint. These items normally served to identify them and their usual functions. However, when they were for some reason performing the duties of another supernatural, they could borrow the gear of any other supernatural except that of Xiuhtecutli. He was unique, original, from whom the other supernaturals derived their being. He is depicted as wearing a paper fire serpent as a backpiece and a stylized turquoise butterfly, the symbol of fire, on his breast (Figure 15). No other supernatural could wear this butterfly. The human personator of Xiuhtecutli was painted a golden yellow all over, with two black bars across his face (Brundage 1979:22,52). The male Northern Oriole duplicates this coloration. Their occurrence in archaeological avian collections may be the result of ceremonial or ritual use connected with the veneration of Xiuhtecutli.

There is no Aztec day name glyph for Raven, as there is for the symbols of many Mesoamerican supernaturals. However, there is a glyph for Vulture (Figure 16). Vultures are large, heavy-bodied carrion birds that have a hard time making a living. They must conserve their energy, so they remain on their perches until the sun is high enough to generate thermals to lift them from their roosts. They soar all day, and only flap their wings when taking off after feeding. In the evening vultures may be seen converging from all directions to their communal roosts. Vultures arrive in the Southwest at about the spring equinox. They remain until the fall equinox. Then they gather in huge "cauldrons" of circling birds and drift south to winter in Mexico.

Seasonal movements of ravens are complementary to those of vultures. At the fall equinox many ravens flap in from the north, scavenge throughout the winter, and then depart at about the spring equinox. At these points of interchange, ravens and vultures may be observed circling together. A few ravens remain through the year as nesting residents.

Vultures are so closely connected with the equinoxes that they fall naturally under Xiuhtecutli's patronage. Turkey Vulture bone occurs throughout the Southwest in small quantities at all time levels. The habit of Turkey Vultures of vomiting carrion when frightened might discourage approach, but they, like condor nestlings, are easily raised.

Michael Lacapa recounts a tale of the bringing of fire to mankind, who were at that time living in thick gloom. After other animals had failed in the task, Turkey Vulture succeeded in bringing fire to provide heat and light to man "from the east, where the fire is." In the

36

Figure 16. Left, Mimbres Black-on-white pottery fragment painted with a vulture. After Snodgrass, 1975:270. Right, day sign for Vulture. After Vaillant 1950:191.

process, his head and neck feathers were burned off, leaving only reddened skin. This tale is reminiscent of the Southern Athapaskan story of Raven's theft of the sun which resulted in creation.

Some archaeologists specializing in the Anasazi area have tended to equate cardinal and quartering directions and astronomical observation facilities with the development of the Katsina Cult. The study of avian remains, especially the documentation of birds of sacrifice, has led me to the opinion that directional and astronomical factors are far more basic, far earlier, and far more widespread than the Katsina Cult. It is not until after A.D. 400 at the earliest, that regional variations in avian remains begin to crystalize out of the early uniform basis of use which is typical of Whittlesey's Plain Ware horizon as discussed in Cordell (1984:233).

Perhaps the most succinct expression of the Raven Complex is a riddle the Aztecs asked of Sahagun (Sorensen and Dibble 1993:52):

"What is the Scarlet Macaw leading,
the Raven following?
The conflagration."

CHAPTER 7

THE MYTHICAL MOAN BIRD

One of the earliest, if not the earliest, South American and Mesoamerican supernatural was the Moan Bird, also known as the Muan Bird, or the Principal Bird Deity. It was variously pictured as resembling an owl, a macaw, or a vulture.

From Tierra del Fuego on the south, north along the Andes through Chile to Bolivia and Peru, the venerated bird was the condor. Condors are large black and white vultures with ten foot wingspans. The males weigh up to 25 pounds; females are slightly smaller. They nest every other year. The single whitish egg is laid on the ground, usually in a mountain cave. Incubation takes two months. The dark brown, downy young stays in the cave for two months after hatching, and must be provided with food by its parents for much longer, even after it is fledged. Condor chicks adapt well to captivity (McGahan and McGahan 1971:687,689, 691-692, 699).

Inca mythology held that at each dawn a condor carried the sun aloft from its nocturnal home in the sacred Lake Waynaqocha (McGahan and McGahan 1971:699). The condor was a symbol of power and health throughout the area. The wing bone was made into a ceremonial flute. Its ground bones were used to treat rheumatism and paralysis. The eyes were roasted and eaten to sharpen the sight. The stomach lining was used as a cure for breast cancer. The flesh was considered a general panacea, especially good for epilepsy and cardiac defects. Drinking the blood was reputed to lengthen life. Even the feathers were placed under the sleeping blanket to ward off nightmares (McGahan and McGahan 1971:690, 700).

Farther north in Mesoamerica, the Screech Owl is an early form of the Bird Deity. In Guerrero, a painting above the entrance to Oxtotitlan Cave depicts a man costumed as a green, horned owl. Green owls also occur in the art of Teotihuacan, and are frequently used to ornament mirrors, which were used for scrying or crystal gazing. Mirrors are the way of the shaman to another reality, and stand for supernatural caves or passageways. A cache from the Temple of Chac Mool at Chichen Itza contained a pyrite mirror placed beneath the remains of a burrowing pygmy owl and a finch (Miller and Taube 1993:128).

Owls, like other birds, were considered messengers between man and the supernatural. Because of their nocturnal activity and cave-dwelling habits, they stood in special position to the night and the underworld. The owl is depicted occupying the temple of the Aztec Death God, Mictlantecuhtli, who often wears an owl-feather crest. The Aztecs designated the feared, form-changing sorcerer as tlacatecolotl, or "owl-man" (Miller and Taube 1993:128).

Figure 17. Left, light colored Ocellated Turkey with "eyes" on its feathers like those of a peacock. Its neck is entwined with that of a King Vulture. A water spiral is used to indicate the eye of the vulture. Madrid Codex, after La Fay 1975:752. Right, the altar supports a head and blood sacrifice, presumably to the water god Tlaloc. Nuttall Codex, after Di Peso 1974: Vol. 2, 568. Below, a similar design showing what appears to be a Small Indian Domestic Turkey head sacrifice. Design from a Kechipawan Polychrome bowl, after Smith *et al* 1966:Figure 47.

40

The Muan-owl of the Maya was a horned owl which was connected with both fertility and corn, and with death and the underworld. The Codex Borgia depicts the horned owl with a skull for a head (Miller and Taube 1993:128,129).

A very early form of the Mayan Moan Bird, garbed in quetzal plumage with a serpent-like head, was a manifestation of Kukulcan, the local name for Quetzalcoatl. It also appears on a stele at El Castillo, which is on the west coast of Guatemala (Burland and Forman 1975:48).

By far the most common identification of the Mayan Moan Bird is the King Vulture, *Sarcorampus papa*. This impressive vulture is almost as large as the Harpy Eagle, and has a wing-spread of 6.5 feet. The adults are mainly pinkish-white and black. The bare skin of the head and upper neck are banded with orange, red, and blue. The bill is orange and black, with a conspicuous fleshy caruncle on the cere. The juvenile is sooty brown or blackish, with a small caruncle (Blake 1953:62, 63). This species occupies a range below 4000 feet, so it was important in areas outside central Mexico. The Zapotec deity, El Ave de Pico Ancho, which was identified by Alfonso Caso and Ignacio Bernal as a vulture, is identical to the Maya Principal Bird Deity. Protoclassic kings of La Mora and Kaminnaljuyu assumed the costume of this god. The King Vulture head, often with a headband, may be used for the word *ahau* in Mayan writing, signifying both the day sign and the word "lord" (Miller and Taube 1993:182).

The Madrid Codex pictures an Ocellated Turkey and a King Vulture facing each other with their necks intertwined (Figure 17- left). The body of the Ocellated Turkey is shown in white with "eyes" spotting its plumage, a fleshy caruncle falling over its beak, and its head crowned with a fleshy protuberance. The King Vulture is shown with its gaudily colored neck, a caruncle at the cere, and a black coloration (La Fay 1975:752). At first glance, the colors of the birds give the impression of being reversed. One usually thinks of turkeys as dark, and the King Vulture as pinkish white. However, the plumage of the immature vulture is dark. In the past, sacrificial meleagrids pictured in codices have simply been identified as "turkey". Now it appears that the crowned turkeys which are shown being sacrificed in Mayan codices are actually light-colored Ocellated Turkeys (Figure 18).

This brings me to the Small Indian Domestic Turkey. It has always troubled me that there was no readily apparent reason for a mutant, dark, feather-necked turkey to have been valued by the aboriginal inhabitants. However, after years of seeing this drawing of the juvenile King Vulture intertwined with the Ocellated Turkey, I am struck by the resemblance of the Small Indian Domestic Turkey to the juvenile King Vulture. Both had feathered necks, both had caruncles, both had gaudily colored heads, both had markedly dark plumage.

Lyndon Hargrave was fond of remarking that turkeys feathers in a cave meant human activity, not natural turkey nesting habits. He always finished his remarks by noting that "Vultures nest in caves, not turkeys." Hargrave was right. Vultures do indeed nest in caves. As cave nesters, vultures, like owls, are appropriate to associate with Tlaloc, the old rain god who inhabited mountain-top caves. The only reasonable model I have been able to devise to explain the careful culture of small Indian Domestic Turkeys for nearly 1900 years is that they were an easily propagated substitute for the juvenile vulture (Figure 17 - right and below).

41

Figure 18. Top, Maya turkey sacrifice. Dresden Codex, after Di Peso 1974:Vol. 2, 576. Below, Ocellated Turkey with cordage about the neck. Tro-Cortesianus Codex, after Di Peso, 1974:Vol 2, 602.

CHAPTER 8

THE SMALL INDIAN DOMESTIC TURKEY
AS TLALOC, RAIN SPIRIT OF TEOTIHUACAN

The development of Teotihuacan as a ceremonial and cultural center began in the second century B.C. Of their deities, Tlaloc, spirit of gentle rain falling on the fields, was most important (Burland and Forman 1975:13-14). The Jaguar God of the Olmecs is considered to be ancestral to Tlaloc because of a similarity of visage. Tlaloc is readily identifiable from about the beginning of the Christian Era, and was later adopted by other groups (Burland and Forman 1975:138). Tlaloc continued as a very important deity into Aztec times. The great pyramid at Tenochtitlan was topped by two temples, one to Tlaloc, the rain god, and one to Huitzilopochtli, the war god patron of the Aztec state (Burland and Forman 1975:23).

The homes of Tlaloc were within the tops of mountains where he gathered the rain clouds and sent them forth to water the fields (Burland and Forman 1975:26). The snow-capped mountain tops were not approached by travelers, since they were considered sacred to Tlaloc and his wife, Lady Precious Green, as the places from which rain came (Burland and Forman 1975:99).

Tlaloc (Figure 19) was also Lord of Tlalocan, a heaven where dwelled those who died from drowning or from diseases associated with water. It was full of lush vegetation supported by a constant light rain. Enlivened by butterflies and rainbows, it was a heaven full of singing and rejoicing for the inhabitants of the arid Plateau of Mexico (Burland and Forman 1975:30). Tlaloc was represented by four lesser forms of the rain spirit that were directional and seasonal in nature. The rain of the north brought destruction in the form of thunder storms, hail, and snow, white as dead man's bones. The rain from the east was thought of as golden, like corn, sprinkling the fields and bringing up the shoots of newly planted grain. The rich rain of summer fertility came from the south. It was considered blue, the sacred color of Tlaloc himself. Fall rain, which came from the west, was red to symbolize the evening sunset and the fruitfulness of harvest. It was also associated with wealth and success (Burland and Forman 1975:39). The Aztecs associated the constellation and astrological sign Aquarius, the Water Bearer, with Tlaloc (Burland and Forman 1975:103).

Di Peso (1974:Vol 2, 565-569; Vol. 8, 289) excavated burials of 121 headless turkeys from Paquimé. His research indicated that the development of the Tlaloc concept began much earlier with the old Olmec water deity. As time passed this deity was venerated among the Maya as Chac, among the Mixtec as Cocijo, and among the Totonac as Tajín. In his unmasked guise, Tlaloc's face was blackened with liquid rubber, spotted with white amaranth seed paste, and crowned with heron feathers. Tlaloc is most often depicted as garbed in a blue case mask distinguished by large round, flat eyes, much like those of a fish, a volute over the upper lip resembling the whiskers of a catfish, and four downward projecting teeth like those of a jaguar. A copper crotl in this form illustrates the

Figure 19. Left, Tlaloc, Bringer of Rain, in his masked form. After Vaillant 1950, Plate 59. Right, Day Sign symbol of Tlaloc. After Vaillant 1950:191.

presence of the Tlaloc concept at Paquimé (Figure 20).

Another symbol for Tlaloc, found throughout the Southwest Culture Area, is the stepped cloud terrace which appears in three dimensional stone carvings, in pottery designs, and on ceremonial headdresses and ritual paraphernalia. Tlaloc is further depicted in the form of the turkey. Di Peso found that the Mayans early offered sacrifices of turkeys to their rain spirits during the five intercalary days. Later, turkey gobblers were offered to Tlaloc on the Central Plateau. Gobblers may have been deemed especially appropriate, since their normally red heads and necks turn a bright turquoise blue when they are agitated, producing Tlaloc's own sacred red/blue color combination. Blood and cornmeal may have formed part of this ancient sacrifice, but the only portion we can document archaeologically is the isolated head, or the headless carcass. Codices depict the decapitated carcass, the sprinkled blood, and the turkey head offered on an altar (see Figures 17 and 18). Decapitated turkeys form offerings accompanying house dedications and death ceremonies at Paquimé. Di Peso points out that the people of the Western Pueblos regard speckled turkey feathers to be symbolic of rain, and the light tips on the tail feathers to be symbolic of foam. However, I believe that the change in color from red to blue of the gobbler's head is the trait which dictates the use of the head or head and neck as a suitable sacrifice to Tlaloc in particular.

Less frequent than turkey sacrifices, but still present at Paquimé, were child sacrifices which commonly honored Tlaloc farther to the south. The Tlaloques, the four directional avatars of Tlaloc, were portrayed as dwarves. Small children were sacrificed to personify these aspects of Tlaloc. It was considered especially propitious if they shed tears on their way to sacrifice. These children were sometimes walled up alive in caves on mountain tops, further depicting the Tlaloques.

The earliest turkey sacrifice in the Southwest Culture Area of which I am aware is the fully feathered natural mummy of a Small Indian Domestic gobbler which was recovered from a Basketmaker II deposit at Canyon del Muerto (McKusick 1986c:4, Figures 16, 17.) It is dated at ca. A. D. 250, or perhaps earlier, which makes it contemporaneous with the early occupation of

44

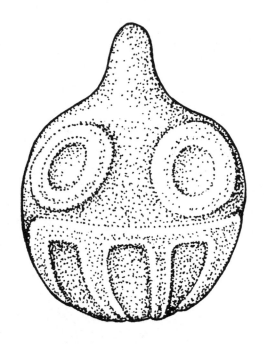

Figure 20. Copper crotl with the visage of Tlaloc from Paquimé. After Di Peso *et al.*, 1974: Vol. 2, 565.

Teotihuacan. The desiccated carcass has a piece of vegetal cordage about the neck (see Figure 18). Since this is a Small Indian Domestic or "Tularosa" Turkey, the neck is feathered to the base of the skull (Figure 21). This mutation makes it appear similar to the Ocellated Turkey depicted in Mayan codices, which has a neck feathered almost to the base of the skull, and a blue head with red caruncles and red eye ring. Like the Ocellated Turkey, the Small Indian Domestic head would have displayed Tlaloc's red/blue color combination even though the neck was concealed.

Basketmaker III levels at Tseahatso, a large cave in Canyon del Muerto, yielded the desiccated carcasses of approximately 300 turkeys (McKusick 1986c:6). They were probably Small Indian Domestics, but were not saved. Jonathan Reyman tells me that Frank Roberts' field notes at the National Anthropological Archives for 1932 and 1933 discuss a fair number of turkey burials from the White Water District which often had jewelry around their necks and other grave goods with them. Breed is unknown. All of these burials are early. Nothing like them has been recovered from Pueblo III and later sites, nor is their mention of such in the ethnographic literature.

Late evidences of turkey head or head and neck sacrifice are the 121 found at Paquimé and one each at Casa Grande and Gila Pueblo in Arizona. The specimens from Paquimé were headless burials. Those from Casa Grande and Gila Pueblo were neck bones of immature females that had received special burial. The Casa Grande turkey was a Small Indian Domestic; the Gila Pueblo turkey was too young for definite determination of breed, but was more like the Small Indian Domestic. Both of these birds had to have been imported during their first fall, when their first black plumage edged with white was mature, since it is too hot at both sites for successful turkey breeding. It is important to note that male turkeys of this age still wear their brown-toned juvenile plumage. The females mature much earlier than the males, and would have been a beautiful glossy black at this stage of their development. Perhaps their fresh black plumage, with its white margins, was desired because it duplicated the black and white coloration of the face paint of the unmasked Tlaloc personator. These females died in their first fall, in late October or November, which coincides with the Aztec ceremony of Tepeilhuitl, The Feast of the Mountains, honoring Tlaloc (Vaillant 1950:196).

TURKEY MYTHOLOGY

Michael Lacapa, Hopi/Tewa/Apache story-teller, has offered the following story for use in this chapter:

A long, long time ago, Turkey was a proud upright bird. Then one day something hit him on the head. He ducked. What was that? Something hit him on the head again, and he ducked to the other side. It was the rain! Turkey kept ducking, but the rain drops kept hitting him on the head. Even today, Turkey bobs his head from side to side.

Soon water began to rise. Turkey flew up into a pine tree, but still the rain drops fell on his head and the water rose higher. Turkey flew from one tree to the next, higher and higher as the water rose, until he came to the top of the tallest mountain. There was only a little land left, just big enough for him to stand on. The brown flood water swirled around him, covered with foam. By this time turkey was very tired. First one wing drooped, then the other wing drooped, and finally his tail drooped, falling into the water. This woke Turkey up, but ever since then, the tips of his tail feathers have been the color of foam.

Even more interesting than feather color is the posture of Turkey. At first he had been upright, but dodging raindrops, he had become stooped. This is a perfect description of the Small Indian Domestic Turkey which was conspicuously hump-backed. Pre-columbian pottery designs depict the three turkey breeds present in the North American Southwest, the Small Indian Domestic, the Large Indian Domestic, and Merriam's Wild Turkey (Figures 21, 22).

SMALL INDIAN DOMESTIC DISTRIBUTION

The earliest evidence of the Tlaloc Cult was among the Olmecs, and Mayan influence was felt in Southwestern iconography right down into the historic period. The Small Indian Domestic is a small, short-shanked, hump-backed intensely black feather-necked turkey. Its intense black coloration indicates that it was domesticated from a stock living in moist lowlands. The Small Indian Domestic Turkey was presumably domesticated in response to the needs of the Tlaloc Cult in the moist coastal lowlands extending from eastern Mexico to southwestern Texas, and was introduced from that direction, moving across southern New Mexico, from southeast to northwest, to the Tularosa Cave area and thence northward to the Four Corners. It became the basic stock at what was to become the trading center of Yellow Jacket by Basketmaker III times. It persisted as a separate breed at Antelope House in Canyon de Chelly for its entire occupation, and was the specialty of the Tompiro Pueblos until the fall of Gran Quivira in 1672, when the breed was extinguished.

All turkey sacrifices to Tlaloc north of Paquimé involved the Small Indian Domestic. At Paquimé, where the turkeys were of mixed breed, the feather-necked individuals would have been obvious, regardless of whether their bones were pure Small Indian Domestic or not. This preference for the Small Indian Domestic for sacrifice to Tlaloc may explain why such effort was made through almost 1200 years to keep the breeds separate, and why they were maintained in the areas where they have been found.

The Small Indian Domestic is first known in large numbers from Basketmaker II levels at Canyon del Muerto, Arizona, and on Black Mesa in the Lolomai Phase, 100-300. Rain on the fields was important at this stage of horticultural development. In Basketmaker III times, when the hardier Large Indian Domestic was introduced to the Four Corners Area, during the 500s, the Small Indian Domestic was displaced, but remained the preferred breed on Black Mesa where rain on the fields is so important. The largest stronghold of the Small Indian Domestic was the Tompiro Pueblos of the Eastern Periphery. The sandy land was so dry there that water shortage was a continuing problem. The Salinas, or salt pans, to the east, held water only intermittently. Like Black Mesa, rain was of the greatest importance. From these sources, it appears that limited numbers of Small Indian Domestics were dispersed to other areas. At Antelope House in Canyon de Chelly, one section of the settlement kept Small Indian Domestics, while the majority of the settlement kept Large Indian Domestics.

Of particular interest are three Small Indian Domestic Turkeys recovered from the excavation of Arroyo Hondo Pueblo. They date to the 1330s, a time of peak population. About 1335 a drought began, as evidenced by an absence of aquatic birds. The occurrence of the Small Indian Domestic Turkeys at this time may indicate an attempt to propitiate the rain god, Tlaloc. These turkeys are coincidental in time with the importation of pottery from the Socorro, New Mexico, area, which indicates their most probable point of origin is the Tompiro Pueblos (Lang and Harris 1984:95, 135).

There were even a few Small Indian Domestic Turkeys on Mesa Verde which may have been traded in from Yellow Jacket, another Small Indian Domestic source. Small Indian Domestics turn up at a variety of sites in southern Arizona in late prehistoric times such as Reeve Ruin, University Indian Ruin, Casa Grande, and probably Gila Pueblo. These could have come from the Tompiro Pueblos or from Paquimé. A confirmation of the worship of Tlaloc among the Hohokam is the recovery of a Chac Mool figure from the second Snaketown excavation dating to the 600s or 700s according to Dean's 1990 dating (Haury 1976:346; Dean 1991).

SMALL INDIAN DOMESTIC TURKEY FETISH

The Small Indian Domestic Turkey sacrifice recovered from the Basketmaker II cave in Canyon del Muerto has been examined by Gary Nabhan. He reports (1989:156-157) that after the head of the turkey was severed from the cordage-wrapped neck, a corn cob was thrust into the body in the area of the crop, between the furcula (wishbone) and spine, resulting in a turkey fetish. Approximately 900 years later, this same motif appears in a Mimbres Classic bowl design which depicts a small, dumpy turkey with a corn cob for a neck (Figure 22).

SMALL INDIAN DOMESTIC TURKEY SUMMARY

In summary, the contemporaneous appearance in the Southwest of the Tlaloc Cult and the Small Indian Domestic Turkey is relevant to an increased interest in farming. The Southwest is marginal at best for the survival of turkeys, and there were no wild turkeys before the introduction of the domestic breeds. The Small Indian Domestic was completely dependant upon human husbandry. Its very presence implies a surplus of corn and/or beans which could be used for

Figure 21. Turkeys raised by the Pre-columbian inhabitants of the Southwest Culture Area. Front center, Small Indian Domestic, hump-backed, short-shanked, and feather-necked. Back, Large Indian Domestics of aberrant colorations: Left, Silver Phase; Center, Erythristic (Smoke Gray); right, Pied Mutation.

turkey feed. It did not have the genetic diversity to survive in the wild, and needed to be fed by its keepers. One does not independently invent a fragile turkey breed in the hinterlands where there are no turkeys at all. Therefore, I believe it is reasonable to suppose that the presence of Small Indian Domestic turkeys, plus turkey sacrifices, indicates the presence of at least a few people who knew how to produce a luxury item like a specialized ceremonial turkey breed, and the food to feed it. The simplest explanation is that this phenomenon was a complex involving improved seed corn, the songs to sing to make it come up, a patron supernatural to oversee its growth and productivity , and a suitable sacrificial bird to keep that supernatural happy.

When these turkeys became more abundant, they were used for feathers to make robes and for other purposes as well as for sacrifice. The Small Indian Domestic Turkey has not previously been seen as elite goods, but it was. Elite goods are generally considered necessary to keep elite persons in power. I cannot picture elite personages in power during these early centuries. The idea of the importation of elite goods to propitiate the supernatural is much more palatable. Perhaps we should take a second look at what elite goods are really intended to accomplish.

Figure 22. Top left, Merriam's Wild Turkey, Mimbres Classic bowl design. After Cosgrove and Cosgrove 1932. Plate 216. Top right, Large Indian Domestic Turkey, Mimbres Classic bowl design. After Brody 1977: Figure 3. Lower left, Small Indian Domestic Turkey, Ramos Polychrome, design file card, The Amerind Foundation. Lower right, Turkey with a corncob for a neck, similar to the Basketmaker II turkey sacrifice/fetish, Mimbres Classic bowl design. After Cosgrove and Cosgrove 1932: Plate 215. The necks of the top two examples are bare. The lower examples show only the heads to be bare.

CHICKENS AS A SACRIFICE TO TLALOC

George Carter has traveled extensively in Mexico collecting specimens of various chicken breeds, chicken linguistic material, and chicken usage. He tells me that the Tarahumara are still walling up small black chickens in caves as sacrifices which parallel Pre-columbian sacrifices of children to Taloc. In addition, if a person is ill, a chicken is placed in a pit in the floor of their room covered with a mat. As the chicken slowly dies from lack of food and water it complains piteously, which is considered effective in drawing the attention of the supernatural to the needs of the patient. After the chicken dies, the hole is filled in with dirt. Carter suggests that early historic burials of chickens beneath room floors, and prehistoric burials of turkeys beneath room floors, and burials of turkeys beneath beds at Paquimé may be instances of this practice.

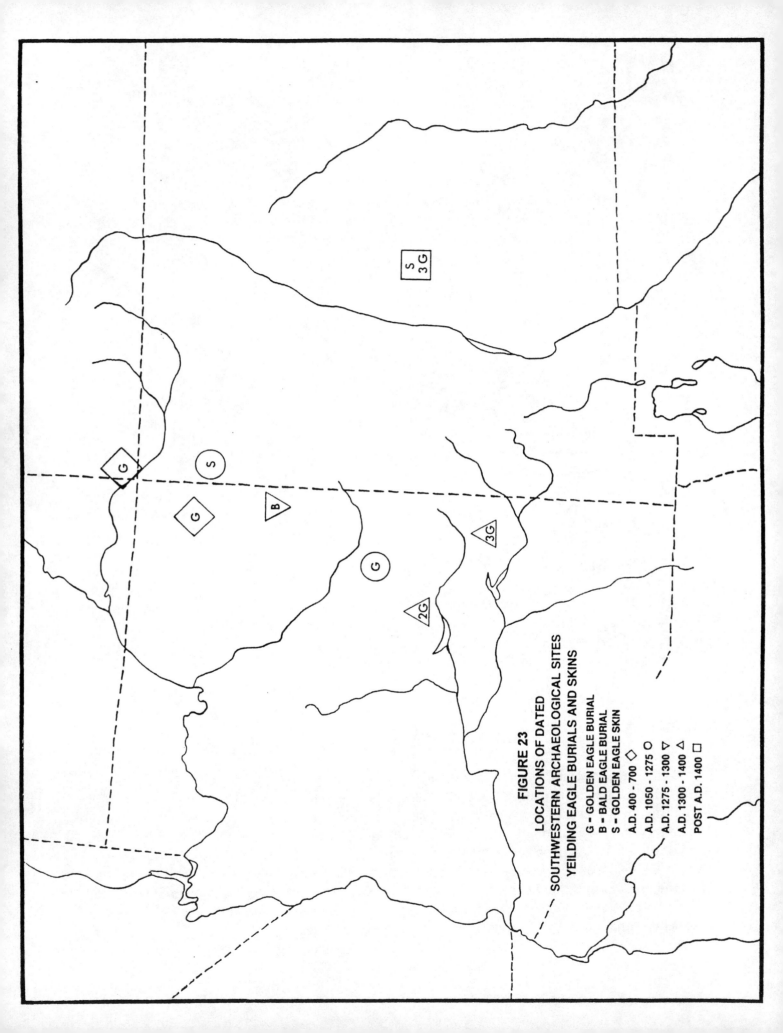

FIGURE 23

LOCATIONS OF DATED
SOUTHWESTERN ARCHAEOLOGICAL SITES
YEILDING EAGLE BURIALS AND SKINS

G = GOLDEN EAGLE BURIAL
B = BALD EAGLE BURIAL
S = GOLDEN EAGLE SKIN

A.D. 400 - 700 ◇
A.D. 1050 - 1275 ○
A.D. 1275 - 1300 ▽
A.D. 1300 - 1400 △
POST A.D. 1400 ☐

CHAPTER 9

EAGLE AS SUN AND TONATIUH

To discuss eagles in ceremonial, ritual, and sacrificial contexts, it is necessary to know something about eagles: the kinds, their distributions, and some of their attributes valued by Native Americans, and eagle-related attitudes and practices of Native Americans (see Figure 23, opposite). For these and other reasons a comparative osteology of eagles is presented in the taxonomic and osteological portion of this volume. A general discussion is presented here. The comparative osteology study was undertaken to serve several purposes:

1. Due to the endangered species status of eagles, it was no longer possible to borrow eagle skeletal material for comparative purposes. The drawings go a long way toward enabling the North American eagles to be identified to species without borrowing skeletons.

2. Lyndon Hargrave was of the opinion that modern wild eagles are much smaller than those found in archaeological sites because of some recent climatic change. This hypothesis did not hold up. It was demonstrated, after the age stages had been established, that the small specimens in his collection were small because they were immature, and had not yet realized their full growth potential.

3. I hypothesized that Bald Eagles have been "endangered" for a very long time. This hypothesis was verified by examining the proportion of Golden Eagles to Bald Eagles in Pleistocene collections from the La Brea Tar Pits, from archaeological collections, and from modern collections. It is apparent that Bald Eagles have been very few compared to Golden Eagles since the Pleistocene. One reason for this is no doubt that while they do fish and hunt small animals, they are opportunistic scavengers, and there is only so much carrion to go around. The reason they are so scarce in archaeological sites may have to do with their color, range, and nesting habits.

Immature Bald Eagles and Golden Eagles both have brown mixed with white on their tails. Tail feathers of immature Golden Eagles are splotched with white. Tail feathers of immature Bald Eagles are clouded with brown, and only become uniformly white with adulthood. Tail feathers of immatures of both species have been recovered from dry sites in the Southwest. However, the golden mantle over the head and shoulders of Golden Eagles is more reminiscent of the sun, to which it is sacrificed.

Golden Eagles are not only holarctic, but they range down into Mexico as well. Bald Eagles are found in more northerly regions of North America. Bald Eagles were not present in Mesoamerica to become incorporated into their religious ceremonies, but Golden Eagles do appear in

Mesoamerican myth and legend. As Mesoamerican religious concepts moved northward into the Southwest, they would have involved only the Golden Eagle.

Another factor in prehistoric eagle usage was undoubtedly the difficulty of obtaining Bald Eagles. Bald Eagle nests are often in the tops of dead snags. The nests, which grow year by year until the tree collapses from the accumulated weight, are inaccessible. On the other hand, Golden Eagles nest in cliffs, from which it is relatively easy to obtain eaglets.

ARCHAEOLOGICAL EAGLE SPECIMENS

Archaeological occurrences of Golden Eagle and Bald Eagle burials, skins, bones, bone artifacts, feathers, and feather artifacts are presented in Table 10 at the end of Chapter 20.

Eagle as Sun first appears in the osteological record in Basketmaker III deposits dating between A.D. 400-700 (Figure 23). The simultaneous occurrences of eagle feather artifacts, eagle bone artifacts, and an eagle burial with offerings suggest that a long tradition of eagle usage existed previous to the deposit of these specimens. A later indication of a preoccupation with Sun as an important supernatural is found at Sunflower Cave at Marsh Pass, west of Kayenta, Arizona, and at Bonita Creek Cave, which is located in southeast Arizona on a tributary of the Gila River. At these sites carved and painted wooden sunflowers were found associated with carved and painted wooden birds and cones; the latter were interpreted as plume holders (Haury 1958:4; Wasley 1962). Sunflowers turn to follow the sun's east to west path across the sky. In the morning they again face east, greeting the sun as it rises.

It is likely that the beginning of ceremonial usage of eagles in the Southwest is contemporaneous with the beginning of ceremonial use of the Small Indian Turkey in the veneration of Tlaloc, since sun and rain are both essential for dry farming.

EAGLE ARTIFACTS

Excavators are sometimes reluctant to risk damage to fragile artifacts which might occur during their transportation to a faunal specialist for identification. There are no doubt many eagle bone artifacts in museum collections which are not identified to species. Eagle bone artifacts are most commonly tubes made from the ulna, which was a major trade item from Taos, Picuris, and Pecos to the Plains. Eagle claws are also fairly common trade items. Fipple flutes made from eagle ulnae are probably the next most common eagle bone artifact (Figure 24).

EAGLE SACRIFICE

Eagle burials appear in small numbers, particularly associated with ceremonial structures, through Southwestern prehistory (Figure 23). Because eagles have generally been buried in special eagle cemeteries remote from settlements they are rarely encountered by archaeological excavations, and these small numbers are probably an under-representation. Eagles are still sacrificed by the Hopi today. The following transcript is from an interview with an aged Hopi informant who was born

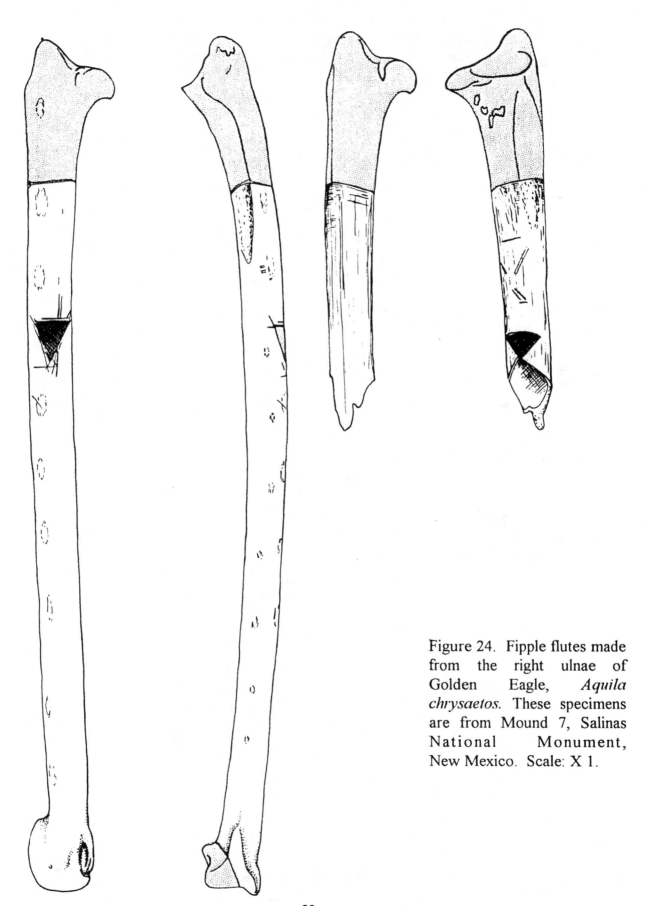

Figure 24. Fipple flutes made from the right ulnae of Golden Eagle, *Aquila chrysaetos*. These specimens are from Mound 7, Salinas National Monument, New Mexico. Scale: X 1.

around 1905. I prefer to withhold his name, since in the past he and his wife have suffered extensive property damage as the result of his assistance to anthropologists. When I mentioned this to Michael Lacapa, he nodded in agreement and said "There are those who do that." He paused thoughtfully, and then continued "It's their job to do that."

The photographs in Figures 25 and 26 are from the Voth Collection, and are roughly contemporaneous with the period described below:

Q. I'm working on birds, and I think there were two different groups. One they go out and hunt or snare and use the feathers. And then, there's another group that they took home as babies, and raised up, and then sacrificed in the old days. Now, does this seem reasonable to you? Like ravens, and owls, and hawks, and eagles, and parrots were all raised up, and then they were sacrificed. But if you go out and get a Blue Jay or something, that isn't something you raise with your family. Does that sound reasonable? Am I crazy, or is that two different groups of birds?

A. It is an entirely different type of thing, different tribes - the Hopi only sacrifice at the Home Dance.

Q. The only thing you have ever seen raised for sacrifice, or sacrificed at all, is eagles?

A. That's right.

Q. Have you ever seen a parrot sacrificed?

A. No. That part I haven't, but I have been told by one of my elders at a time when I was questioning, he was Bow Clan, so they know, he is the one that told me that, that they, because of their katsina dance, the reason why they do that, was because we have a Parrot Clan. Due to that respect, when they raise them up and they could no longer go on to produce their feathers, then is when they sacrificed.

Q. How did they kill them?

A. They kill them just like [eagles], first of all they suffocate them. There's no bones broken. It's the same thing that we do with the eagles. My father, I've seen them, because I've participated, and I've also participated in taking them to the burial. It's a very, very deep ceremonial, because they are the same birds we are going to get next year. No life is ever destroyed.

Q. How are they buried? They're picked, there's no feathers on them?

A. There's no feathers on them, that's right. And you see, at that time they've made all these preparations. With a blanket like I've told you.

Q. A blanket they got when they were first brought home? To be buried?

54

A. [The informant brought out two small blankets, white with red stripes.] Now this is the difference in the patterns. Now this is for the girls, if a baby died. Now I've got my blanket from my grandfather. If a baby dies, it's wrapped in it. Now this is for a boy.

Q. Yes, I see the difference. The boys' have three bands of white and the two narrow in the middle, whereas the girls' have four bands of white and then the two narrow bands in the middle. How do they catch the eagle? Do they take it out of the nest?

A. I went on a couple of them. My father and my brother, in secret, went out all together out west from Oraibi, where they call it the Bear Spring. I haven't seen that ruin at Bear Spring, but it was right up from there on the cliffs. We put a gunny sack on the rope, and then teased the eaglets with a rock in it so we could swing it back and forth. Finally, they got a little bit mad and they grabbed at that gunny sack and got caught.

Q. It caught their claws?

A. Yes. Then we shook it out, and they all fall down there, so we just went down and picked them up. [Another time we went out west of Moencopi] and did the same thing. And then we bring them home on a blanket. They used to have a cage they put those eaglets in, if they were lucky enough. They were lucky to get so many. So they used to make a cage out of willow, when they're green they bend up, and put them on a burro. And they bring them home on a burro.

Q. What do they feed them? Who goes out and catches the rats and mice and things for them? Little boys?

A. Boy, oh boy! Have I had that experience! I had about - many of my friends, rabbits! We went out trapping squirrels, prairie dogs! Ha! Anything that we could get! And then we bring them home. We took the skins off. And then each boy had his own place, we had this volcanic rock, and we started pounding this meat up. And then each would go to his pal and give him that early in the morning. When they get to love you, they don't bother you at all.

The least number when I did, I guess about 1912, was about 17 eagles. And then the next largest crop we had was, I think, about 21. It was just covered up on top! I can hear them calling right now!

After they're done, my father and all our uncles would be there, the Bear Clan would be there, and each would bring their eagle. First we laid them out. And my grandmother would give them food on their journey, cornmeal to eat, all laid down in a row. They would do that. And my father and all the rest of them make a little bow. And they could tell the male from the female, and they laid the little dolls [indicting the flat type of katsina doll], they would make that. And they laid them in front of them, the little dolls and the little bows. Sometimes there were more dolls than bows. Those are the male and the female eagles. When the chief picks them up for burial, he picks the one up at the head, he fixes it up with cornmeal in his hand, and wraps it up, each in its own blanket.

When they bring them in, they lift up the tail. There is one special fluffy; it is the

Figure 25. Upper left, an eagle sits on its rooftop roost at Hopi. Upper right, removing the tethered eagle from its perch prior to sacrifice. Lower left and right, plucking the sacrificed eagle. Photos from the H. R. Voth Collection. Prints courtesy of the Southwest Archeological Center, Gila Pueblo, Globe, Arizona.

Figure 26. Feathers from the sacrificed eagle utilized in an altar arrangement. Hopi. Photo from the H. R. Voth Collection. Prints courtesy of the Southwest Archeological Center, Gila Pueblo, Globe, Arizona.

most perfect feather in the whole world. It is the first one they pull out. After all these other ceremonies, that is the one they pull out. That is the one that they use at the time of So-yal. That was the one, and they make - my father's chief kiva, they spun a long cord. It came up from the fire place, all the way up the kiva, all the way to the plaza, all the way to the east, at the end, that's the one [feather]. It's life everlasting.

Then each one takes their eagle, we go out to a certain place for burial. And then when we get over there, they've already been out there to prepare for it, for the number of eagles we have, they've got it all ready, and each one puts in their own place and gives them food for their journey, and for male and female, they put the bows and dolls on top, to propagate life of eagles. So, according to our story, each year, we have the same eagle back. No life ever dies.

Q. What about the Red-tailed Hawks? Were they treated much the same way?

A. Yes, they're treated just the same way. It works to give us everlasting life, nothing else. I'm a great believer in it.

TONATIUH

The earliest bird associated with Sun in Mesoamerica appears to be the King Vulture, which is as large as a Harpy Eagle. In early Maya times this is equated with the Principal Bird Deity (Miller and Taube 1993:182). This early concept connects Raven's stealing the sun with Vulture bringing fire to man, and the later view of the sun as a flying eagle. The next bird associated with the sun is the Scarlet Macaw (see Macaw as the Mayan Old Sun God which follows). The association of the Golden Eagle with Sun may have developed in the North American Southwest and traveled south in late prehistoric times. In Aztec mythology, the highest heaven was populated with those who had given their lives to benefit the nation such as slain warriors, sacrificial victims, and women who died in childbirth. This was a glorious place where eagles accompanied the warriors and carried messages from the sun to the earth.

Sun, in the person of Tonatiuh, He Who Shines Forth, was depicted in sculpture as a diving eagle (Burland and Forman 1975:31, 102-103). He is also the deity carved into the center of the famous Calendar Stone. In paintings he appears with red body paint, an eagle feather headdress, and a large, rayed, solar disk (see Figure 27; Miller and Taube 1993:172).

QUAIL AND DOVES

The bird associated with Tonatiuh in his day hour aspect was the Mearns Quail (Miller and Taube 1993:54). The males of this species are black with white spots, which in Mesoamerican symbolism signifies the night sky. Quail, like doves, vocalize at sunrise. Quail are also very vocal at sunset. This is probably an important factor in making them appropriate temple sacrifices (Hultkrantz 1979:278).

Figure 27. Upper left, The Sun as Tonatiuh, showing the sun disc behind his head. After Krupp 1983:66. Upper right, Eagle Day Sign symbol of Tonatiuh. After Vaillant 1950:191. Lower, the sign for Tenochtitlan is the eagle upon the cactus growing out of the Earth Mother. The ripe, red cactus fruit are symbolic of sacrificial human hearts. After Brundage 1979:146.

Figure 28. Mimbres Classic bowl design of a quail hunter garbed as a deer may illustrate a myth of solar renewal. After Brody *et al.* 1983:98.

Quail play an important part in the myth in which Sun, the posthumous son, resurrects his father, the sun of the previous day. In this myth, the son stops to hunt quail, at which moment the bones of the old sun turn into a deer which springs away into the north, streaming rays of light. The deer was a mammalian personator of the sun (Brundage 1979:38). A painting on a Mimbres bowl depicting a quail hunter with deer antlers may depict a version of this myth (Figure 28).

The face of the personator of Tonatiuh was painted white with bands of black across the forehead, nose, and chin. Several species of quail found in Mesoamerica wear these markings (Leopold 1959:232-233, 238, 258), but the Mearns' quail is most conspicuous. The Mearns' Quail is illustrated in the Codex Mendoza (Time-Life 1992a:43) and in Mimbres Pottery (Bradfield 1931:302) (Figure 29 - top).

Random bones of quail, which occur throughout Southwestern archaeological sites from early to late, have until now been considered as food remains. However, a burial of a sub-adult quail has recently been reported for the Mimbres Area (Shaffer 1991:169). Many realistic depictions of all three Southwestern species are found on Mimbres pottery: Scaled Quail, *Callipepla squamata*; Gambel's Quail, *Lophortyx gambellii*; and Mearns Quail, *Cyrtonyx montezumae*. Both Gambel's Quail and Mearns Quail males have black and white facial markings. In addition to realistic depictions of quail, there are quail ornamented with radiating floral designs, which may have solar significance (Figure 29 - bottom center). According to Florence Hawley Ellis, modern Rio Grande Indians consider that flowers are the gifts of the sun. They are especially associated with initiations involving the sun, which she believes is probably a Mesoamerican concept (Ellis 1975:81).

The radiating designs on another Mimbres quail (Figure 29 - bottom right) are reminiscent of astronomical symbols. The four-pointed star is a symbol for Venus; the flower-like design is more appropriate to the sun. This particular flower appears to be an Evening Primrose. These conspicuous yellow flowers unfurl themselves in a matter of a few seconds at sundown. They are visited by late-

Figure 29. Top Row, The Male Mearns Quail, *Cyrtonyx montezumae*, has the black and white facial markings of the personator of Huitzilopochtli. The body is black, spotted with white, symbolic of the night sky and of Tezcatlipoca, of whom Huitzilopochtli is an avatar. Left, Mimbres Classic, Eby Site. After Brody 1977:159. Middle, Mimbres Classic, Cameron Creek Village. After Bradfield 1931: Plate LXXVI. Right, Codex Mendoza 1978:33.

Bottom Row, Radiating designs on quail. Left, Evening Primrose, *Oenothera hookeri*, has four petals with a central fold, a pistil with four divisions, and eight stamens. Center, a Quail ornamented with the sunburst or Evening Primrose design which signifies the sun. The bars on the petals painted on the center quail are apparently depictions of the male stamens, and form the same design as the eight-spoked solar wheel of the Old World, as well as a solar design in the New World. Right, quail decorated with the four-pointed star signifying the planet Venus. Both designs from Swarts Ruin in the Mimbres Valley. After Cosgrove and Cosgrove 1932: Plate 215.

Figure 30. Top left, male Mearns Quail surmounted by a tomato hornworm. Mimbres Classic. After Brody 1977:199. Above right, adult Tomato Worm Moth, *Protoparce sexta*, with spread wings. This is a member of the Hawk Moth or Hummingbird moth Family, Sphingidae. After Storer 1943:499. Below, Hawk Moths with folded wings and quartered directional symbols which may signify solstices and equinoxes. Lower Left, Matsaki Polychrome, 1475-1600, Hawikuh. After Smith *et al.*, 1966: Plate 72. Lower right, Hawikuh Polychrome, 1630-1680, Hawikuh. After Smith *et al.*, 1966: Pl. 77.

flying hummingbirds and Hawk Moths.

A Mimbres bowl design of a Mearns Quail is surmounted by a Hornworm, the larval form of the Hawk Moth (Figure 30). The quail stands on a line from which sprouts an Evening Primrose as it appears in the daylight before the flowers open for their nocturnal blooming. From the line hang a feather and a rattle; this combination of symbols is associated with sunset. The body of the quail is filled in with the design that represents corn, instead of simple dots. Larval hornworms pupate underground, only to emerge again as adult moths, recalling Sun's nightly journey through the Underworld. And the stripes on the hornworms's neck are not the markings of a real hornworm, but may be an allusion to those on Tezcatlipoca's face.

Adult Hawk Moths themselves have markings that may represent the Sun's sojourn in the Underworld: conspicuous yellow spots separated by black bars parallel the face paint coloration of Tezcatlipoca, the late solar warrior. And the spots may also represent the sun in the underworld, the way those of the jaguar do, and perhaps those on Mearns Quail (see additional discussion in Chapter 14). Other Southwestern depictions of Hawk Moths may have additional astronomical associations (Figure 30-bottom).

Mimbres sites are on a main north-south trade route. Mesoamerican association of quail with the sun would not be out of place there. Quail are an obvious choice of symbol for the sun, since they are rather quiet during the day, but vocalize extensively at sunrise and at sunset.

HUMMINGBIRD

The hummingbird is associated with the Sun as Huitzilopochtli. Since this is an aspect of the southern Tezcatlipoca, and is connected with warriors, hummingbirds are considered in that section, following (Chapter 14).

Figure 31. Mayan Macaw holding torches from the Schellhaus God List published in 1904. After Miller and Taube 1993:147.

CHAPTER 10

SCARLET MACAWS AS THE OLD SUN GOD

The Scarlet Macaw, *Ara macao*, from its earliest to latest appearances is associated with two astronomical bodies, the sun and the planet Venus. The earliest occurrence of Scarlet Macaw is among the Maya in the centuries shortly before A. D. 1. It was a symbol of the sun god. Figure 31, opposite, is noted in print as a Military Macaw-man. This is improbable. The beak of the Military Macaw is black, but the upper beak of this personage is white like that of the Scarlet Macaw.

In this time and place the Old Sun God was pictured in profile as an old man with a Roman nose and a large eye (Coe 1975:10). As well as being the sun god, he appears to be identical to Itzamná the "god of the heavens" who was also the "learning god" or the "wise god" (Helfritz 1968:144). In these early times, Macaw symbolizes the patron of an agricultural society composed of small villages.

After 400, when strong centralized government was developing, Scarlet Macaw became the patron of a whole dynasty of Mayan Rulers. This occurred at Copán, which can be translated "Macaw Mountain." The first in the dynasty, Xax Kuk Mo, "Resplendent Quetzal-Macaw," ascended to power in 430. The first part of the dynastic art work dealt with the sun and Venus. Later, art work reflected a preoccupation with war as the social organization disintegrated. The last king in the dynasty, Yax Pac, "Rising Sun," held power until the beginning of the ninth century (Stuart 1988:147-152).

Yax Pac erected an impressive altar depicting the entire 16 rulers of the dynasty circling about it so that he was pictured receiving the insignia of office from his ancestor, Yax Kuk Mo. Behind the altar were crypts, a large one containing the bones of 15 jaguars, and smaller ones containing macaw bones (Stuart 1989:497).

The association of the deity symbolized by the Scarlet Macaw with rulership, which developed among the Mayas, continued through time and space, and became very important among the Toltecs and Aztecs.

The connection of the sun with Venus is linked to eclipses and astronomical convergences. When the sun is wholly or partially eclipsed by the passage of the moon between the sun and earth, Venus is sometimes seen transiting that portion of the sky. The sun, according to Mesoamerican mythology, was devoured by a monster during the eclipse. The Mesoamericans suffered from a continuing fear that the sun would go out and all would be lost. It must have been very impressive to the ancients to see Venus remain brightly illuminated when the sun was wholly or partially dark.

Figure 32. Left, the old Maya Sun God, Dresden Codex. After Coe 1975:2. Right, Itzamná, the learning god or wise god. After Helfritz, 1970:144.

CHAPTER 11

ASPECTS OF QUETZALCOATL

The planet Venus was very important in the Mesoamerican calendric system. Venus was known as Tlauixcalpantecuhtli, "Lord of the House of Dawn" (Burland and Forman 1975:35). Venus, however, appears to us as both the Morning Star and the Evening Star. The ancients realized this, and honored both aspects. Quetzalcoatl was the gracious, kindly, Morning Star which was the patron of art, poetry, song, craftsmanship, and the conscious, intellectual side of mankind. He was known as the "Precious Twin", the "Feathered Serpent." Neither of these translations really express the full implications of the name as expressed in Mesoamerican art work and tradition. The serpent is not adorned with mere feathers; it is garbed in precious plumes. The "Plumed Serpent" is probably the best English translation for the Morning Star aspect of the deity. The plumes, the green tail feathers of the male Quetzal, or the central tail feathers of the Scarlet Macaw, formed priestly headdresses and ceremonial paraphernalia.

The confusion in translation between Quetzal Birds and Scarlet Macaws in reference to Quetzalcoatl is brought about by the Nahuatl word for macaw tail feathers, *cuezalin*, which signified "flame." Macaws hold flaming torches in the Maya Madrid and Dresden Codices. The name for macaw in Quiché Maya is *cacquix*, or "fiery feather" (Miller and Taube 1993:132).

The Scarlet Macaws traded throughout the North American Southwest were usually sacrificed to Quetzalcoatl at the time of the Spring Equinox, when their first long tail feathers were mature, and were completely plucked before burial (Hargrave 1970:34).

The Evening Star was personified as Xolotl, an animal-headed monster with long tusks, slavering jaws, and one eye out of its socket, pendant on the cheek. His back was hunched, and the feet twisted, if not turned backwards. He brought trouble and misfortune (Burland and Forman 1975: 35). Even Xolotl, however, had his place as a benefactor. When Huitzilopochtli became dominant sun god as patron of the Aztecs, he demanded that all the other gods, the stars, be sacrificed before he would move across the sky. Finally, all the gods were sacrificed but Xolotl, the evening star. He used sorcery to resist the darts of Huitzilopochtli. First he changed into a double or monstrose maguay, next into a doubled Teocentli (maize), and finally into the Axolotl or Water Dog, the aquatic stage of the Tiger Salamander, *Ambystoma trigrinum*. The feathery external gills of the Axolotl may be the origin of some feathered-serpent sculptures. Thus Xolotl is the patron of the genetic doubling of monstrose forms characteristic of some improved domestic crops (Crosswhite 1985:114-116).

The beneficient Morning Star brought the sun up. The malevolent Evening Star brought the sun down. There were two Venus cycle periods when the planet was not visible, one for eight days and one for 180 days. During these periods, Quetzalcoatl and Xolotl were believed to be struggling with each other in the Underworld. Only at these times were human sacrifices made to Quetzalcoatl.

Figure 33. Top, Water Dog or Axtolotl. After Cochran, 1930:Plate 37. Center, Tiger Salamander, *Ambystoma tigrinum*. After Storer, 1943:593. The water dog is generally considered to be the model for the "feathered serpent" personification of Quetzalcoatl. The water dog is the larval form of the Tiger Salamander which is mainly black with yellow markings, a pattern symbolic of the starry sky, just like the male Mearns Quail and Jaguar. Water dogs do not always turn into salamanders, and may reproduce in the larval state. Cochran believed that the Axolotl, which the Spanish Conquistadores found the Aztec eating roasted or broiled with chili, was a closely related species which never developed into the adult form.

Bottom left, the Muscovy Duck, *Cairina moschata*. After Arthur Singer illustration in Zim 1961:68. Lower right, Day Sign icon for Ehecatl, Wind. After Vaillant 1950:191. This icon represents the red buccal mask of Ehecatl, which some consider to be a representation of a toad. I see it as a representation of the red featherless face of the Muscovy Duck. The males of this species, which has marked sexual dimorphism, are large, aggressive, and often fight to the death.

Figure 34. Top left, round temple of Quetzalcoatl with conical roof and conch shell at the apex. The bird is a Quetzal, the Elegant Trogon. After Brundage 1981:89. Top right, tan chert four-pointed star from Cherry Creek, east central Arizona, 32 X 6 mm. Bottom left, Quetzalcoatl in unmasked form with two four-pointed stars, symbolizing Venus as Morning Star and Evening Star, on his cloak. He wears a tall, conical Huastec cap. After Codex Telleriano-Remensis, 16th Century Aztec, Warren and Ferguson 1987:4. Bottom right, Quetzalcoatal as Ehecatl, with red buccal mask and Huastec cap. A sharp bone pierces his forehead. From the wound flows penitential blood which nourishes a Quetzal bird. The conch shell pectoral ornament, or "wind jewel" signifies the whirlwind. After Brundage 1979:103.

If conditions were very bad, a noble of Toltec descent was chosen by lot to be secretly sacrificed. In more normal times, when the Morning Star was to be seen, two drops of blood were drawn from the ear lobe with a thorn and cast to the east at sunrise as a personal sacrifice (Burland and Forman 1975:36). The most common sacrifices to Quetzalcoatl were flowers and butterflies. The Scarlet Macaw, sacrificed at the Spring Equinox, became associated with the Morning Star aspect of Quetzalcoatl at a very early date.

Another important aspect of Quetzalcoatl is Ehecatl, "Lord of the Winds." In this guise he is shown wearing a red mask which projects in a pointed snout over the lower part of his face. Some believe this wind mask depicts the Mexican Whistling Toad, *Rhinophyrne dorsalis*. There is also an allusion to the Earth Monster which myth portrays as a cross between the alligator and the toad. I believe the mask more strongly resembles the Muscovy Duck, *Cairina moschata*, which is found in Mexico and south to Peru and Argentina. This large, aggressive duck displays marked sexual dimorphism, and a bare red face, eye-ring, and caruncle, which is strikingly similar to the Day Sign icon for Ehecatl.

The Ehecatl aspect was worshiped in round temples, since the wind blows where it wishes, and cannot be contained within four walls. The round plan is also reminiscent of the whirlwinds which are such a conspicuous feature of hot, arid lands. Ehecatl dried the fields to prepare for planting. Quetzalcoatl as Morning Star, who died, and who will return, came to symbolize the coming of springtime and the return of vegetation, which explains the sacrifice of Scarlet Macaws at the Spring Equinox. In the Southwest Culture Area, Quetzalcoatl appears to have come to represent water flowing in channels during the Classic Period, whereas Tlaloc continued on as patron of gentle rain on the fields. To quote Burland and Forman (1975:46-47):

> Firstly, he was a god of springtime, and the beneficent winds. Secondly, he was an astrological deity of the Morning Star. Thirdly, he came to be regarded as the founder of kingship. At each stage the god symbolized a further advance in civilization. In his final position as the king who was and is to be, Quetzalcoatl had become the highest expression of divine kingship that had yet been evolved in Central America.

This rose-colored view of Quetzalcoatl leaves out a baleful aspect of this supernatural which is very important in the North American Southwest. This is Ce Ácatl, One Reed, the war dragon and warrior who was so prominent in Tula and Chichen Itzá. The supernatural appears in this case as a warrior companion of the Sun. He is, on one hand, the warrior who defeats the stars and sacrifices them to resurrect the sun; and, on the other hand, is himself the sacrifice.

The most likely evidence of the veneration of the Ce Ácatl aspect of Quetzalcoatl in the Southwest would be human bone artifacts, especially any inscribed with the four-pointed Morning Star, a trait with which he is associated in Mesoamerica (Figure 35-top). Such artifacts have been found in such late period sites as Pecos, Gran Quivira and Paquimé. Mimbres pottery designs include quail with radiating patterns on their bodies which may have solar significance. One quail displays the four-pointed Morning Star (Figure 29-bottom right), suggesting Ce Ácatl as a companion of Tonatihu. I have also been given a flaked stone four-pointed star which was a surface find along Cherry Creek in east-central Arizona (Figure 34-top right) (cf. Johnson 1971:188-194).

Ce Ácatl is equipped with atlatl and darts, and may wear the red vertical striped face paint of a warrior who risks capture and sacrifice. Alternatively, he may be shown with the face of a skull, signifying his periods in the Underworld (Brundage 1981:115, 170-175). A Mimbres bowl design depicts a decapitation scene in which the perpetrator wears a Horned Serpent/Ehecatl mask (Figure 35-bottom). It seems to combine the main avatars of Quetzalcoatl: water patron, wind god, and warrior, which were most prominent in the prehistoric Southwest.

Figure 35. Top, Ehecatl plays music on instruments made of human bone while God 7 Flower eats hallucinogenic mushrooms. Codex Vindobonensis, Late Post Classic Mixtec. After Miller and Taube 1993:91. Bottom, Mimbres bowl design in which a man in Ehecatl-Water Serpent costume decapitates a victim. After Brody *et al.* 1983:118.

TABLE 2. DISTRIBUTION IN TIME AND SPACE OF MACAWS OF KNOWN AGE

SITE	JUVENILE	IMMATURE	NEW FLEDGED	ADOLESCENT	BREEDING	AGED	TOTAL
600s							
Snaketown			2				
Total	0	0	2	0	0	0	2
Est. 700-900							
Pueblo Grande			2				
Total	0	0	2	0	0	0	2
Late 1000s-ca.1150							
Gatlin Site			1				
Galaz Ranch Site			1				
Old Town					1		
Wind Mountain			1				
Pueblo Bonito (Pepper)		1	9	2		1	
Pueblo Bonito (Judd)			9	3			
Pueblo del Arroyo			3				
Kin Kletso				1			
Total	0	1	24	6	1	1	33
1150-ca.1200							
Wupatki		4	15		1		
Nalakihu				1			
Montezuma Castle			1				
Jackson Homestead				1			
Tuzigoot		2	1				
Ridge Ruin		2					
Total	0	8	19	2	1	0	30
HIATUS							
ca. 1275-1300							
Kiet Siel			2				
Houck			1				
Pollock's Ranch			1				
Turkey Creek		2	6	3			
Point of Pines		4	17	1	2		
Gila Cliff Dwellings				1			
Total	0	6	27	5	2	0	40
1300s							
Arroyo Hondo			2				
Grasshopper	1	1	4		1	1	
Kinishba			3	1			
Total	1	1	9	1	1	1	14
Post-1400							
Pecos			2				
Gran Quivira			1				
Reeve Ruin			1				
Freeman Ranch			1				
Pinal Pueblo			2				
Total	0	0	7	0	0	0	7
Grand Total	1	16	90	14	5	2	128

The Newfledged macaws were 11-12 months old. the majority of the Immature macaws were 10-11 months old. The majority of the Adolescent macaws were 12-13 months old. From this clustering of ages, it is apparent that the primary use of these macaws came at the Spring Equinox, presumably as seasonal sacrifices to Quetzalcoatl.

CHAPTER 12

SCARLET MACAWS
IN THE SOUTHWEST CULTURE AREA

The Southwest Culture Area during the last 2000 years may be visualized as an area remote in distance from the more developed areas of Mesoamerica, but not necessarily remote in influence. The notion of new ideas trickling, one at a time, into a quiet cultural pool would be a comforting model, but such a model is a very bad fit for faunal remains recovered from the excavation of Southwestern archaeological sites. Rather, new ideas, as expressed in occurrences of faunal remains, arrive as parts of complexes cast like rocks with different trajectories, with large splashes, and with many ripples. The first such event was the sudden importation into the Late Archaic/Early Agricultural Southwest of the Small Indian Domestic Turkey, apparently part of a Tlaloc/Sun Cult, associated with a new reliance on dry farming.

The setting for the second event was Whittlesey's (1995) Plain Ware Horizon, an unusually uniform regionwide beginning brownware period in which seed storage appears to have been the primary objective of pottery making. Birds utilized throughout the area in the 400s include such tender, edible, native species as ducks, geese, quail, and doves, plus the Sparrow Hawk which is actually a tiny falcon with colorful tail feathers. During the 500s two new birds were imported into the Southwest, the Large Indian Domestic Turkey into the Four Corners Area, and the Scarlet Macaw into the Hohokam Area. The Large Indian Domestic Turkey is considered in detail in the chapter on Tezcatlipoca and in the Taxonomic and Osteological chapters. The introduction of the Scarlet Macaw (*Ara macao*) is considered here as a part of the complex which grew into the Hohokam regional system of agriculture, including canal irrigation, and the introduction of new squash, new beans, cotton, and loom weaving.

Table 2 summarizes the distribution in time and space of macaws of known age north of the international boundary. In addition to these specimens, there were also macaws with remains so fragmentary that they could not be aged, as well as the macaws recovered from the excavation of Paquimé. From the Viejo Period came a single bone of a macaw, but from the excavations of the Medio Period came 100 macaws of undetermined species (many of which could now be identified), 81 Military Macaws, and 322 Scarlet Macaws for a grand total of 504 (McKusick 1974:247, 274-275). Current dating indicates that the trading center of Paquimé took commercial advantage of an already existing trade in macaws, rather than initiating it. Total macaws of both species, Military and Scarlet, which I have examined may be compared as follows:

	NORTH AMERICAN SOUTHWEST	PAQUIMÉ
600S	2	0
Est. 700-900	2	0
Late 1000s-ca. 1200	95	1
Hiatus		
1275-1400	71	474
Post 1400	10	29
Total	180	504

The Scarlet Macaw is not entirely scarlet. It also has brilliant yellow and blue feathers. By providing feathers of the three primary colors, it can be used for a variety of ceremonial purposes. Probably many macaw feathers were imported into the Southwest in early centuries, just as they were in the early historic period, and as they are today. Nevertheless, Table 2 demonstrates that the primary sacrificial use of Scarlet Macaws coincided with the Spring Equinox ceremony honoring Quetzalcoatl when the 11 to 12 month old Newfledged macaws achieved their adult plumage which included the precious long, central tail feathers (McKusick 1974:Vol. 8, 276-280). Table 2 also demonstrates that Scarlet Macaw occurrences parallel the development or acceptance of water control devices through time and space.

The earliest known introduction of macaws into the Southwest Culture Area was among the Hohokam at Snaketown, perhaps as early as the Estrella Phase, in the 500s, but definitely by the Sweetwater Phase, during the 600s (McKusick 1976:375; Dean 1991). Another Snaketown macaw deposited during the Snaketown-Gila Butte Phases dates between 700 and 900. Two Pueblo Grande macaws are estimated to be dated ca. 700 to 900 (McKusick 1991). A single macaw from the Gatlin Site dates in the 1000s (Wasley 1960; Dean 1991).

Schroeder (1977:44) states that by the middle 1000s there was a "relatively sudden development of water control devices" among the northern Sinagua. Sinagua macaw use began in the 1000s and extended through at least the mid-1100s if not a little later. Schroeder further notes trade contacts that supplied shell, copper bells, and parrots (1977:42), which some suggest indicates that the Sinagua macaw supply, and perhaps ideas of macaw usage, were coming up the Verde River. I am convinced, from many years of experience in keeping parrots, that bells and shells can be traded from hand to hand, but that attempting to do this with macaws would have inevitably resulted in the loss of a number of fingers.

The recovery of skeletal remains of 41 macaws from Wupatki (Hargrave 1970:36-39) makes this the largest concentration of macaws north of Paquimé at any time in the prehistory of the Southwest Culture Area. The reason for this concentration of macaws, and perhaps the reason for the location of Wupatki itself, may be the blow hole adjacent to that site. The blow hole is a vent leading to an enormous subterranean cavern. During the day the air in the cavern expands, rushing vertically out of the vent. During the night, the air in the cavern cools, drawing air down into the vent. It is as if the earth itself were breathing. As noted above, the most conspicuous aspect of Quetzalcoatl in the North American Southwest is Ehecatl, the Wind God. Ehecatl manifests himself as the whirlwind. The draft from the blow hole may have been venerated as evidence of the operation of the deity as he breathed the breath of life and beauty upon the earth. In any case, a ball court, a Mesoamerican feature (Di Peso 1974: Vol. 2, 551), was built next to it. Near Wupatki is Montezuma Well, which would have been an ideal site for the veneration of Chalchihuitlique. The prolonged volcanic activity of nearby Sunset Crater (Reid and Whittlesey 1997: 215) must have attracted the attention of most of the inhabitants of northern Arizona to the area as a special province of Xiuhtecutli. In other words, Wupatki was a perfect place for religious pilgrimage over many, many years. These factors, as well as the avian remains, lead me to connect the large concentration of Scarlet Macaws at Wupatki not with the Hohokam regional irrigated agricultural system, but with an entirely different frame of reference: the Mimbres settlements and the Chaco sphere of influence.

The setting in northern Arizona and New Mexico which is relevant to the macaw problem is adequately outlined by the distribution of the Large Indian Domestic Turkey which had been introduced in the 500s, probably from the east up the Canadian River, and went feral along the Mogollon Rim during the 600s. By the 900s, this distribution is a T-shaped area occupied largely by unit pueblos from Picuris on the east to the Great Falls of the Little Colorado on the west, and the trading center of Yellow Jacket on the north to a pre-Paquimé site at Casas Grandes on the south. The north-south axis of this distribution runs through the Chaco Canyon and Mimbres settlements. Steven Lekson (1999) has interpreted this phenomenon as the "Chaco Meridian" an esoteric construction which was deliberately surveyed to connect Chaco Canyon to its later outlier, Aztec, to the north, and the even later site of Paquimé, to the south. I am seeing the same phenomenon in bird bones that he sees in the distribution of great houses and directional relationships, but have interpreted it differently. I consider this line to be an early south-to-north trade route which ran through the Casas Grandes area, through the Mimbres settlements, north to Chaco Canyon, and on to Yellow Jacket (McKusick 1986c:7-8). The early macaw trade along this route is outlined by a single macaw bone at Casas Grandes on the south (McKusick 1974:247), remains of 22 macaws from at least seven sites in the Mimbres Area (Creel and McKusick 1994), to Chaco Canyon on the north, where we find the second largest aggregation of macaws north of the international border, with 29 macaws at Pueblo Bonito alone. The macaw trade did not pass on to Mesa Verde, but appears to have branched west to the Sinagua Area. It appears most probable that the Wupatki macaws, and those from nearby sites, were brought in by professional bird merchants via this route rather than being traded "hand to hand" up the Verde River at this time level. The Chaco Canyon sites begin slightly earlier than the Sinagua sites, but their macaw use appears to be roughly contemporaneous, that is, during the 1000s to the mid-1100s, lasting a little later among the Sinagua. Cordell (1984:246) lists water control features as one of the diagnostics of the Chaco Phenomenon. Other listed diagnostics include macaws and copper bells. To these I would add large amounts of shell and artifacts made from the bones of large carnivores such as bears and mountain lions occurring together in caches, as well as a host of non-faunal artifacts of Mesoamerican origin.

Macaws, in order to be kept successfully, must be removed from their nest in the wild at an age of about seven weeks. They are fed, often by mouth, such foods as chewed hominy. They must be kept warm in baskets, and quickly become human-imprinted. Parrots are usually very attached to their keepers, but are jealous birds with long memories. They will launch vicious and sustained attacks on strangers or on those who have offended them. Nestlings need lots of care in a quiet environment. Scarlet Macaws appear so often in Mimbres art, as do Military Macaws

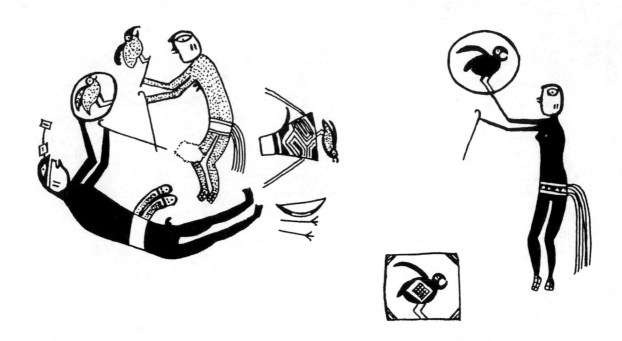

Figure 36. Left, Mimbres Polychrome bowl design depicting a trader delivering juvenile macaws to a Mimbres aviculturalist, Mattocks Site. After Brody 1983:72. Right, aviculturalist with crook, hoop, and cage. After Brody 1977:187.

and small parrots of the genus *Amazona*, that it appears probable that some of the inhabitants of the Mimbres settlements were actually raising nestlings to marketable age as a commercial activity. Especially interesting are Mimbres Classic pottery depictions of macaw keepers, both male and female, with juvenile macaws (Figure 36). They are equipped with hoops, crooks, and rectangular cages. Some have staffs and baskets, which suggest that one person in the picture may be a trader delivering juvenile macaws to a local aviculturalist to be raised to a marketable age when they would be carried north to Chaco Canyon and west to the Sinagua settlements.

The live macaw trade was rather quiet during the early 1200s, but a sudden flurry of activity occurred between 1275 and 1300. Sites of this period include Kiet Siel, Houck, Pollock's Ranch, Turkey Creek, Point of Pines, and Gila Cliff Dwellings. Gila Cliff Dwellings is located on a creek which empties into the West Fork of the Gila River. It seems like a very remote and inconspicuous site to be included in the macaw trade. However, there was a beaver dam during its occupation (Anderson *et al.* 1986:260-261), which made the immediate vicinity more suitable for raising crops than it is now. Manipulation of water from the beavers' pond may be the reason for a desire to propitiate Quetzalcoatl by obtaining a Scarlet Macaw.

The revival of the macaw trade during the late 1200s and early 1300s draws attention to the relationship between Grasshopper and Point of Pines in east central Arizona and Paquimé to the south. Both Grasshopper and Point of Pines had reservoirs. Point of Pines also had an elaborate system of agricultural terracing on the slopes above the site. Paquimé had complex water control devices ranging from simple check dams to indoor plumbing (Di Peso 1974:336-356).

Another possible association of Scarlet Macaw occurrences with water control devices may be found at Arroyo Hondo Pueblo which is located about five miles south of Santa Fe, New Mexico. The occupation of Arroyo Hondo stretches from about A.D. 1300 to shortly after 1420, with population peaks at about 1335 and in the very early 1400s. The Scarlet Macaw material from Arroyo Hondo is among the best dated in the Southwest. Of the two well-documented burials, one dates to the late 1320s and the other to the early 1330s, and are thus coincidental with Arroyo Hondo's period of highest population and most active commerce. Both burials of 11 to 12 month old macaws were in Plaza G, which was also used for human burials. One was placed east of the ventilator tunnel of Kiva 12-14-6 in the southeast corner of the plaza. The other, accompanied by a chip of turquoise, was on the east side of the plaza. A single quadrate bone from a third bird was deposited in Plaza C in the 1380s, but may have originated in an earlier stratum (Lang and Harris 1984:115-117).

During the late 1320s and early 1330s, when the two well-preserved macaws were buried, there was also a noticeable increase in water-dependent birds such as Canada Goose, Yellow-headed Blackbird, the loon, and a water-dependent mammal, the raccoon (Lang and Harris 1984:34,37,123). On the bases of these data, Lang suggests that water impoundments, or stream damming for irrigation purposes, is probable. It is worth noting that the same types of water birds were associated with the presence of a reservoir at Point of Pines, and their presence in the Grasshopper Pueblo avian collection actually led to the discovery and testing of an ancient reservoir at that site.

Lang points out that in historic Pueblo religion, the Scarlet Macaw is associated with the Sun Deity, which in turn is associated with turquoise. The predominant color of the Scarlet Macaw is red, the historic Pueblo color for south and southeast. Further, parrots are associated with summer and such summer aspects as the rainbow, the Corn Maidens of Pueblo myth, and the "Germinator" or *Muyingwu,* an underworld supernatural who served as Lord of Crops (Lang and Harris 1984:117). This historic Pueblo association of Scarlet Macaws and turquoise parallels the early historic Pima custom of raising Scarlet Macaws for feathers to trade for turquoises far to the north (Hargrave 1970a:1).

The third greatest concentration of macaws in the prehistory of the Southwest Culture Area north of the international border was found at Point of Pines. The recovery of 29 macaws is noteworthy by itself, but the circumstances of their recovery are even more illuminating. The large site at Point of Pines, AZ W:10:50, had a dual population. The main part of the pueblo was occupied by local people. One section, however, was occupied by a Kayenta Anasazi contingent. The macaw remains in the Kayenta section were closely concentrated, usually buried under room floors. The macaw remains in the main portion of the pueblo were more scattered, most often buried in trash dumps like humans, suggesting a difference in macaw usage (Avian files, Southwest Bird Laboratory). Even more interesting is the trade relationship between Point of Pines and Paquimé which can be documented osteologically. Some of the macaws at Point of Pines and at Paquimé share cranial abnormalities which do not occur among specimens from any other sites (Hargrave 1970a:34-35; McKusick 1974:281). Apparently macaws were traded to Point of Pines in exchange for the enormous Large Indian Domestic Turkeys which were raised only at Point of Pines.

The Mimbres aviculturalists were gone by this time. Juvenile macaws were now being raised to a marketable age primarily at Paquimé, in four sections of the city set aside for that purpose

(McKusick 1974:276-278). From Grasshopper Pueblo come the fragile remains of the only juvenile macaw recovered at an archaeological site north of the international border. It is too young to have been imported from the tropical Mexican lowlands where Scarlet Macaws occur wild. It was probably bred at Paquimé, but it is possible that it was bred at Grasshopper Pueblo (McKusick 1982:87-90). During the peak of the Southwest trade in live macaws one adult macaw was found at each of three sites, Pueblo Bonito, Wupatki, and Old Town in the Mimbres Area. During the late 1200s and early 1300s revival of the macaw trade, two adult Scarlet Macaws were recovered from Point of Pines and three were found at Grasshopper Pueblo. Whether this increase in adult birds represents an attempt to breed macaws locally or not, it is certainly a variation in the customary pattern of usage. Macaw breeding in Arizona is possible, but extremely unlikely. First, the adult macaws may not have been present at the sites where they were found at the same time. Second, macaws are not easily sexed unless they happen to lay an egg. Third, even if a pair is correctly sexed, they may have to be associated for as much as five or six years before they mate. Fourth, and probably most important, human-imprinted birds often do not recognize members of their own species as potential mates.

The post-1400 macaws present quite a contrast in that all seven specimens complete enough to age are in the 11-12 month Newfledged age stage associated with sacrificial use. Picuris Pueblo, Garcia Site (Pojoaque Pueblo), and Pecos are in the Rio Grande Area. Pecos and Picuris, along with Taos, were the gateway to the Plains Culture Area, and were prominent trading centers. Gran Quivira was a prominent trading center on the Eastern Periphery. Through Gran Quivira flowed dried meat from the east in exchange for Pueblo corn from the west. In addition to foodstuffs, Gran Quivira was on an east-west trade route which carried pearly fresh-water mussel shell from the rivers of Texas to as far west as Gila Pueblo in east central Arizona. Gran Quivira was in an area so dry that it could not have existed without its trade activities and its exploitation of the Salinas, or salt pans, to its east. There were clay-lined pits which seem to have been cisterns (Howard 1981:13-14), but water was so scarce it hardly needed control devices. It is probable that the worship of Tlaloc was much more important than was the worship of Quetzalcoatl at Gran Quivira, as evidenced by the presence of 944 Small Indian Domestic Turkeys to only two Scarlet Macaws. However, the presence of a human bone artifact, a disc made from the right parietal with two perforations like a button, similar to one from Pecos which was incised with the four-pointed Morning Star pattern (McKusick 1981:59-60), points to the presence there of the Quetzalcoatl Cult.

SCARLET MACAWS BURIED WITH HUMANS

About 1973, pot hunters gave me the osteological remains from two high status Salado burials under the impression that the human burials were accompanied by those of dogs as well as many polychrome vessels and painted wooden artifacts (McKusick 1992:86-91). The burials were from Pinal Pueblo, a fifty-room communications center site located across Six Shooter Canyon from Besh-Ba-Gowah, south of Globe, Arizona. When, after 20 years, I finally unpacked the boxes in anticipation of measuring dog bones, I was surprised to find that there were no dogs, but that one of the two burials was an adult female whose skull was covered with green paint. Instead of dogs, she was accompanied by infants and small children. There were a neonate, two infants under two, a three to four-year-old, and two children under six. Major elements of a Scarlet Macaw, including the right ulna, were found among the remains of the main mass of children. The three to four-year-old child was packaged separately. Among its bones was another right ulna of a Scarlet Macaw. Since the remains were removed by pot hunters in search of salable artifacts, it is not possible to determine how complete the macaw skeletons were when buried. Macaws may have been present in the area because of Quetzalcoatl's aspect as a patron of water control devices. There are at least three reservoirs in the canyons which converge at Pinal Pueblo which I believe to be ancient. In addition there were stone-lined Salado irrigation ditches leading from year-round streams in the canyon bottoms.

The two macaws were about 11 months old, which means that they probably died during February or March. The questions left by this mass burial are: Did the woman, children, and macaws die of the same ailment? Were the macaws sacrifices accompanying this high status burial? Or were the woman, children, and macaws all sacrifices at the Spring Equinox when Newfledged birds could have been delivered by aviculturalists? Sacrificial Macaws are a little younger in the south, and a little older in the north. It seems likely that birds were shipped to the farthest points north as soon as their tail feathers matured because the trip was so long, and that those fledging later were kept to deliver slightly later to nearby southern pueblos. This plan would have worked well so long as all deliveries were made before the Spring Equinox.

About 1970 I examined Bird Burial 9, resting directly above the chest of a boy, Human Burial 130, found in Room 22, which forms part of the south wall of the Great Kiva at Grasshopper Pueblo. Although it appeared to be an articulated Scarlet Macaw (Olsen and Olsen1974:Figure 2), the sample proved to be the head, wings, and sternum of a large aged bird, reassembled with the pelvis and legs of a small immature bird about 11 months old, to look like a single Scarlet Macaw (McKusick 1982:95). This burial complex, with a child and an 11 month old macaw, is reminiscent of that found at Pinal Pueblo.

A number of macaws accompanied human burials in the Mimbres Valley, but they were excavated so many years ago that information on the age of the macaws at death is insufficient to draw any conclusions. So far as I am aware, all were at least 11 months of age or older. This raises questions of whether macaws were sacrificed to accompany burials, whether they were pets kept to supply feathers and were killed upon their owners demise, or whether the human and macaw were both sacrifices.

MACAW FEATHER ARTIFACTS

The most beautiful examples of ceremonial use of macaw feathers come from eastern Arizona and southern Utah. From Antelope House came a "Corn Mother" fetish, a perfect ear of corn with red, yellow, and blue Scarlet Macaw contours caught into its wrappings; and a fragment of cotton band into which were finger-woven forty-seven small, red contour feathers (McKusick 1986b:148, 156). Another outstanding artifact is a circlet of red Scarlet Macaw contours recovered from Gila Cliff Dwellings (Fenner 1986:237-243). The most conspicuous artifact is an apron made of cords completely covered with Scarlet Macaw feathers. The main part of the garment was bright red, with a central figure in blue. The apron was attached to a thong tie and topped with the skin of an Abert's Squirrel. It was recovered from a rock shelter at Lavender Creek, San Juan County, Utah, and is estimated to date between 1275 and 1300. Time-Life books pictures both this artifact from Utah

(1992b:126), and one made in the same technique from Mexico (1992a:131). The Mexican illustration shows Netzahualcoyhotl, poet-king of Texcoco, garbed in an entire kilt made from cords covered in red, yellow, and blue feathers.

Lyndon Hargrave had a color snap-shot of an apron made of the red central tail feathers of the Scarlet Macaw which the owner called a "chin mask". Hargrave believed it was probably a dance skirt similar to those formerly made of eagle feathers by Indians in the San Diego area. However, after recovering the remains of a high status woman from the ceremonial room at Gila Pueblo who was wearing a scarlet fiber apron adorned with a stomacher of 6-7,000 fine shell beads (McKusick 1992:89) I am inclined to consider these aprons as possible ceremonial garb of female religious functionaries. The Gila Pueblo woman was costumed exactly the same way as a female depicted on a Mimbres bowl (Bradfield 1931: Plate LXXIX). Two high status men from this same complex wore sets of hair pins identical to those worn by a man in a bat costume, thought to be a personator of Tezcatlipoca, pictured on another Mimbres bowl (Figure 44). From the avian and iconographic evidence at hand, I believe the full pan-Southwestern socio-politico-religious complex was in place by no later than 1000, and continued into the historic period in areas not invaded by the Pueblo Katsina Cult.

CHAPTER 13

MILITARY MACAWS AS CHALCHIHUITLICUE

As noted in Chapter 1, the predominantly green Military Macaw, *Ara militaris*, and the similarly colored Thick-billed Parrot, *Rhynchopsitta pachyrhyncha*, were birds of sacrifice to an unknown supernatural at Paquimé. The macaw appears in Mayan codices as a lightning beast depicted in semi-human form brandishing torches. This personage was associated with ceremonies pertaining to childbirth and baptism (Figure 31; Di Peso 1974:Vol. 2, 554).

This association of the Military Macaw with childbirth and baptism brings us back to the Wife of Black God who entered the New World with the Paleo-Indians. She was the one who gave the wild animals the sense of smell by a symbolic rebirth. It is apparent from examining art expressions from both sides of the Bering Strait that such conventions as the whirlpool water spiral, the inverted triangle as a sign of the female, and the lunar association of the maiden, matron, and hag came into North America along with the Wife of Black God (Figure 37-left).

At Paquimé, Military Macaws were sacrificed at the Spring Equinox when they had achieved their first adult plumage along with Scarlet Macaws. The ratio overall was about one Military Macaw to four Scarlet Macaws (McKusick 1974:Vol. 8, 274-275). There is growing acceptance of the interpretation that Scarlet Macaws were sacrificed to Quetzalcoatl; however, there is no attempt in the literature of Southwestern archaeology, to my knowledge, to determine to what supernatural the Military Macaws were sacrificed. The only Military Macaw from an archaeological site north of the international border was recovered from the Mimbres excavation at Galaz Ranch Site. It had been wrapped in strings of turquoise and shell beads, and buried under a green stone next to the fire pit of Kiva 73 (Hargrave 1970:48-49).

A spherical greenstone manuport the size of a bowling ball was resting on the A.D.1440 floor of Room 98 at Gila Pueblo, near a sub-floor storage pit which held the neck bones of a Small Indian Domestic Turkey, a presumed sacrifice to Tlaloc. Frank and Carol Crosswhite of the Boyce Thompson Arboretum, Superior, Arizona, tell me that the O'odham ceremonialists at Quitobac displayed a sacred basket at a ceremony re-enacting the creation of the world. The basket contained half of the Earth Monster's heart, a green stone. This appears to be the same sacred, baseball-sized green stone reported by Davis in 1920 (pp.162-164) which was kept nested on eagle feathers in a deerskin bag lashed in a basket.

Russell (1908:221-224), recorded a Pima oral tradition which connects green stones and parrots. Among the people living north of Picacho, Arizona, was a man named Tarsnamkam, Meet the Sun. He saw the turquoises used for ornaments at Casa Grande, and wished to obtain some. He made a fine green parrot and told it to fly to Casa Grande and swallow all the green stones it could find in the Big House there. The daughter of Si'al Teu'-utak Si'van found the bird, but it would not

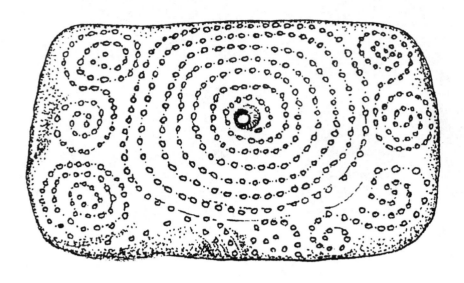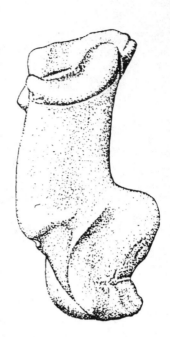

Figure 37. Left, earliest known spiral in the history of art, from a Paleolithic ritual cave burial in Siberia. After Purce 1974:100, Figures 13, 14. Right, squatting goddess figure, generally associated with birth, carved in ivory from the Aurignacian Period, perhaps as early as 27,000 B.C. Sireuil, Dordogne, France. After Torbrügge 1968:18, 51; Time-Life 1973:98.

eat. After several days it was turned loose, and was observed eating turquoise. The people gathered to see the curiosity of a bird eating stones, and gave it all the turquoises they could find. When it was full to the beak it flew home and disgorged the turquoises which Tarsnamkam gave to all the people. Si'al Teu'-utak Si'van was very angry when he learned he had been taken in. He sent rain for four periods, which is equivalent to sixteen days, to destroy Tarsnamkam, but he survived the flood. This feud continued with reciprocal retaliations culminating in the advent of Ha-ak, a female child-eating monster that had to be killed by Elder Brother. Some of Ha-ak's blood was gathered by an old woman who kept it until it turned into two eggs which eventually hatched into parrots. The people wanted the beautiful birds, but the old woman sent her two grandsons to carry the parrots to the mountains where they took shelter. When the grandsons returned, they found that the disappointed people had killed their grandmother. They buried her, and in four days the first tobacco plant grew from her grave.

The beautiful parrots, the turquoises, and the child-eating female monster are a pattern which repeats over and over. Since Earth Monster is the original form of Earth Mother, the green stone suggests one of her aspects, Chalchihuitlicue. Chalchihuitlicue, was variously known as Our Lady of the Turquoise Skirt (Vaillant 1950:171), She of the Jeweled Robe (Vaillant 1950:183), She of the Skirt of Jade (Gilmore 1949:14), or Lady Precious Green (Burland and Forman 19795:39). Chalchihuitlicue is associated with precious green stones such as jade and turquoise, and wears a cloud terrace nose ornament of turquoise mosaic. She is a water goddess, the beautiful adolescent consort of Tlaloc. Chalchihuitlicue is patroness of lakes and streams, but manifests herself in her destructive, hag mode as a whirlpool (Figure 38-upper right).

Figure 38. Upper right, Chalchihuitlicue depicted on an Aztec feather disc in her whirlpool aspect. After Burland and Forman, 1975:93. Left center, Chalchihuitlicue seated on a birthing stool, with infants in the birth stream. Codex Borbonicus, 16th century Aztec. After Miller and Taube, 1993:61 Lower left, figure scratched on the back wall of Room 529 at Awatovi. This Figure is a representation of the whirlpool manifestation of Chalchihuitlicue, complete with round eyes, jagged teeth, whirlpool water spiral on the abdomen, and an issue of amniotic fluid. After Smith 1952: Figure 92. Lower center and right, head detail and entire Soyokmana depicted in kiva mural from right wall of Room 529 at Awatovi. The figure is rendered in black outlined with white. Red lips and tongue set off the jagged white teeth. The figure parallels the goddess seated on the birthing stool and the squatting goddess in figure 37. After Smith 1952: Figure 51.

Figure 39. Top left, the Ce Àcatl aspect of Quetzalcoatl wounds the leg of Chalchihuitlicue who offers herself naked upon the waters. After Codex Borgia in Coe 1975:21. Top right, Chalchihuitlicue, pierced (impregnated) by a dart, with the womb indicated by a water spiral, from which issues an umbilical cord. She holds a large centipede (see "Shrines to Chalchihuitlicue"). Bidahochi Polychrome bowl design, 1320-1400. After Pilles and Danson 1974:21. Below, Ce Àcatl, with the Morning Star on his shield, and skeletal garb, casts a dart, wounding the water goddess's breast. The milk which gushes forth is a simile for corn in the milk stage. Codex Cospi. After Brundage 1979:109.

Figure 40. Awatovi Kiva Mural, Room 529. The inverted figure at the top is identified by Black God's insignia, the Pleiades, on the mask. At left, the naked Chalchihuitlicue offers herself to Ce Àcatl in her typical posture. At center, the warrior Ce Àcatl casts a dart at Chalchihuitlicue's leg. At right, the dart has passed through (impregnated) her womb; the birth canal is visible below. After Smith 1952: Figure 53.

Quetzalcoatl is an early patron of flowing water and, by association, of reservoirs, canals, and ditches. In his guise as Ehecatl, Quetzalcoatl can be observed as a whirlwind. The parallels between the patronages and visible forms of Ehecatl and Chalchihuitlicue are obvious. Their fertility functions appear to be similar also (Figure 39).

As whirlwinds are violently destructive, so are whirlpools. It has been customary to blame disastrous flood, in the form of the great water serpent, upon Quetzalcoatl. However, since he is the patron of water control devices, and Chalchihuitlicue is the patron of springs, lakes, and rivers, it seems more logical to blame violent floods upon her. Indeed, one of the most serious effects of flooding is the destruction of water control devices of which Quetzalcoatl is patron. Both modern Pueblo and O'odham legends recount the sacrifice of children to stop floods. Mother earth, in whatever guise, always takes back whatever she has given.

As principle Central Mexican Goddess of lakes and springs, Chalchihuitlique was patron of the day, Serpent, which coincides with the great water serpent of the Pueblos. She is also the patron of the thirteen day period of 1 Reed or Ce Acatl, the day name associated with the warrior aspect of Quetzalcoatl. Although legally the spouse of Tlaloc, it was a May-December relationship. Chalchihuitlicue was the budding adolescent, Tlaloc the aged cave-dwelling rain god. She wears the cloud-stepped nose ornament of Tlaloc, but she spends a large amount of time with Quetzalcoatl in his generative role. In Figure 39, Quetzalcoatl casts a dart at the water goddess. As Ce Acatl, the warrior, he wounds her, he impales, he impregnates, he fructifies. As Ehecatl he breathes upon the growing corn, he pollinates, he fertilizes. The milk swells in the growing kernels of corn as in the budding breasts of Chalchihuitlicue. Clear parallels in the depiction of Chalchihuitlicue, in both her benevolent and malaevolent aspects, and as the consort of Ce Acatl, can be seen in images from Mesoamerica and in protohistoric Hopi pottery and kiva murals (Figures 38, 39, 40).

In Figure 41 Chalchihuitlicue is seen as the patron of a year. In her year corn is expected to grow well. She pours forth her waters upon the corn; she becomes the green, growing corn. In contrast, as whirlpool (Figure 38) Chalchihuitlicue is terrible to behold. She is powerful, awe-inspiring. She cannot be resisted. She draws life-giving waters back into herself. She emerges as the ever-hungry Earth Mother who eventually devours all of her own children.

Multiple macaw burials at Paquimé indicate that some Military Macaws were sacrificed at the Spring Equinox along with a greater number of Scarlet Macaws. Rains can be expected at the Spring Equinox, so a sacrifice to Chalchihuitlique as well as to Quetzalcoatl would have been appropriate.

THICK-BILLED PARROTS

Thick-billed Parrots look like smaller editions of the Military Macaw. Thick-billed Parrots measure 15 to 16 inches in length, contrasted with 27 to 30 inches for the Military Macaw (Blake 1953:191, 193). I am unaware of any mention in the literature of their being associated with, or sacrificed to, any supernatural. Of the 15 Thick-billed Parrots known from Southwest archaeological excavations, all have been found at sites which also produced bones of the Scarlet Macaw. While the Scarlet Macaw is an easily tamed bird with a generally good disposition, both the Military Macaw

Figure 41. Chalchihuitlicue, with her turquoise cloud terrace nose ornament, pouring water on a corn plant. After Burland and Forman 1975:75.

and Thick-Billed Parrot tend to be disagreeable. Military Macaws were available at Paquimé. Thick-Billed Parrots, however, used to range farther north into southeastern Arizona and southwestern New Mexico until deforestation in northern Mexico diminished the pine nut supply upon which they depend for food. It may be that prehistoric proximity was the reason they were used instead of Military Macaws. Thick-billed Parrots may not have been sacrificed. They may have been kept over long periods of time as a source of feathers for ritual objects.

Both Military Macaws and Thick-billed Parrots, as well as the small green, short-tailed *Amazona* parrots are depicted in Mimbres pottery designs (Creel and McKusick 1994). Hibben reports that Pottery Mound kiva murals depicted Military Macaws and Thick-billed Parrots as well as a great many Scarlet Macaws (Hibben 1975:63). An Awatovi kiva mural shows a Military Macaw and a Scarlet Macaw of equal size in the same scene (Smith 1952: Plate E).

SHRINES TO CHALCHIHUITLICUE

Wupatki had the highest number of both Thick-Billed Parrots and Scarlet Macaws. Nearby are two enormous limestone sinks which hold water seasonally, and may be the type of natural feature that require the propitiation of Chalchihuitlicue. More impressive than the limestone sinks near Wupatki is Montezuma's Well. As you approach this natural feature, it looks like a barren, breast-shaped hill in the desert. However, once you reach the summit of the path, the hill has no top. Instead, it is an impressive water-filled limestone sink. The waters of Montezuma's Well travel one hundred and fifty feet underground, and then gush forth from the base of the hill in a powerful stream which supplies a Pre-columbian irrigation system. This configuration is reminiscent of depictions of a great torrent of amniotic fluid carrying fully-dressed boy and girl children which flows from beneath Chalchihuitlicue as she sits on a birthing stool (Fig.38). This awe-inspiring natural feature was probably a focus of veneration of Chalchihuitlicue. Montezuma's well

Table 3, Prehistoric Occurrences of Thick-billed Parrots and Military Macaws

600s			
Snaketown		1	0
	Total	1	0
900s			
Snaketown		1	0
	Total	1	0
Late 1000s - 1100s			
Wupatki		4	0
Pueblo Bonito		2	0
Cameron Creek Village		1	0
Galaz Ranch Site		2	1
Treasure Hill		1	0
	Total	10	1
1275 - 1300			
Gila Cliff Dwellings		1	0
	Total	1	0
Post-1300			
Paquimé		2	80
	Total	2	80
	Grand Total	15	81*

*A Military Macaw feather was found at Tularosa Cave.

is also similar to the cenote adjacent to the Temple of Tlaloc at Chichen Itza'. Chichen Itza' was an important place of Mesoamerican pilgrimage even into historic times (Miller and Taube 1993:23). Jade carvings, gold discs, and humans, especially adolescents, were common sacrifices. The green, algae-colored waters of the cenote would have been an ideal place of sacrifice to Chalchihuitlicue.

A man-made shrine was probably Awatovi Kiva Room 529. Unfortunately, the painted murals and incised designs from this room were treated by Smith (1952) as individual design elements, rather than as a cohesive whole. Among the scattered depictions of motifs are classic renditions of Ce Àcatl impregnating Chalchihuitlique, pregnancy, birth, a cluster of female triangle motifs, and ceremonial paraphernalia. Particularly interesting are bowls of what Smith terms "flowers". Informants identify these as end views of piles of corn ears which are still used in ceremonies. Chalchihuitlique, like Quetzalcoatl, is definitely associated with the cultivation of corn.

A painting of a small animal probably represents the Ring-tailed Cat, a nocturnal riparian mammal. Its favorite food is the giant centipede, one of which is depicted with Chalchihuitlicue in a pottery bowl design (Figure 39-upper right). And centipedes are common along rivers and streams, of which Chalchihuitlicue is patron.

Other shrines to Chalchihuitlicue may include the large, round green stone and storage pit in Room 98 at Gila Pueblo, and the Military Macaw buried beneath a green stone next to the hearth in Kiva 73 at Galaz Ranch Site. This raises the question of whether these rooms were kivas in the usual sense, or if they were the rooms of a Women's Society. Another Salado-Mimbres parallel is the discovery of female high status functionaries at Gila Pueblo at A.D. 1440, and the depiction of similarly clothed women on Mimbres pottery more than 300 years earlier.

The inclusion of Chalchihuitlicue is the most innovative part of the four-part model. There is no other deity which even remotely fits the known facts, and Chalchihuitlicue fits them very well indeed. Since she is one of the five important supernaturals who supervise the eras of the Aztec world scheme, the model is further reinforced in late Pre-columbian times.

CHAPTER 14

THE TEZCATLIPOCA CULT

Ek Chuah, a deity with properties similar to the later Tezcatlipoca, appeared early among the Mayas in southern Mexico (Burland and Forman 1975:11-12). Tezcatlipoca was above all the ruler of the surface of the earth. Aztec myth tells us that in the beginning the earth monster was submerged below the waters. Tezcatlipoca tempted her with his foot. She rose and tore off his foot, but he tore off her lower jaw in turn. She was unable to sink back beneath the waters, and now all mankind lives upon her back (Burland and Forman 1975:55-56).

As there were four Tlalocs and Four Quetzalcoatls, so there were four Tezcatlipocas. The color of the eastern Tezcatlipoca was the yellow of the rising sun and maize. The southern Tezcatlipoca was the blue of Huitzilopochtli, the midsummer sun, known as The Blue Hummingbird, Hummingbird on the Left (Burland and Forman 1975:55-56), or Hummingbird Wizard (Vaillant 1950:88). The Tezcatlipoca of the west was the red of Xipe Totec, Our Lord the Flayed One, symbolizing suffering and the blood of sacrifice. The Tezcatlipoca of the north was the black of the evil whisperer, witchcraft, and black magic (Burland and Forman 1975:55-56).

All aspects of Tezatlipoca were associated with magic and sacrifice. All of his forms were patrons of war and warriors. Tezcatlipoca was a dangerous and deadly being, but the Aztecs did not regard him as evil, for he brought them material gain and the glory of conquest. In the day he was the sun at zenith, Huitzilopochtli. At night he was seen as the constellation we know as the Big Dipper or Great Bear, Ursa Major. The portion of the sky surrounding Polaris is a field of stars which never dip beneath the sea. In Mesoamerica Ursa Major was variously seen as the single footprint of Tezcatlipoca as he hopped around Polaris, or as the Great Jaguar who prowled endlessly around the pole star. In the North American Southwest where the jaguar, *Felis onca*, is seldom seen, the bear took its place as dominant predator. Caches of Black Bear, *Ursus americanus*, and Mountain Lion, *Felis concolor,* ceremonial or high status bone artifacts probably have some connection with Tezcatlipoca. In the Eastern Pueblos today, bear is a powerful healer connected with the warrior society, and Mountain Lion is important in hunting shrines. As the mammalian predators contemporaneous with the introduction of the Tezcatlipoca Cult include Jaguar, Black Bear, and Mountain Lion, so avian predators associated with Tezcatlipoca include the eagle of Huitzilopochtli, the owl of the northern Tezcatlipoca, and the hawk associated with warrior initiation.

While the war god concept is early in Mesoamerica, the Tezcatlipoca Cult does not appear until the Tenth Century, toward the end of Toltec Rule. According to Burland and Forman (1975:14, 58), the warrior cult so closely connected with Tezcatlipoca is very similar to the warrior societies of the Plains Indians (Bernal 1975:79-84; Vaillant 1950:201). They suggest that the Tezcatlipoca Cult may have been brought into Mexico by tribes moving down from the north, possibly those who eventually became known as the Chichimecs.

During the early agricultural period of the Southwest, Quetzalcoatl, the Morning Star Venus aspect, is balanced in attributes by Xolotl, the baleful Evening Star Venus aspect. This balance continues until the late 900s, when things suddenly change. Into the relatively quiet Pueblo II pool of unit pueblo culture is cast our third Mesoamerican stone. This time it is not a small group bringing a new agricultural complex which gave the local people more options for survival. It is rather, a strong, centrally organized political system which consolidates the population into larger, more easily controlled communities. This system appears to enter along a trade route through the Casas Grandes Area, up the Mimbres River Valley, to Chaco Canyon. Presumably, at least a few people must have come from Mesoamerica to transmit this new mode of organization. From the viewpoint of avian remains, Chaco Canyon had been rather slow on the uptake before this event. Perhaps a developmental vacuum gave the new system a good place to take root. The importation of exotic goods, including macaws, suggests that there was at Chaco Canyon a market for sacrificial birds, and something of value, probably turquoise, for which they could be exchanged. The cessation of raiding, which had been endemic since the late Archaic (LeBlanc 1999), the beginning of cannibalism (White 1992), and the presence of personages with high status burials and filed teeth (Turner and Turner 1999:472-477) reinforces the supposition that the perpetrators of this new system were Mesoamerican.

If we accept the practitioners of the Tezcatlipoca Cult as Mesoamericans, it is reasonable that they would have chosen the Large Indian Domestic Turkey as a bird of sacrifice. Not only was it the only turkey breed available at Chaco Canyon when they arrived, but it also looked like the South Mexican Turkey with which they would have been familiar. The Small Indian Domestic Turkey not only has a feathered neck, but is a dumpy little bird with a humped back and short legs. In contrast, the Large Indian Domestic is a handsome, tall, long-legged bird with a naked neck like the South Mexican Turkey.

Macaws were imported in large numbers, indicating the presence of Quetzalcoatl. However, the former balancing supernatural, Xolotl, is replaced at this point by the new Toltec sorcerer/war god, Tezcatlipoca, around whom had grown up a powerful cult. Just as Quetzalcoatl, the Plumed Serpent, represented art, literature, music, trade, and the conscious side of the human psyche; so Tezcatlipoca, the Smoking Mirror, was the balancing power, representing war, suffering, sacrifice, witchcraft, and the subconscious side of the human psyche. The Smoking Mirror symbol for Tezcatlipoca depicted an obsidian mirror used for scrying, much as some modern psychics use a crystal ball as a focus for meditation (Figure 42-left).

Pseudo-cloisonné, a Mesoamerican decorative technique, occurs among the elite goods recovered from Pueblo Bonito. In addition, Woodward discovered pseudo-cloisonné mirrors and mirror fragments during his 1930 excavation of the Grewe Site near Casa Grande, Arizona. Of these specimens, the reverse of one depicted Tezcatlipoca as an animated figure wearing a headdress with feathers projecting at the front, and the hand grasping a ceremonial object or weapon. The dancing figure wears a circular pectoral ornament and a mirror at the temple. The leg wraps around the edge of the mirror so that the amputated foot is replaced by the actual mirror on the obverse (Holien 1975:162, 171).

Figure 42. Left, Tezcatlipoca with his smoking mirror in his hand. His foot, which was severed during his fight with the Earth Monster, has been replaced by his smoking mirror name glyph. After Krupp 1983: 71. Center, Tezcatlipoca in turkey costume. He used the ring pendant on his chest to spy on the activities of mankind from afar. After Helfritz 1970: 43. Right, pottery turkey leg censer bearing glyph of Tezcatlipoca. After Burland and Forman 1975:61.

Another guise of Tezcatlipoca was Chalchiuhtotolin, the Jeweled Fowl, who was depicted in turkey form (Vaillant 1950:184)(Figure 42-center). The skin-covered turkey leg with claws attached is a common symbol for Tezcatlipoca. Mesoamerican pottery censers bearing the Smoking Mirror symbol were formed in the shape of the spurred leg of a turkey (Figure 42-right).

ARCHAEOLOGICAL OCCURRENCES

The first turkeys in the Southwest were the Small Indian Domestics which are associated with the worship of Tlaloc. Much later, during the 500s, the Large Indian Domestic was brought into the Four Corners Area, probably from the east. It spread from settlement to settlement, becoming the dominant breed by Pueblo II times. By the 600s the Large Indian Domestics had gone feral in the mountains adjacent to the pueblos where they were kept as domestic fowl, resulting in Merriam's Wild Turkey, *Meleagris gallopavo merriami*. Of these three available alternatives, the Large Indian Domestic is the only turkey which was used for sacrifice to Tezcatlipoca. Skin-covered turkey leg and foot offerings were secreted in dark crevices or rock shelters shortly before 1100 at Tularosa Cave, in the mid-1100s at Chaco Canyon, before 1277 at Antelope House, and post-1400 at Upper Tonto Ruin (Southwest Bird Laboratory Avian Files). The five desiccated male turkey legs secreted in the rock shelter at Antelope House were all xanthine orange (a standardized true orange), indicating that they were from birds only a year old. Apparently they were sacrificed when they attained their first black adult plumage. The specimen from Tularosa Cave was also xanthine orange. The censer illustrated by Burland and Forman (Figure 42-right) is painted orange. Presumably these legs and feet are meant as substitutes for the foot Tezcatlipoca lost to the Earth Monster during the creation of the surface of the earth.

The severed, skin-covered turkey leg with foot dries to resemble a desiccated human arm with a closed hand. A Mimbres bowl from the McSherry Site in the Gila Drainage depicts a pair of turkeys with a pair of human forearms in negative (Brody 1977:166). These offerings may have a lot in common with the remains of desiccated human trophy limbs recovered from late sites such as Ash

Creek. Conversely, a post-1400 female skeleton from Pinal Pueblo had a skull fracture and its hands removed. The victim lived long enough for the skull fracture to infect before she died, and the body was in a state of decomposition, as indicated by fly pupae, when buried in a shallow trench.

An unpigmented turkey leg and foot was recovered from Chaco Canyon. The original find of the feather-necked "Tularosa Turkey", dating just before 1100, was accompanied by the severed, xanthine orange leg of a male Large Indian Domestic Turkey, several small unpigmented poults, and larger poults with unpigmented legs which appeared to be developing erythristic (gray and red) plumage. Unpigmented turkey poults and turkey legs may not have been from all-white fowl. Feathers from silver phase, pied mutation, and erythristic turkeys have been found in a number of cave sites and rock shelters over a period extending from the earliest introduction of the Large Indian Domestic in the 500s to 1300 or perhaps even later. All of these aberrant colorations are forms of partial albinism (Figure 21). Turkeys are generally thought of as black birds with brown markings. In actuality, the basic color is white, a schemochrome or structural color. Over this a wash of reddish-brown melanin is deposited in appropriate areas such as the tail feathers. The patterning of black melanin is inherited and formed independently. Erythristic birds lack black melanin. The areas where it would normally be deposited are altered, giving them a pale, grayish cast. The result is a turkey with a pale gray body, white, gray-barred wings, and a rufous tale tipped with gray and cream. Erythrism is by far the most common aberrant coloration of turkeys raised by the inhabitants of sites where feathers are preserved. Rufous tail feathers would be especially appropriate for Xipe Totec (McKusick 1986c:12-14).

Pied Mutation results in turkeys in which the primary and secondary wing feathers are glossy white with a few black splotches. Body feathers are splotched with white. Tail feathers are banded with white. Predominantly white feathers may have been desired to honor the northern Tlaloc, patron of winter snows, which are so important to successful farming in the Southwest.

Silver Phase turkeys are the result of the loss of metallic brown and non-metallic buffy brown pigmentation. The resulting fowl are cool gray to white with black-tipped body feathers in the male, pale wing feathers, and pale, white-tipped rump and tail feathers.

Turkeys of aberrant colorations were also raised in Mesoamerica. According to the Florentine Codex (Dibble and Anderson, 1963:53) "Some turkeys are smoky, some quite black, some like crow feathers, glistening, some tawny, some smoky." The reference to turkey feathers like crow feathers and "smoky" feathers is reminiscent of Xiuhtecutli. It may be that raising turkeys of aberrant coloration was meant to honor several different supernaturals.

Aside from desiccated legs and feet, and erythristic turkey feathers, probable evidence of additional offerings of turkey legs to Tezcatlipoca are the distal ends of Large Indian Domestic Turkey tibiotarsi and proximal ends of tarsometatarsi (drumstick and shank bones) with what are called "butchering marks" (cuts made on the bone when the tendons were severed to remove the lower leg and foot). These specimens have been recovered from pueblos where Large Indian Domestics were not raised and turkeys were not eaten. One late example is an enormous male Large Indian Domestic which was recovered from Mound 7, Gran Quivira, in central New Mexico, where only Small Indian Domestics were raised. The turkey is so large that it could only have come from

Figure 43. Left, Burrowing Owl, a bird associated with the dead and the Underworld. After Brundage 1979:50. Center, Burrowing Owl with a human skull for a head. Codex Borgia, late Post-Classic. After Miller and Taube 1993:129. Right, Owl with a temple of night, Codex Cospi. After Brundage 1979: 86.

Point of Pines in east-central Arizona. The proximal articular head of the tarsometatarsus shows butchering marks where the tendons had been cut to free the shank and foot from the carcass, forming the unit traditionally dedicated to Tezcatlipoca (McKusick 1981:52). In a number of past reports, particularly Gran Quivira and Antelope House, I have reported these butchering marks as a suggestion of possible infrequent food use. This interpretation, although widely accepted among archaeologists, has always bothered me, and I have now abandoned it as extremely improbable. Given that Large Indian Domestic Turkeys were commonly eaten on Mesa Verde after 960, and Merriam's Wild Turkey was hunted and apparently eaten at a number of sites along the Mogollon Rim from the 600s on (McKusick 1986c:18), most domestic turkeys in the Southwest were kept for feathers to provide warm, twined robes. I have come to believe that they were considered too valuable to eat at most sites.

OWLS

In some areas, which are unsuitable for turkey breeding, other birds may have been used as sacrifices to Tezcatlipoca. One likely example is the concentration of owls recovered from the excavation of Nalakihu (King 1949:141). The avian remains from this site consisted of one each Scarlet Macaw, *Ara macao*, Great Horned Owl, *Bubo virginianus*, Long-eared Owl, *Asio otus*, Short-eared Owl, *Asio flammeus*, Burrowing Owl, *Athene cunicularia*, and the American Raven, *Corvus corax*. Owls occur in collections from a great many Southwest archaeological sites. They are generally considered nocturnal predators, but the Burrowing Owl is a diurnal burrow dweller. As such it is especially appropriate as a representative of the Underworld, and may even be portrayed with a human skull mask instead of an avian head. The owls, like the macaws and ravens, can be hand-raised, and are suitable as birds of sacrifice. The owl is one of the symbols for the Black Tezcatlipoca of the North, the patron of warfare, trickery, and sorcery (Figure 43).

Early Mayan codices depict owls colored green. Since there are no green owls in nature,

95

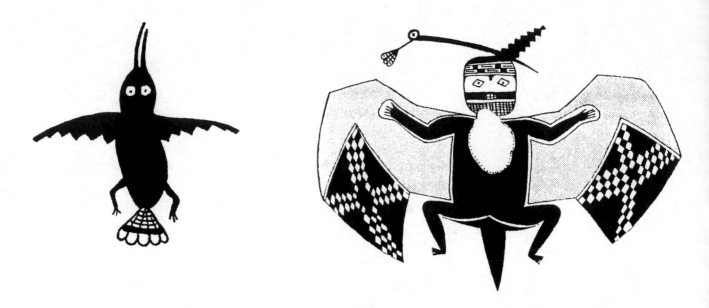

Figure 44 Left , Hummingbird, Mimbres bowl design, Swartz Ruin. After Cosgrove and Cosgrove 1932: Plate 212. Right, man in bat costume design from Mimbres Polychrome bowl. The tassel pendant from the larger hair pin is probably the rufous tail of a female hummingbird. After Brody *et al*. 1983: Figure 6.

this is a conventional communication of youth. That is, the owls are shown Newfledged, the age at which hand-raised birds are usually sacrificed.

HUMMINGBIRDS

The hummingbird is associated especially with the Aztec Sun/War God, Huitzilopochtli, the Tezcatlipoca of the South. Hummingbirds, particularly males, fight constantly for territory. Aztec myth states that slain warriors become hummingbirds to hover around the sun in the most glorious heaven. In Mesoamerican imagery, the hummingbird is seen as sipping from flowers which symbolize the supernatuals feeding on the blood of war and sacrifice. The sipping hummingbird may symbolize a range of ritual bloodletting, including human sacrifice (Miller and Taube 1993:98).

Hummingbird bones are so tiny that they are not yet represented in faunal collections from archaeological sites. However, a tassel made from the entire tail of a female Broadtailed Hummingbird, *Selasphorus platycerus,* was recovered from the excavation of Inscription House in northern Arizona. It is rufous in color. Hummingbirds are depicted frequently in Mimbres pottery design, and a tassel such as was found at Inscription House is shown attached to a hairpin on a man wearing a bat costume (Figure 44). Like the hummingbird, the bat is associated with Tezcatlipoca.

HAWKS

The feathers of Accipiters, or bird hawks, and the feathers of falcons, are considered especially desirable by modern Pueblo ritual specialists because their great speed during life is appropriate where a fast response to prayer is important.

Large buteonine hawks, such as the Red-tailed Hawk, may be raised for sacrifice like Golden Eagles if eaglets are unavailable. However, the primary event with which the sacrifice of newfledged hawks is associated, is the second, or tribal, initiation of young men by which they formerly became warriors, of which hawks were symbols. This usually took place in the November during the lunar periods called the Sparrow Hawk Moon or the Moon of Young Hawks, and in some groups involved a new fire ceremony preceding the Winter Solstice Ceremony (Ellis 1975:65).

Hawk remains occur in most large Southwest archaeological sites, but a particularly dense concentration of hawks buried in and around an isolated structure at Point of Pines may indicate the presence of a Warrior Society. Evidence of four societies was found at Grasshopper Pueblo, the members of which were identified by burials involving arrowheads, shell pendants, shell tinklers, and bone hair pins (Reid and Whittlesey 1999: 126-130). This is reminiscent of the two large men who were killed in the ceremonial complex at Gila Pueblo, one ca. 1340, and one ca. 1440. Both appear to have worn chaps fastened with shell tinklers. Because of their stature, special costume, and association with the ceremonial/ redistribution complex, I have speculated that they may have been leaders of a hunt or war society enjoying achieved high status.

Two other men wearing bone hairpins of the same size and shape, and worn in the same position as the man in the bat constume shown in Figure 44, were also killed in the ceremonial/ redistribution complex in ca.1440. I am inclined to interpret their presence as an indication of a hereditary organization on the basis of the post-1385 presence of high status infant burials in the floors of the ceremonial/redistribution complex. The parallels between Mimbres pottery designs and the clothing of functionaries at Gila Pueblo suggest a very conservative and ancient organization which is more like a deity cult than a society.

Dutton expresses the opinion that the warrior societies came into Zuni from the Eastern Pueblos (Dutton 1963: 205-206). If the warrior societies of the Plains Culture Area are considered to be the ultimate origin of the Tezcatlipoca Cult, it is entirely reasonable the warrior societies lingered on in the Southwest. This leaves us with three types of entities in the late prehistoric period, Deity Cults, the Katsina Cult, and the Societies.

CHAPTER 15

DISCUSSION OF THE MODEL

The avian evidence from the archaeological record fits the proposed model to a surprising degree; however, there were three deficiencies discovered and remedied:

1. Lack of differentiation of breeds in turkey sacrifices.

The original model listed the sacrifice of the turkey head to Tlaloc and the turkey shank and foot to Tezcatlipoca. It was not until I was marking these two types of turkey sacrifices on the maps that I realized that all sacrifices to Tlaloc were Small Indian Domestic Turkeys, and that all sacrifices to Tezcatlipoca were Large Indian Domestics.

Since sacrifice of Small Indian Domestic Turkeys is known from Canyon del Muerto at about A.D. 200 or perhaps earlier, 300 fully-feathered natural turkey mummies were found in the Basketmaker cave known as Tseahatso, in Canyon de Chelly, and a smaller number were found in pre-ceramic levels at Tularosa Cave, it appears that ceremonial use was a major factor in the introduction of the Small Indian Domestic. Sacrificial use of the turkey head also began at least 800 years before the sacrificial use of the turkey shank and foot. Once I had arrived at this conclusion, it was immediately apparent that the introduction of the Large Indian Domestic Turkey during the A.D. 500s was one event, and that the beginning of the sacrificial use of the Large Indian Domestic Turkey shank and foot was an entirely different event taking place 500 years later. I was sure the shank and foot sacrifice was connected to the Tezcatlipoca Cult because of iconography, but had not really connected the entry of the Tezpatlipoca Cult into the Southwest with the Chaco Phenomenon. Once this connection was made, the one early Casas Grandes macaw bone from Paquimé and the Mimbres preoccupation with macaws fell into place as indicators of a route of entry of the Tezcatlipoca Cult, and also of a continuing path of trade from Mesoamerica.

2. Failure to account for sacrificial use of the Military Macaw, and possible similar use of the Thick-billed Parrot.

The original model did not make any provisions for the Military Macaws or Thick-billed Parrots even though Military Macaws had been sacrificed along with Scarlet Macaws at Paquimé. The single Military Macaw from Galaz Ranch Site was also a puzzle. The remains of two Thick-billed Parrots in the small avian sample recovered from the second Snaketown excavation, should have alerted me to their probable early significance in Hohokam ceremonialism. The original model was deficient in that it did not account for the presence, much less the sacrifice, of these two large green parrots. After reviewing the published attributes of a large number of Mesoamerican deities (Vaillant 1950, Burland and Forman 1975) it became obvious that Chalchihuitlicue was the missing supernatural.

3. Failure to account for variation in avian sacrifice on Mesa Verde.

While Tlaloc and Sun were very likely venerated by Mesa Verde agriculturalists, as indicated by the importation of a small number of Small Indian Domestic Turkeys, and a relative abundance of eagle remains, there is to date no clear evidence of avian sacrifice to Tezlicatlipoca, and no evidence at all of avian sacrifices to Quetzalcoatl or Chalchihuitlicue in Mesa Verde avian collections which I have studied. McGuire (1986:243-269) contrasts the single, large, centralized economic network of Chaco Canyon with Mesa Verde, where there were a number of competing centers, each within its own support areas. Presumably, the Mesa Verde centers were composed of an indigenous population, with a socio-politico-religious organization which met its local needs. The late-arriving southern supernaturals served no integrative purpose in this system, and so were not adopted. In contrast, at least the leadership of the Chaco System appears to be Mesoamerican, even to the point of having filed teeth (Turner and Turner 1999:472-476), with its own socio-politico-religious system complete with appropriate Mesoamerican supernaturals.

CHAPTER 16

NEW PERSPECTIVES

The original model supposed that Mesoamerican influence was present in the North American Southwest more or less continuously, but that it was difficult to trace because of differences in Southwestern and Mesoamerican artistic traditions. As the testing of the model progressed, it became clear that not all areas were recipients of Mesoamerican influence from the same source or at the same time, nor did they all adopt this flow of culture in the same manner. Neither was Mesoamerican influence constant; it ebbed and flowed.

SEPARATENESS OF THE HOHOKAM AREA

The Hohokam Area received macaws considerably earlier than did the Mogollon or Anasazi Areas. The dates of perhaps the 500s, but definitely the 600s, are far in advance of the 1000s, when macaws began to be moved through the trade corridor where Paquimé would eventually be built.

Foster (1986:58) points out that in prehistoric times there was no cultural gap between the heartland of Mesoamerica and the North American Southwest. Further, there is a continuity of vegetation zones, including plateau and basin and range lands, which produced similar cultural adaptations. Into this setting Haury (1976) projects an influx of Mesoamerican traits, and perhaps people as well. To quote Foster (1986:59) "Not only were the developing societies of the Southwest bounded to the south by Mesoamerican cultures, there was a heavily Mesoamericanized society - the Hohokam - in the heart of the Southwest."

At this early period, long distance trade may have come through the Chalchihuites (Foster 1986:93). Kelley (1986:93) states that the goods which mobile merchants brought into the Chalchihuites Culture originated along the West Coast of Mexico, not in the Valley of Mexico. The differences in Hohokam Area adaptations and adoptions of this early culture flow set it aside from the Mogollon and Anasazi Areas.

APPARENT SCARCITY OF MACAWS AND PARROTS IN THE HOHOKAM AREA

Nelson (1986:171) notes the scarcity of macaw remains in the Hohokam Area, and suggests a number of possible explanations. After having reviewed both bird and animal remains from several Hohokam sites, it is apparent to me that avian remains in general are very scarce. Further, remains of mammals from Hohokam sites are also very sparse indeed. Most Southwestern settlements depend on the production of one growing season a year. Hohokam settlements could have availed themselves of up to three crops a year. Avian species identified from the second Snaketown excavation suggest a close association all year with the river, the canals, and the fields. While hunters ranged abroad to secure the Mule Deer and Desert Bighorn, which provided most of the animal

Table 4. Macaw Percentages in Selected Sites.

Site	Macaws	Total Birds	% Non-Turkey	% Total Birds
Long House	0	1,590	0.00	0.0 0
Gran Quivira	1	2,298	0.24	0.04
Picuris	1	2,146	0.61	0.05
Grasshopper	13	645	3.32	2.02
Snaketown	3	68	4.41	4.41
Point of Pines	28	697	5.68	3.87
Gila Cliff	1	49	6.25	2.04
Turkey Creek	15	243	10.09	6.00
Nalakihu	1	6	16.67	16.67
Paquimé	504	1,212	90.47	41.58

Table 5. Golden Eagle Percentages in Selected Sites.

Site	Golden Eagles	Total Birds	% Non-Turkey	% Total Birds
Snaketown	0	68	0.00	0.00
Paquimé	10	1,212	0.12	0.08
Grasshopper	6	645	1.53	0.93
Long House	3	1,590	2.42	0.19
Point of Pines	23	697	8.33	2.44
Gran Quivira	196	2,298	14.48	6.62
Picuris	645	2,146	40.45	30.07

Table 6. Owl Percentages in Selected Sites.

Site	Total Owls	Total Birds	% Non-Turkey	% Total Birds
Snaketown	0	68	0.00	0.00
Paquimé	10	1,212	0.19	0.08
Picuris	30	2,146	1.84	1.40
Point of Pines	26	697	5.61	3.73
Gila Cliff	1	49	6.25	2.04
Grasshopper	28	645	7.16	4.34
Gran Quivira	2	2,298	8.03	0.09
Long House	10	1,590	8.06	0.63
Nalakihu	4	6	66.67	66.67

Table 7. Common Raven Percentages in Selected Sites.

Site	Common Ravens	Total Birds	% Non-Turkey Birds	% Total Birds
Gila Cliff	1	49	0.00	0.00
Paquimé	6	1,212	0.69	0.50
Snaketown	1	68	1.47	1.47
Gran Quivira	78	2,298	5.76	3.43
Long House	13	1,590	10.48	0.82
Point of Pines	57	697	12.45	1.75
Nalakihu	1	6	16.67	16.67
Grasshopper	80	647	20.46	12.40

protein throughout the occupation of Snaketown, the people appear to have been more preoccupied with farming than those of any other area of the Southwest. In addition to corn, beans, and squash, the Hohokam raised cotton in quantity. This provided them with a source of oil and protein from cotton seed. Many archaeologists consider cottonseed inedible, but it was used as a food beyond the Hohokam Area at sites throughout the Southwest as distant as Antelolpe House, Inscription House, Glen Canyon, and probably Gila Pueblo. It is still used among the Pima, and by the Hopi to oil their piki stones (Morris 1986:111, 177; McKusick and Young 1997:91).

Tables 4 through 7 are offered in order to provide a basis for comparison of the Snaketown collection with collections from a sampling of other sites from various areas in the Southwest. Nalakihu is included because 100% of the avian collection from that site was composed of species used for sacrifice. Percentages are given relative to total birds and non-turkey birds because turkeys constitute such a high percentage of avian remains from most sites that the relationships of birds of sacrifice species to other non-domestic species is obscured.

It is apparent from these tables that there are more macaws in the Snaketown collection numerically than at Gran Quivira or Picuris, and more percentagewise than at Gran Quivira, Picuris, or Grasshopper. There are no Golden Eagles or owls. There are more eagles than turkeys at Picuris, and more macaws than turkeys at Paquimé. Turkeys constitute 93.12% of the Antelope house collection, and 92.2% of the Long House collection. Commercial activity, such as agricultural specialization among the riverine Hohokam, raising macaws for trade at Paquimé, the manufacture of bird bone tubes at Picuris and at Gran Quivira, the production of feather robes at Antelope House, and the food use of turkeys at Mesa Verde, is usually the most conspicuous feature of an avian collection. Ceremonial, ritual, and sacrificial usage is generally of secondary magnitude. An exception to this commercial concern is Nalakihu, where 100% of the avian collection is species used for sacrifice. King correctly noted that something peculiar was going on there. In the present state of knowledge of avian usage, Nalakihu would have been interpreted as a special use area which served some integrative purpose in Sinagua society. Considering the Hohokam preoccupation with irrigated farming, the scarcity of macaws in the Hohokam collections does not disprove a strong Mesoamerican influence.

EFFECTS OF SETTLEMENT AGGREGATION AND THE DEVELOPMENT OF THE KATSINA CULT ON AVIAN SACRIFICE

Following the conspicuous peak in the macaw trade at the Mimbres, Chaco Canyon, and Sinagua sites, ceremonial activity involving the importation of Scarlet Macaws for sacrifice slowed, or perhaps virtually stopped by 1200. Then, about 1275, something happened. There is evidence of the beginning of a revival of the trade of live Scarlet Macaws at such scattered sites as Kiet Siel, Pollock's Ranch, Houck, Turkey Creek, Point of Pines, and Gila Cliff Dwellings. This secondary peak in the live macaw trade then shifts to Kinishba and Grasshopper during the 1300s. Post-1400 macaw remains are again few in number and widely scattered.

E. Charles Adams (1991) outlines the origin and development of the Katsina Cult as beginning in the middle Little Colorado Valley about 1275. According to Adams, the Katsina Cult activities were planned in rectangular kivas, performed in enclosed plazas, expressed in katsina representations in asymetrical pottery designs, advertized through katsina depictions in rock art, and intended to increase intramural cooperation and extramural trade involving agglomerated communities. It apparently proved successful in these purposes, because it crosscut groups with divergent interests and backgrounds.

Both Grasshopper and Point of Pines are large agglomerated sites. From avian and mammalian remains I would characterize the inhabitants of the eastern Room Block 1 at Grasshopper as incoming Anasazi folk who were taking advantage of a good climatic period to practice farming in the mountain meadows. Their focus was farming and raising Large Indian Domestic Turkeys like those at Kinishba. Numerous waterfowl suggest that they had control of the reservoir just upstream of the village. The avian and mammalian remains from Room Block 2, just west of the old bed of the Salt River Draw, were more Mogollon in character, and the people were more active in hunting Mule Deer and gathering wild upland foodstuffs. This group also hunted and ate far more Merriam's Wild Turkeys than any other group with which I am familiar. Previously (McKusick 1982), I suggested that the dual division of the pueblo might indicate a moiety system. After I passed on to other projects, subsequent excavation revealed that there was another area, Room Block 3 on the west side of the site, which was different yet. Burials indicate that the inhabitants of Room Block 1 practiced Anasazi cranial deformation, the inhabitants of Room Block 2 practiced Mogollon cranial deformation, and that the skulls of the burials from Room Block 3 were not deformed (Reid and Whittlesey 1999:117-119). While the cranial deformation practices agree with the avian collections of Room Blocks 1 and 2, the presence of a third unidentified group indicates that village organization was the result of agglomeration rather than of a moiety system.

In plotting occurrences of sacrificial bird species for Grasshopper Pueblo, there is a clustering of 17 individuals around an unnamed plaza-like area between the upstream end of Room Block 1 and the small Room Block 5. More conspicuous however, is a concentration of 43 individuals in and around Plaza 3/Great Kiva in Room Block 2.

Point of Pines has an even more conspicuous division of population. One section of the south end of the pueblo was occupied by a group of settlers from Kayenta. Here, the differences in avian usage were not so much in species, but in disposal of carcasses. The Kayenta people tended to bury hawks, macaws, and ravens under the floors of their kiva or rooms adjacent to it. The larger, local group tended to deposit the carcasses of their birds of sacrifice in the trash dumps among human burials more often than they buried them under floors. Like Grasshopper, the Great Kiva at Point of Pines had a sprinkling of birds of sacrifice buried under it or under adjacent rooms, suggesting that it was a center for activities which integrated the entire community. If the Katsina Cult was present at Grasshopper and at Point of Pines, as seems likely, it may be the stimulus for the revival of the trade in live macaws evident at those sites.

As time went on, the Katsina Cult spread to many pueblos. One that escaped its influence is Picuris. Herbert Dick (personal communication June 1991) described Picuris as composed of local people rather than as an agglomerated site populated by groups moving in from other areas. As such, the pueblo would have been united in history, custom, and purpose, and there would have been no need to adopt the Katsina Cult as an integrating agency. According to Dick, the Picuris people have a long history of eating domestic turkeys, and do not today use feathers of any sort. This is in sharp contrast to pueblos where the Katsina Cult is prominent and requires the planting of prayer feathers for hundreds of purposes, and where turkeys were not generally eaten.

DIFFERING VIEWPOINTS ON THE LATE PREHISTORIC RELIGIOUS COMPLEX IN THE SOUTHWEST CULTURE AREA

Frank Crosswhite (personal communication) has compiled a vast array of botanical information based on the association of Mesoamerican supernaturals with the introduction of corn farming into the Southwest. He calls this complex "Quetzalcoatlism", and visualizes the varying dominant forces such as Ehecatl, Xolotl, and Tezcatlipoca as avatars of Quetzalcoatl.

Lange (1992:325-333) leans toward a view based partly on the distribution of redware pottery in which Quetzalcoatl is associated with the Pueblo Katsina Cult, and Tezcatlipoca is associated with the Hohokam Platform Mound. He points out that the distribution of the Scarlet Macaw and platform mounds are nearly mutually exclusive in the post-Classic.

From my viewpoint, based mainly on the presence of bones of birds of sacrifice, the supernaturals in the Southwest ultimately hark back to Raven (Xiuhtecutli), the primal flux. I agree that the Mesoamerican ceremonial complex arrived in the Southwest contemporaneously with the beginning of corn culture, an opinion offered by Reyman in 1971. Whereas Lange sees Quetzalcoatl and Tezcatlipoca as separate, even opposed, I see them as the necessary parts of a whole, maintaining a dynamic balance, especially in the post-Classic.

Taking the Globe Area Salado as an example, it appears that there were far too many people for the carrying capacity of the land. Gila Pueblo suffered from episodes of armed conflict in 1260, in 1340, and in 1440, when the pueblo was destroyed for the final time. Extensive woodcutting had resulted in the irrigated agricultural fields being subjected to sheet erosion from the denuded hillsides. In spite of this, a lively export was being carried on of turquoise jewelry, fine cardium shell beads, ground pigments, nests of five polychrome bowls, and fine cotton cloth. The personal adornment of two groups of high status persons, both male and female, killed in the final attack suggests that Quetzalcatl was the patron of one moiety, and that Tezcatlipoca was the patron of another moiety, both of which were valuable to the governing of the pueblo (Figure 45).

Figure 45. Left, Tonto Polychrome human effigy jar from Gila Pueblo depicting a medicine pouch worn on right hip similar to those of two high status men at Gila Pueblo. The star suggests Quetzalcoatl. Right, detail of Mimbres Polychrome bowl design of man costumed as a bat, an animal associated with Tezcatlipoca. The hair pins are identical to those of two other high status men killed in the ceremonial complex in 1440. After Brody *et al* 1983: Figure 6.

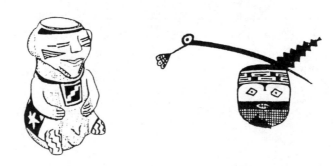

CHAPTER 17

SUMMARY AND CONCLUSIONS

The place of birds in human ceremonialism has a venerable history. Depictions of birds first appear in Upper Paleolithic cave paintings at Lascaux, Montignac, Dordogne, France. Interestingly, the birds are not depicted for their own sake, but as part of ceremonial apparatus. A man wearing a bird headdress lies inert before the horns of a bison which has been disemboweled by a spear wound. Beside him lie a spear thrower and a staff topped with a bird. A nearby rhinoceros does not seem to be part of the scene. The painting, at the bottom of a 23 foot shaft, has been interpreted as a fatal hunting accident; as a dispute between bird, bison, and rhinoceros clans; and, most commonly, as a shaman who has fallen into a trance. The shaman hypothesis is supported by the fact that the bird-topped staff or spear thrower is associated with the paraphernalia of modern Siberian shamans (Prideau 1973:130-131). A reindeer antler artifact of this type topped with a beautiful heath cock carved in full round was recovered from Le Mas d'Azil, Ariege, France. This cave is also noted for its numerous bird figures, which has led to speculation about early totemism (Torbrügge 1968:20-21).

The study of birds of sacrifice in the North American Southwest was begun in 1963 in order to attempt to make order out of the chaos of thousands of avian identifications from sites extending through a period of more than two thousand years. The idea of tracing Mesoamerican influence in the Southwest by plotting birds of sacrifice on maps representing different periods in history grew out of the identification studies of Paquimé, Point of Pines, and Gran Quivira. The trade connections of Point of Pines with the other two sites was verified by comparison of the bones of imported turkeys, and by duplication of cranial aberrations in Scarlet Macaws. Following Mesoamerican influences in the Southwest through expressions of widely distributed archetypal concepts led to a consideration of the deities which personified some of these archetypes. Tracing Mesoamerican deities by means of birds of sacrifice was necessitated by the differences in artistic traditions of Mesoamerica and the Southwest.

This study has demonstrated a remarkable consistency in ritual practice for over 11,000 years. Raven, venerated by the Paleo-Indians, is still important. The Golden Eagle has been used as a sacrificial bird from extremely ancient times into the present. The Small Indian Domestic Turkey, which was so fragile that it never went feral, was maintained as a separate breed, even in the presence of the much more numerous Large Indian Domestic Turkey, from perhaps as early as 300 B.C. until A.D.1672 when the breed was extinguished with the fall of the Tompiro Pueblos. The Large Indian Domestic Turkey was used in sacrifices as least as early as the A.D. 1000s until about A.D. 1723, when it disappeared as a domestic breed due to the decline of the Rio Grande Pueblos. Macaws have been used from the A.D. 500s-600s to the present.

It has been suggested that, for all practical purposes, "birds ARE gods". They are not, of course, but the necessity of having the proper bird to sacrifice to maintain the harmony of the universe for human survival does make it possible to trace holarctic and Mesoamerican ceremonial activity through time and space in the Southwest Culture Area.

Two factors have emerged which help to explain the state of the Pan-Southwestern Socio-politico-religious Complex at the time of European contact. First is the breakup of central control in the Salado and Hohokam communities. Armed conflict is present at Gila Pueblo in 1260, but the ceremonial/redistribution complex was restored to use as a single, unchanged center of activity. However, when the 1340 destruction overtook the inhabitants of Gila Pueblo, central control ended. The reconstructed ceremonial/redistribution center had two foci by 1345. In 1440, when Gila Pueblo was finally wiped out, there were at least five foci of ceremonial artifacts in the south dozen rooms.

Teague (1993:435-454) outlines Pima oral traditions which recount an actual war in which one Hohokam platform mound community after another was destroyed. Warriors from the southern border area of Arizona moved northward striking one community after another, ending the war with the decimation of Casa Grande about 1358.

The second event which had a major impact upon the Pan-Southwestern Complex is the spread of the Katsina Cult. Ferg (1982) points out that there is a katsina representation on a polychrome bowl from Besh-Ba-Gowah, which is certainly part of the Katsina Cult pattern. Other parts, however, are missing or perhaps developmental. Tonto Cliff Dwelling does not seem to have a recognizable ceremonial room. Besh-Ba-Gowah has a very deep rectangular ceremonial room, which has many kiva-like characteristics. Gila Pueblo has an early large ceremonial room with looms and what appears to be a permanent slat altar set in a rectangular floor-level aperture. After about 1345 two sipapus are built in a new floor, one for each half of the room, and a balancing pair of looms are added. The effect is like twin, mirror image kivas set side by side in the same large room. Besh-Ba-Gowah and Gila Pueblo each have a large plaza which is divided in two. They would have been very useful as moiety-controlled market places, but were not really suitable for the performance of large masked dances. Avian remains from all three sites are rather sparse, in contrast to the abundant avian remains characteristic of sites where the Katsina Cult was practiced, and vast quantities of feathers from a large number of species were required to make prayer sticks to keep the affairs of the community running smoothly.

However scant the avian remains are in these three communities, they still indicate a continuation of the veneration of Mesoamerican supernaturals, unobscured by the Katsina Cult, up to about 1450. Tlaloc is indicated by the Small Indian Domestic Turkey neck bones specially deposited at Gila Pueblo and Casa Grande. The Sun is indicated by bones of the Golden Eagle at Besh-Ba-Gowah and at the Geronimo Ruin, a Salado site to the east. Quetzalcoatl is indicated by Scarlet Macaw feathers at Lower Tonto, and by the bones of two Scarlet Macaws accompanying a high status burial at Pinal Pueblo, across Sixshooter Canyon from Besh-Ba-Gowah. Tezcatlipoca is represented by a deposit of spurred shanks and feet of the Large Indian Domestic Turkey at Upper Tonto. Correspondences with the Classic Hohokam avian remains from Casa Grande and other sites (Ferg 1985: Table 3) suggest that a common religious background continued to be shared by the late Salados and the late Hohokam.

PART II

TAXONOMY AND COMPARATIVE OSTEOLOGY

CHAPTER 18

TYING UP LOOSE ENDS: TURKEYS

This chapter and the next deal with areas of debate on Pre-columbian avian remains which include everything from confusion to consternation among the ethnobiological community. I would have preferred to ignore all these issues, but so many of my colleagues have insisted that I attempt to defend the data, that I have at long last, and very reluctantly, agreed to do so.

I vigorously support the freedom of any investigator to formulate hypotheses, no matter how far-fetched they may seem, since proper, objective testing of these hypotheses will quickly eliminate those which are invalid. However, when scientific data are manipulated to produce results which are false, the data deserve defense to preserve the integrity of the scientific record.

My view of research can be likened to an attempt to cross a flowing stream dry-shod by jumping from rock to rock. The rocks are hypotheses which can be tested by various means such as archaeological testing or statistical analysis. If an hypothesis proves invalid, one simply retreats to the solid stepping stone preceding it, and formulates a new hypothesis which is susceptible to testing. It does not matter that a great number of hypotheses produce negative results, since negative results are as valid scientifically as positive results. Properly done, the stated test conditions must be such that the hypothesis can be confirmed or negated; i.e., one must state the conditions under which the hypothesis is denied, as well as the conditions under which it is satisfied or confirmed. What really matters is that a workable model is eventually developed -- that we finally reach the opposite bank, damp but undaunted.

I do not consider the model presented herein to be my, or anyone else's, last word on the subject. Each identification project I undertake brings new information which changes my view of Pre-columbian avian usage. Just as hypotheses are formulated and tested, models are modified and improved to fit additional data. Any given model is merely a stage in the progress of scientific enquiry; it is not an end result. This leads to the consideration of the first problem which my colleagues have urged me to discuss.

TAXONOMY:

Meleagris gallopavo coltoni

In the 1960s I was employed as an assistant to Lyndon L. Hargrave who was at that time

Collaborator in Archaeo-ornithology at the Southwest Archeological Center of the U. S. National Park Service in Globe, Arizona. One of the identification studies involved feathers from Sand Dune Cave, a Basketmaker site near Navajo Mountain, Utah. In the resultant publication, Hargrave (1970b:24, 25) presents an excellent discussion of the relevance of the Sand Dune Cave specimens to our knowledge of domestic and wild turkeys in the North American Southwest. Hargrave was troubled by the presence of a group of feathers (#D2116) from a small male turkey which had brown-toned vanes and quills. He had me prepare Table I comparing the brown-toned feathers with those of *Agriocharis (Meleagris) ocellata, Meleagris gallopavo merriami*, and *Meleagris gallopavo silvestris*. Shortly after the completion of this project, Hargrave accepted a position with Prescott College, and I continued working for the National Park Service. When the Museum of Northern Arizona decided to publish the Sand Dune Cave material, the finished manuscript with which they were provided described the brown-toned turkey feathers, but did not attempt to identify them as other than "Common Turkey".

About this time one of my daughters brought me four domestic turkey poults to raise as pets. It soon became apparent that the brown-toned feathers were nothing more than the first fall plumage of a normally pigmented male turkey.

When the Sand Dune Cave publication was released, I was startled to find that Hargrave had inserted three paragraphs naming a new subspecies, *Meleagris gallopavo coltoni*, in honor of Harold S. Colton, well-known archaeologist and founder of the Museum of Northern Arizona. Considering that Hargrave had in his collection the skin of a brown-toned turkey poult, there is uncertainty as to how this came about. Hargrave did admit to me before his death to having realized that the brown-toned turkey was a normally pigmented juvenile. When I asked him why he had named a new subspecies, he replied that he had wanted to honor Dr. Colton.

However altruistic the motive behind the naming of this new subspecies may have been, it is still invalid. Subspecies are not named without actual specimens which can be demonstrated to be different from already existing subspecies. Further, subspecies are not named on the basis of domestic breeds, they are only named when a wild population can be demonstrated to exist, or to have existed. The juvenile turkey feathers upon which the new subspecies, *M. g. coltoni*, is based do not meet these requirements. Therefore, *M. g. coltoni* does not exist; and I have assigned the brown-toned feathers to juvenile Large Indian Domestic, *M. g. merriami*, on a basis of the broad white bands on the wing feathers.

TAXONOMY:

Meleagris gallopavo tularosa

This consideration of turkey subspecies brings up the problem of *M. g. tularosa*, named by A. W. Schorger (1961, 1970). This name was given to fully-feathered mummies which differed in plumage, size, and osteological characters from turkeys recovered from the main body of Southwestern archaeological sites. Briefly, the turkeys were very small, short-shanked, hump-backed, unusually dark in color, with feathers extending up the neck to the base of the skull. The narrow white bands on the primary and secondary wing feathers give them a conspicuously dark appearance. Schorger believed that the Dragon's Blood Red coloration of the legs was indicative of recent domestication. I have since found that this is the normal coloration for the legs of fully adult male Indian Domestic Turkey of both breeds, and so is an indication of age rather than of recent domestication.

While Schorger was studying his short-shanked mummies, I was studying skeletal remains of a large population of small, hump-backed, short-shanked turkeys from excavations at Gran Quivira, New Mexico. Schorger and I were corresponding about these unusual fowl, and soon realized that we were working with the same form. As a result, I began to refer my Small Indian Domestic Turkeys to *M. g. tularosa*, but was promptly taken to task for this by Amadeo M. Rea, who correctly pointed out that no wild population of this bird can yet be demonstrated to exist or to have existed. Accordingly, I have subsequently referred the Small Indian Domestic to *M. g. silvestris (tularosa)*, to acknowledge that it is the same as Schorger's mummies on one hand, and to concede that it cannot be established as a valid subspecies on the other. Indeed, it is osteologically closest to western *M. g. silvestris*, from which it was apparently domesticated.

M. g. osceola, the wild turkey native to Florida, is also small, and dark in coloration. Small, dark-colored subspecies are usually found in warm, wet environments. Since Florida is a long way from the North American Southwest, and *M. g. osceola* (Olsen 1968:107-137) differs in character from *M. g. silvestris (tularosa)*, I have suggested the coastal lowlands of southwestern Texas or extreme northeastern Mexico as a possible source for the Small Indian Domestic.

COMPUTER MODEL PROBLEM:

EMANUEL BREITBURG'S 1988 DOCTORAL DISSERTATION

In the mid-1980s I received a long distance phone call from Emanuel Breitburg requesting my lifetime accumulation of metric measurements of turkey bones. Since it is my practice to provide students with whatever resources they need, I offered to send the metric data, including several standard measurements on the humerus, tibiotarsus, and tarsometatarsus, location, dating, age, sex, breed, drawings of character differences separating the turkey breeds, a chart indicating the distinguishing characteristics, a graph indicating the probable origin of the Large Indian Domestic, and maps showing routes of introduction into the Southwest. Breitburg declined the offer of all the background data, stating that he only intended to use the metrics to test a computer program which was reputed to consider bones as three-dimensional objects.

When his doctoral dissertation was completed I was dismayed to find that testing the computer program had grown into a larger work, the effect of which was to put forth a model which negates all the contributions to the study of the turkey in the North American Southwest so far amassed by Hargrave, Reed, Schorger, Steadman, Rea, Lang, Harris, and me, as well as many others.

When I provided the measurements, I had expected that all of them would be used. Instead, Breitburg excluded the measurements of the tibiotarsus which reveal conspicuous differences in both proportion and axial rotation and which separate the Small Indian Domestic (SID) from the Large Indian Domestic (LID) and Merriam's Wild Turkey. Further, he added measurements on the portion of the humeral head which articulates the wing to the body. This is a very conservative feature, which one would not expect to vary at all from one breed to the next. All turkeys fly, and do perch at night. Any variation in this articulation which impaired the turkey's ability to fly would result in its loss to a nocturnal predator. It is a self-limiting feature that one would not ordinarily choose to measure.

Briefly, Breitburg eliminated from consideration conspicuous size differences, conspicuous character differences, and the measurements of the tibiotarsus and pelvis which display conspicuous morphological differences, all characters which distinguish the SID from the LID and Merriam's Wild Turkey. He further excluded from consideration the all-important time levels from which the specimens were recovered. The elimination of these important variables has, I believe, resulted in skewed input, which has produced skewed output.

To illustrate further, I believe the reader will agree that turkeys and Sandhill Cranes are very different birds. However, the crane femur is so similar to the turkey femur that in the past they have been confused in identification studies (cf. Hargrave and Emslie 1979). If we entered the measurements for crane and turkey femora into the program in the same manner that Breitburg entered his data, the result would be that turkeys and cranes are identical. No computer program, no matter how well designed, is a substitute for intellectual honesty and scientific rigor. In the last analysis, it is the perspective and discernment of the researcher which is the deciding factor.

The product of this computer procedure and a lack of integration with the published literature have led Breitburg to formulate a model which displays many deficiencies. I will cover the most seriously disputed of these as briefly as possible:

A. Breitburg (1988:34) states that, "...investigators who have studied prehistoric turkey domestication have failed to take an objective approach by assuming a) turkey domestication is originally a Mesoamerican phenomenon...."

This statement can be taken two ways: it may be implying that archaeologists believe South Mexican Turkey, *M. g. gallopavo,* was actually imported into the North American Southwest, or that the idea of turkey domestication was imported into the Southwest. In answer to the first proposition, the South Mexican Turkey, *M. g. gallopavo,* the Rio Grande Turkey, *M. g. intermedia,* and Gould's Turkey, *M. g. mexicana,* are easily eliminated from consideration in regard to Southwest turkeys on character differences (McKusick 1986c: Figures 24, 25, 26, 27, 30, 32, and 33). There is no evidence of any South Mexican Turkeys in the Southwest prior to their introduction as a domestic meat producer in historic farmyards.

In regard to the second interpretation, we usually think of *M. g. silvestris* as inhabiting the northeastern United States, and *M. g. merriami* as inhabiting the Southwest, most of a continent away. These are misconceptions. *M. g. silvestris* extended as far west as Dewy, Major, and Alphalpha Counties in Oklahoma. *M. g. merriami* extended as far east as the drainage of the Cimarron River in the Oklahoma panhandle. Barely 185 miles separates these ranges (Schorger 1966:46-47).

Schorger demonstrated convincingly that *M. g. silvestris* turkeys were locally domesticated in many places, including Oklahoma. These incidents were totally unrelated to the local domestication of *M. g. gallopavo* in Mexico (Schorger 1966:3-18, 42-61). I agree with Schorger that the most probable source of the LID and *M. g. merriami* is the *M. g. silvestris* in Oklahoma. Further, the feather-necked mutation found in the SID is known to occur in *M. g. silvestris* (Schorger 1966:Plates 28 and 29). Both Indian domestic breeds have a purplish sheen on their contour feathers which they share with *M. g. silvestris*. This apparent relationship of the Indian domestic breeds with *M. g. silvestris* is borne out by osteological characters (see. Figures 45-51). In September of 1994, Sean Coughlin of the Department of Anthropology, University of Tennessee, Knoxville, loaned me the skeleton of an adult *M. g. silvestris* from a Mississippi population. This specimen was small, rather short-shanked, and hump-backed. Further, it was intermediate in both size and character between the SID and LID. Size and character indicate that *M. g. silvestris* is the wild progenitor of both domestic breeds known from the Southwest. The SID represents a very early domestication which appears to have selected for the feather-necked mutation, which incidentally accentuated the short, dumpy appearance of the breed. The extreme uniformity of the Small Indian Domestic through its long history suggests very low heterozygosity. This was probably initially the result of selection for the desired feathering, which was later intensified by its having been introduced in very small numbers into the Southwest, where there were no turkeys at all. Very low heterozygosity is probably the reason the SID never went feral (Stangel *et al.*1992:24-27).

The buff rump found in the turkeys of the Southwest may be a result of random genetic drift within a small population, may have been an adaptation of protective coloration appropriate to the desert, or may have been deliberately perpetuated in the domestic form.

Breitburg fails to note the fact that there is no evidence of turkeys in the Southwest before they appear already well integrated into their keepers' economies and ceremonial practices. The SID appears to enter the Southwest via the Pecos River drainage, veering west-northwest at the Guadalupe Mountains, and reaching Tularosa Cave in western New Mexico by about 250 B.C. and Canyon del Muerto in the Four Corners area long before A.D. 250. Turkeys occur in Basketmaker II cultural deposits on Black Mesa in the Lolomai Phase, A.D. 100 to 300 (Whitecotton and Lebo 1980: 168; Lebo and Warburton 1982: 82; Leonard, Belser, Jessup, and Carucci 1984: 371, 387; Leonard 1989:10-11). The SID is the only turkey in the Southwest from 250 B.C. to A.D. 500, a period of 750 years. The SID is found only in association with human settlements.

B. Breitburg (1988:88) states "Size degeneration is evident in the Gran Quivira population, and it is suggested to be a result of isolation and reduced gene flow between parent prehistoric wild and/or domestic Gran Quivira populations".

This statement is contrary to fact. The Gran Quivira turkey population does not degenerate in size with time; it is fully representative of the SID breed at all time levels. Gran Quivira turkeys are neither larger nor smaller than the earliest turkeys brought into the Southwest about 250 B.C. The SID breed is remarkably consistent in size, feathering, morphology, and osteological character for its entire history of more than 1900 years. It was carefully preserved as a separate breed where it occurred, except for the trading centers of Yellow Jacket on the north, Pottery Mound in the middle, and Paquimé on the south. These three sites were commercial centers where hybrid turkey (Text continues on page 122)

Specimens drawn in turkey illustrations include:

A124, *Meleagris gallopavo merriami,* young adult female, collected 1971 near Payson, Arizona. Southwest Bird Laboratory Collection.

A197, *Meleagris gallopavo merriami,* adult female, collected 1982 south of Flagstaff, Arizona. Southwest Bird Laboratory Collection.

#3650, *Meleagris gallopavo silvestris,* adult female, collected 1977 in Mississippi. University of Tennessee Collection.

C1, smallest known Large Indian Domestic, *Meleagris gallopavo merriami,* archaeological adult female turkey buried beneath the floor of Room 50, Pueblo del Arroyo, Chaco Canyon National Monument, New Mexico. Western Archeological and Conservation Center Collection.

#1655, Small Indian Domestic, *Meleagris gallopaveo silvestris (tularosa),* archaeological adult female from Mound 7, Salinas Pueblos National Monument. Western Archeological and Conservation Center Collection.

Figure 46. CHARACTERS OF THE TURKEY PELVIS

Dorsal and caudal views of the pelvis, adult females, Scale: X 1.

A and C, A124, Merriam's Wild Turkey, *M. g. merriami.*

B and D, #3650, Eastern Wild Turkey, *M. g. silvestris.*

The pelvis of Merriam's Wild Turkey is broad and flat in appearance, characters present in the Large Indian Domestic. The depressed area of the interacetabular synsacrum is both large and deep (a).

The pelvis of the Eastern Wild Turkey is laterally compressed in appearance, sloping downward on each side from the synsacrum. The depressed area of the interacetabular synsacrum is very small (a'). This pelvis is similar to that of the Small Indian Domestic (cf. McKusick 1986c: 46, Figure 29).

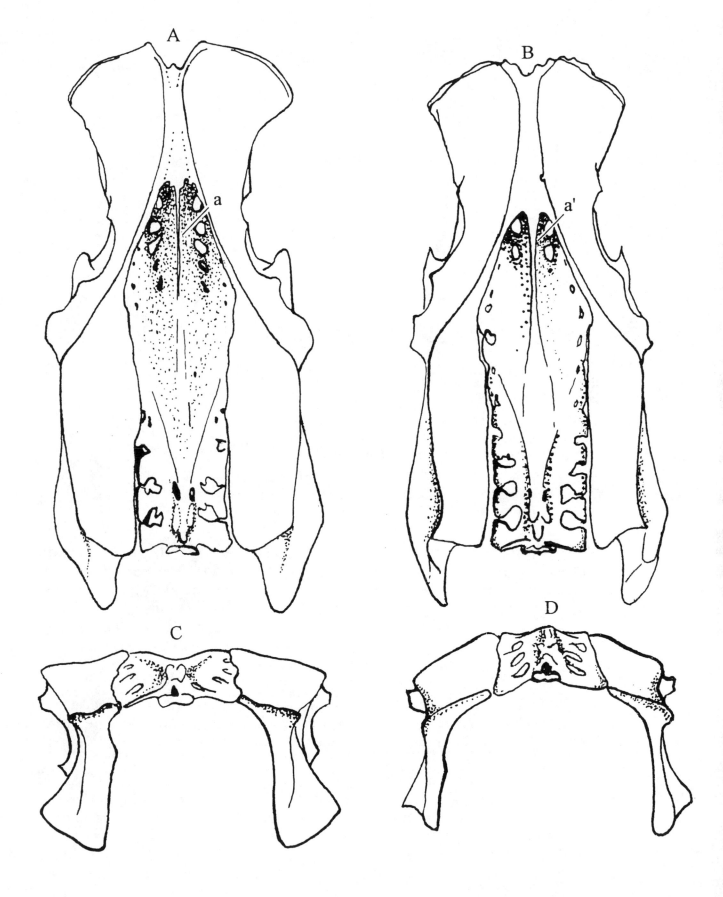

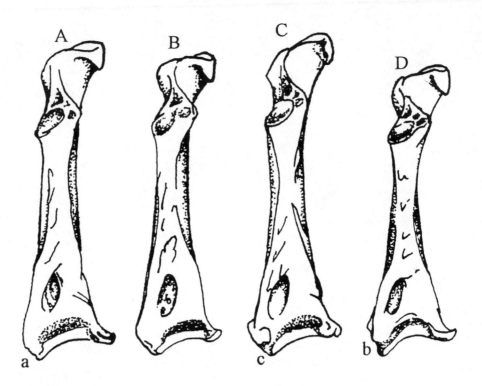

Figure 47. CHARACTERS OF THE TURKEY CORACOID
Left coracoids, dorsal view, adult females. Scale: X1.

A. A124, Merriam's Wild Turkey, *M. g. merriami.*
B. C1, smallest known Large Indian Domestic, *M. g. merriami.*
C. #3650, Eastern Wild Turkey, *M. g. silvestris.*
D. #1655, Small Indian Domestic, *M. g. silvestris (tularosa).*

M. g. merriami specimens have a straight-to-convex area (a) between the sternocoracoidal process and the sternal facet (see. McKusick 1986c: 36, Fig. 24). The Small Indian Domestic is concave in this area with a definite notch (b) which it shares with the surviving mummified specimen from Tularosa Cave, the feather-necked, dark-plumaged, "Tularosa Turkey". The Eastern Wild Turkey, like the Small Indian Domestic, has a definite notch (c) in this area. The modern Eastern Wild Turkey is intermediate in this character between the Small Indian Domestic and the Large Indian Domestic, and is least like the modern Merriam's Wild Turkey.

The Eastern Wild Turkey appears to be the wild progenitor of the Small Indian Domestic, a very early, very homogeneous breed present in the North American Southwest from perhaps 250 B.C. until A.D.1672 when it became extinct with the fall of the Tompiro Pueblos.

The Large Indian Domestic also appears to be derived from the Eastern Wild Turkey. It arrived in the Southwest Culture Area in the A.D. 500s as a recently or partially domesticated fowl, perhaps up the Cimarron River, since early Large Indian Domestics were recovered from Ancho Canyon west of Raton.. A feral form, Merriam's Wild Turkey, first appears in the archaeological record during the A.D. 600s in areas adjacent to settlements where the Large Indian Domestics were kept. The last large herds of Indian Domestic Turkeys were reported in A.D. 1723 (Schroeder 1968: 102-103).

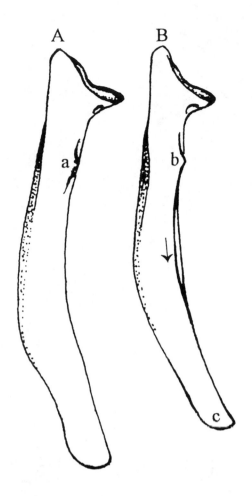

Figure 48. CHARACTERS OF THE TURKEY SCAPULA
Left scapulae, ventral view, adult females. Scale: X 1.

A. A197, Merriam's Wild Turkey, *M. g. merriami.*
B. #3650, Eastern Wild Turkey, *M. g. silvestris.*

The scapular tubercle (a) rises and falls in Merriam's Wild turkey, a character it shares with the Large Indian Domestic. The scapular tubercle rises and continues in a definite intermuscular line (b) in the Eastern Wild Turkey, a character it shares with the Small Indian Domestic.

The caudal limit of the scapular blade is more tapered in the Eastern Wild Turkey (c) and the Small Indian Domestic than is that of Merriam's Wild Turkey and the Large Indian Domestic.

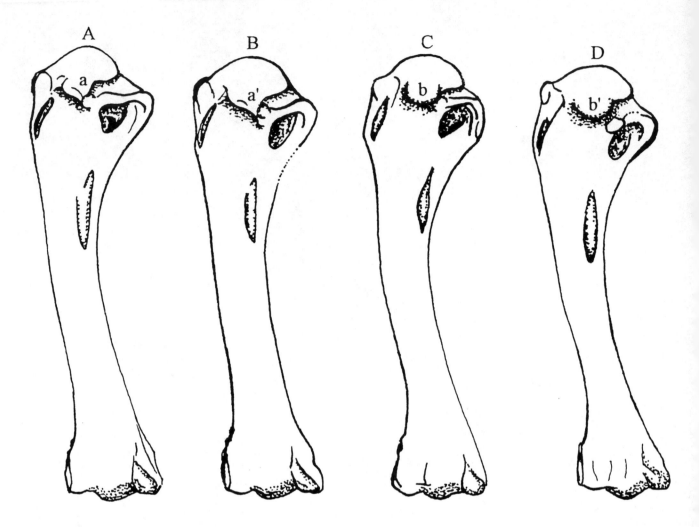

Figure 49. COMPARISON OF TURKEY HUMERI

Left humeri, anconal view, adult females. Scale: X1.

A. A124, Merriam's Wild Turkey, *M. g. merriami.*

B. C1, smallest known Large Indian Domestic, *M. g. merriami.*

C. #3650, Eastern Wild Turkey, *M. g. silvestris.*

D. #1655, Small Indian Domestic, *M. g. silvestris (tularosa).*

The margin of the articular head of *M. g. merriami* is concave to S-shaped (a, a'). The same area in *m. g. silvestris* is bulbous (b, b'). The shaft of the humerus is rather straight and stout in *M. g. merriami.* It is more graceful and gracile in the Eastern Wild Turkey, and even more markedly gracile in the Small Indian Domestic.

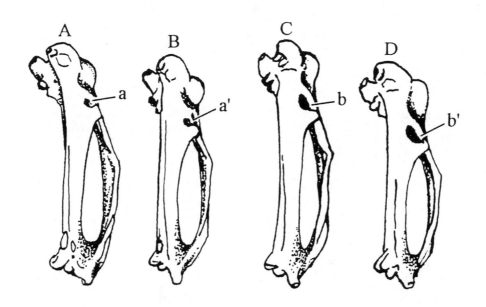

Figure 50. COMPARISON OF TURKEY CARPOMETACARPI

Left carpometacarpi, lateral view, adult females. Scale: X 1.

A. A124, Merriam's Wild Turkey, *M. g. merriami.*

B. C1, smallest known Large Indian Domestic, *M. g. merriami.*

C. #3650, Eastern Wild Turkey, *M. g. silvestris.*

D. #1655, Small Indian Domestic, *M. g. silvestris (tularosa).*

     The area enclosed by the intermetacarpal process is very small and round in *M. g. merriami* (a, a'), but it is larger and more oval in *M. g. silvestris* (b) and in *M. g. silvestris (tularosa)* (b').

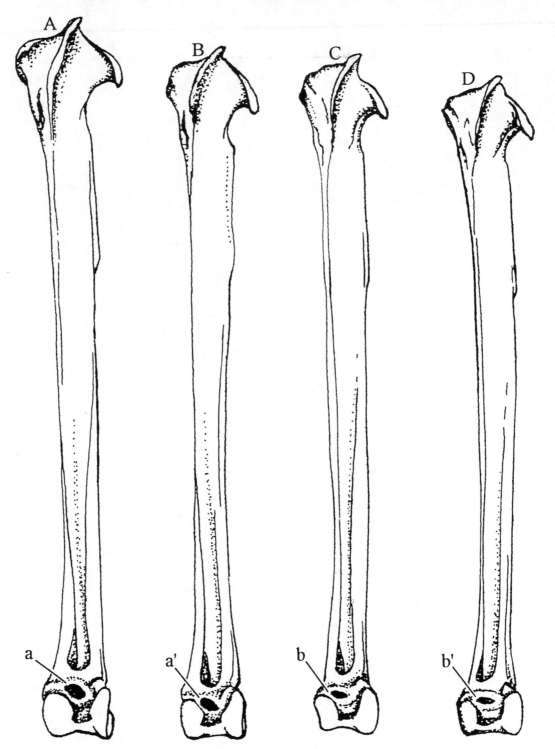

Figure 51. COMPARISON OF TURKEY TIBIOTARSI

Left tibiotarsi, anterior view, adult females. Scale: X1.

A. A197, Merriam's Wild Turkey, *M. g. merrriami.*

B. C1, smallest known Large Indian Domestic, *M. g. merriami.*

C. #3650, Eastern Wild Turkey, *M. g. silvestris.*

D. #1655, Small Indian Domestic, *M. g. silvestris (tularosa).*

      The area enclosed by the tendinal arch is rather large (a, a') in *M. g. merriami,* and is narrower and smaller (b, b') in *M. g. silvestris.* Again, the Eastern Wild Turkey is intermediate between SID and LID, and least like the modern Merriam's Wild Turkey.

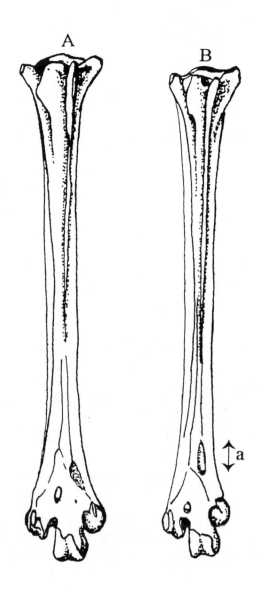

Figure 52. COMPARISON OF TURKEY TARSOMETATARSI
Left Tarsometatarsi, posterior view, adult females. Scale: X 1.
A. A197, Merriam's Wild Turkey, *M. g. merriami.*
B. #3650, Eastern Wild Turkey, *M. g. silvestris.*

  The distal end of the *M. g. merriami* tarsometatarsus is broad, resembling an open hand. The distal end of the *M. g. silvestris* tarsometartarsus is laterally constricted, resembling a more closed hand. This constriction brings the muscular attachment into a position where it is parallel to the long axis of the shaft (a).

populations were the rule. At Yellow Jacket, the hybrid turkeys displayed the small size of the SID and the skeletal character differences of the LID. At Pottery Mound, the turkeys were a more even blend with short but stocky bones. At Paquimé, the hybrid turkeys displayed the large size of the LID and the skeletal character differences of the SID.

C. Breitburg (1988:71) further states, "...even though some investigators continue to suggest that Merriam's turkey is a feral domestic of Mexican derivation, the above analysis suggests that assertion to be unlikely, ...would a domestic animal gone feral show an increase in size?"

First, I do not believe that the Large Indian Domestic came from Mexico, nor do any other avian osteologists that I know of. Second, had Breitburg not rejected the time level data I attempted to persuade him to use, he would have been aware that when the LID entered the Southwest from the east, during the A.D. 500s, it was fully as large as *M. g. silvestris*. *M. g. merriami*, maintained this large size in the wild from its first appearance in the A.D. 600s, to the present day. The peculiarities which distinguish *M. g. merriami*, such as irregular spurring and reduced harem size, appear to me to support a model proposing their derivation from a domestic strain with a somewhat different gene pool than that found among other wild turkey subspecies.

The reduction in size of the late LID, particularly among the hybrid population at the trading center at Pottery Mound, is the result of 1200 years of occasional unintentional interbreeding with the SID. Breitburg did not separate the breeds in his computer input for the various sites, but most prehistoric and early historic turkey breeders of the Southwest did separate them. They used turkey pens to keep them in separate plazas at Antelope House. They also kept turkeys with aberrant colorations separate for hundreds of years. If these separations were so important to the Indians we are attempting to study by accumulating data on turkeys, I believe it is incumbent upon us to make the same distinctions when we are processing these data.

D. Breitburg (1988:37) objects to my statement that, to the best of my knowledge, SID were not normally food items. He cites data from Gran Quivira to support this objection, and attributes my opinion that the SID was not generally eaten to "intuition".

I assure the reader that all of my opinions on turkeys are the result of detailed drawings of character differences, painstaking metric measurements, and meticulous record-keeping over a period of nearly 40 years. Most of the Gran Quivira burials of intact turkeys come from the earliest period, which is what one would have expected of the pan-Southwestern ceremonial complex which was practiced at that time. Most of the broken turkey bone is from trash which accumulated late in the history of the pueblo. During this period the Katsina Cult was practiced at Gran Quivira, as indicated by kiva murals and Katsina representations painted on pottery. The practices of this cult do not involve the burial of those birds stripped of feathers for ritual and ceremonial purposes; they are simply tossed out on the dump. Once there they may have had hot coals thrown over them, which caused burning. However, this evidence of burning was consistent with that occurring when bare bones are subjected to fire, which is unlike that charring which occurs on the portions of bones that project from roasting meat. All evidence indicated that boiling was the customary method of cooking meat at this site. There were also dogs which no doubt scavenged on the dump for at least part of their food, causing breakage of turkey bone in the process.

Alden Hayes, Jerry Greene, and I had several conversations on possible food use of turkeys at Gran Quivira. The cooking jars were so small at this site that we could not devise a way to put a turkey into one for cooking, even if dismembered. Our final decision on the matter was that turkeys were so valuable for their production of raw materials for feather-cord robes and feathers for a variety of other purposes, that most were probably kept for this purpose until they died of natural causes. Cuts made on dead bone at this and other sites suggest that tool stock was removed from dead turkeys before they were consigned to the trash dump.

In spite of the disagreements between our current models, it is worth noting that Breitburg's and my models agree that turkeys domesticated in Central Mexico play no part in the North American Southwest, and that all Southwest domestic turkeys, as well as Merriam's Wild Turkey eventually hark back to *M. g. silvestris*.

DNA STUDIES OF TURKEYS: KAREN E. MOCK

During the 1999-2000 school year at Northern Arizona University, Karen E. Mock performed DNA analyses on modern relict subspecies of wild turkeys in preparation of her doctoral dissertation. The South Mexican subspecies was excluded because there is serious doubt as to its survival. She also attempted to secure DNA material from the two Indian Domestic breeds, but was unsuccessful. Although the results of her study reveal differences between the subspecies, *M. g. silvestris* and *M. g. osceola* are most similar, and *M. g. mexicana* is most divergent (Mock, Theimer, Greenberg, and Keim 1999) . These results agree with the osteology presented herein, and in McKusick 1986c, in spite of the facts that SID has been separated from its wild progenitor for at least 2300 years, LID has been separated from its wild progenitor for at least 1500 years, and that the turkey is considered to be a very plastic species.

WILDLIFE MANAGEMENT PERSPECTIVES: HARLEY G. SHAW

Harley G. Shaw, General Wildlife Services, Chino Valley, Arizona, has presented a model which is a refreshing new view of the Merriam's Wild Turkey/LID problem (Shaw 1995). To simplify, there is no evidence of the Common Turkey, *Meleagris gallopavo*, in the Southwest before 250 B.C., at the very earliest (see. Steadman 1980, Rea 1980, McKusick 1980). To quote Shaw (1995: 4), "Limited evidence exists for a Pleistocene species, *Meleagris crassipes*, that occurred as far north as the Grand Canyon and as far south as Nuevo Leon in Mexico predating the Anasazi cultures. This bird survived after human arrival in the Southwest (until approximately 3000-6000 BP), and the cause of its extinction can only be guessed. Most likely, its habitat simply disappeared as a result of post-Pleistocene climatic, hence habitat, change. *M. crassipes* was probably not a player in the history of *M. g. merriami*."

Shaw , based on the experience of wildlife managers attempting transplants of domestic stock, has serious and reasonable doubts that feral turkeys arising from Indian Domestics could have survived. Southwestern habitats are marginal for turkeys today. In the recent past, forests may have been more open, and thus more suitable for turkeys before they were altered by heavy grazing, logging, and fire prevention. Climatic changes in the recent past are only beginning to be appreciated.

Shaw is understandably uncomfortable with my model which is admittedly influenced by my interest in cultural events which are contemporaneous with the appearance of the LID. Carter (1967:44-45, 50-53) has put forth a model in which 8-rowed flour corn moved into the Four Corners from the east from the area of the Oklahoma panhandle. In contrast, Ford (1981:7-8, 11-17, 21) has proposed a model in which improved corn moved through the same area in a west to east direction. Whichever direction this seed stock is eventually established to have moved, the human contact in the area has certainly been well demonstrated.

Shaw and I both find it very unsettling that Rea's and my model of LID going feral to become Miriam's Wild Turkey was so readily accepted by the biological community without their offering any alternative models (Kennamer, Kennamer, and Brenneman 1992:7). I believe this acceptance is based on the fact that osteological remains of LID in the Southwest are not only earlier than those of Merriam's Wild Turkey, but are far more numerous.

As an alternative model, Shaw has suggested three routes by which wild turkeys might have made their way into the Southwest by other than human agency: first, up the Canadian, Cimmaron, or Arkansas rivers; second, up the Pecos or Rio Grande rivers to the Guadalupe and Sacramento mountains; third, up the Gila and San Pedro rivers. There is no archaeological evidence to support the third route, but the first coincides with my model for the introduction of the LID and Carter's model for the introduction of 8-rowed flour corn, and the second coincides with my model for the introduction of the SID and compares in a more general way with Ford's model for the introduction of Teosinte-introgressed Chapalote corn (Ford 1981:13).

In August of 1994, Wetherbee B. Dorshow submitted for identification samples of turkey bone from the Ancho Canyon Project located in Colfax County, west of Raton, New Mexico. The bones were found in the eastern drainage of the Vermejo River, a tributary of the Canadian River. The earliest site from which these specimens were recovered, KS 60/290, dates to ca. A.D. 640. This site is Late Plains Archaic through middle Terminal Woodland, and was occupied by people of eastern origin, as indicated by diagnostic projectile points, architecture, faunal data, and human osteological data (Dorshow, personal communication 1994). The recovery of these turkey specimens, assigned to LID on size (McKusick 1997), lends weight to Shaw's first suggested route, up the Canadian, Cimmaron, or Arkansas rivers.

Three new models could be based upon the archaeological data at hand that would not do violence to the principles of wildlife management. It is possible that Merriam's Wild Turkey came in from the northeast under its own power, and was immediately domesticated by Basketmaker III people who were already well-qualified as turkey breeders from their centuries of experience with SID. As yet there are no osteological data to support this model. If bones of Merriam's Wild Turkey can be found among collections from the Four Corners Area, or from northern New Mexico, either from human habitational sites or from any other source, the immediate domestication of wild turkeys as they entered woud be the most reasonable model. In spite of many years of seeking such, I know of no bones of wild turkeys in this area from any time period. Merriam's Wild Turkey bones are found in collections from archaeological sites only along the Mogollon Rim and in the Mimbres Valley (McKusick 1986c:3-7).

The second new model might propose that wild turkeys could have been captured with snares, as pictured on Mimbres Classic pottery, and deliberately transplanted to the Mogollon Rim to provide a new resource. At first glance, this seems a really wild idea, but it would have been much easier to accomplish than the importation of Scarlet Macaws from the humid tropical lowlands of Mexico which was taking place beginning at this same time period. A persuasive argument against this model is the low rate of utilization of wild turkeys at this time period. The only site I know of at which Merriam's Wild Turkey was ever an important economic resource is Grasshopper Pueblo, which was occupied during the 1300s.

A third new model is suggested by the 1999 publication of David Keys' *Catastrophe, An Investigation into the Origins of the Modern World*. This volume documents a volcanic event which darkened the entire world for 18 months during A.D. 535-536. This explosive eruption, which occurred in the straits between what are now Java and Sumatra, was chronicled in detail in southeast Asia, and has been verified by studies of tree rings and glacial deposits in both the northern and southern hemispheres. So much water vapor, sulphur, and particulate matter was thrown into the stratosphere, that the sun was darkened except for about four hours per day for 18 months.

This disaster precipitated the fall of the Avar Empire on the steppes of western Asia, which in turn brought about the invasion of eastern Europe by waves of refugees and displaced persons bringing about a period popularly known as "The Dark Ages". There is no written documentation of the effects of this event upon the residents of the Great Plains of North America, but it is likely that as the grass failed to renew itself, the surviving population took refuge in more brushy and wooded areas such as those excavated by the Ancho Canyon Project in northeastern New Mexico. In any case, the groups of people of the Plains Woodland Culture who moved into the Southwest were in possession of the LID, and contact between the Plains and the Southwest has never been severed. Pecos, Picuris, and Taos Pueblos established a specialization in trading eagle bone tubes, eagle claws, and feathers to the Plains Indians which is still active. At this writing, these Plains Woodland settlers appear to be the most probable source for the LID.

CHAPTER 19

TYING UP LOOSE ENDS: MACAWS

The most recent tempest in the ethnozoological teapot was first presented as "Macaws at Casas Grandes: Adventures in the Bird Trade", at the 64th Pecos Conference in Casas Grandes, Chihuahua, Mexico, 1991, by Peter Y. Bullock, Office of Archaeological Studies, Museum of New Mexico, Santa Fe. The paper is currently being circulated under the title "Macaws at Casas Grandes and in the American Southwest."

To quote Bullock (1991:2-3):

> "The major problems addressed in this study are the validity of macaw sourcing through species identification, the implications this has with regard to regional trade, and the possibility of major modifications regarding prehistoric macaw ranges. A critical review of the macaw species identification system developed by Hargrave (Hargrave 1970), and modified by Mckusick (Mckusick 1974b) [sic] casts some doubt on its accuracy. How changes in identification pertain to accepted concepts of Southwestern regional and Southwest-Mesoamerican trade based on this evidence, are examined. Finally, an alternative conceptual view of prehistoric macaw occurrence, habitat, and range within the American Southwest is proposed which challenges the traditional premise of macaws as foreign goods."

In his paper, Bullock cites excerpts from various publications which are not related to macaw identifications in an attempt to establish that it is impossible to identify archaeological macaws to species by any means, including bones and feathers, so that he may put forth a new model of trade in the Southwest which divorces the culture area from direct influence from Mesoamerica. Since his propositions vary so widely from the archaeological record, and attempt to invalidate the scientific data, I will consider these points individually, six sins of commission, and seven more of omission.

A. Bullock (1991:5) states "A review of Hargrave's macaw identification system indicates one major flaw: it is not valid. One truism of ornithology is that related species within a given genus, with similar or overlapping body size ranges and differing only by plumage color, cannot be identified by skeletal remains alone (Pyle *et al.* 1987)."

Pyle's publication is a field guide, not a taxonomic work giving diagnostic, in-the-hand characters. It treats passerines which are small perching birds with many similar races which appear to the casual observer to differ only in the color of their plumage. Nothing could be farther from the truth. According to Amadeo M. Rea (personal communication, 25 September 1991), "There are even Passerine birds that are most easily identified on the basis of their skeletons, rather than skins. One need look no farther than *Tyranus melancholicus* and *T. couchi*, long considered the same species by those who don't pay any attention to skeletons. The same for *Pipilo fuscus* and *P. crissalis*.

These are finally being recognized by the AOU as full species, long after I published on them. And of course, the only safe way to identify most Aimophila (except in unworn plumage), is by the humeri! Avian paleontologists the world round are publishing daily on the specific identification of congenerics."

To return to macaws, Bullock appears to believe that Military and Scarlet Macaws overlap in size range and build. They do not. Blake (1953:191-192) lists live measurements for Military Macaws as 27-30" and Scarlet Macaws as "34-38". There is no overlap in feathered size. In addition, their proportions differ. Military Macaws have shorter wings and legs in proportion to their body size than do Scarlet Macaws. In bones, this is particularly conspicuous in the tibiotarsus (Figure 56).

B. Bullock (1991:6) objects to the use of bone measurements to differentiate macaw species.

Neither Hargrave nor I have ever used bone measurements to determine macaw species. All of our identifications are based on conspicuous character differences of the cranium, premaxilla, quadrate, basihyal-basibranchial, manubrium, sternal profile, humerus, femur, tibiotarsus, and tarsometatarsus (Figures 54-56). These character differences are not a matter of degree; they are a matter of "yes" or "no", | or 0, the current flows or it doesn't flow. This was done to assist the beginning student on the one hand, and to facilitate computer data entry on the other.

Early in the 1960s we recruited Ruins Stabilization Unit personnel at Gila Pueblo who were not experienced with bones to test our criteria. Without exception, they made correct identifications of modern comparative specimens of known species. Bullock's opinion to the contrary, the criteria are valid, and our results have been replicated by a number of other investigators.

C. Bullock (1991:6) objects to determining age by bone measurements.

Neither Hargrave nor I have ever determined age stages by measurements. Progressive stages of ossification are clearly illustrated and discussed in *Mexican Macaws* (Hargrave 1970a: 3-10, 39, 45) and summerized in Figure 53. Apparently Bullock is unaware of the fact that young parrots, like the taxonomically adjacent pigeons, are large, fat, and actually heavier when they leave the nest than they will be at any other time in their lives.

D. Bullock (1991:6) states the archaeological macaw feathers cannot be identified to species on a basis of color, and that little has been done to identify the feathers which have been recovered.

Neither of these statements is accurate. The first part of this assertion contradicts Bullock's own point A, where he feel that feathers must be present for species identification. In actuality, macaw feathers are distinguishable on the basis of the color of the quill, the upper surface, the lower surface, and the down. Even Military Macaw feathers, Thick-billed Parrot feathers, and *Amazona* parrot feathers, all of which are green on their upper surface, may be separated by the differing colorations of the lower surface. The feathers of Scarlet Macaws are even easier to identify.

128

Bullock is apparently also unaware that I long ago identified all the prehistoric Southwestern macaw feathers available for study, and that the results are published (Anderson *et al.* 1986: 241).

E. Bullock (1991:7) suggests the capture and keeping of Military Macaws.

He appears to be unaware that while Scarlet Macaws are relatively docile (but not so docile as Green-Winged Macaws and Blue and Gold Macaws), and are relatively easily kept and transported, Military Macaws tend to be vicious and difficult to keep, much less transport. A wild-caught Military Macaw would simply have bitten its way out of a wooden cage and flown off. Even in a metal cage, wild-caught Military Macaws commonly beat themselves against the bars until all their limbs are broken and they die. Even hand-raised Military Macaws are difficult to keep. Jonathan Reyman has found from experience with the Feather Distribution Project (Reyman 1990) that of the thousands of bird owners and others who contribute feathers, only two have Military Macaws.

F. Bullock (1991:8) seems to imply that the Southwest Culture Area had an inability or unwillingness to absort a large feather production.

There is a still-sacred cave in east central Arizona which contains large quantities of macaw feathers. This is but one accident of preservation. How can one assume that, once the Katsina Cult was established, the immense need for feathers which can be established for many other species did not extend to macaws? Reyman (personal communication) reports that in the first 15½ years of the Feather Distribution Project, he processed 4,000,000 feathers of which 2,100,000 were wild turkey and 1,900,000 were macaw and parrot.

G. Bullock's model does not consider that Scarlet Macaw feathers in the Southwest number in the thousands, in contrast to only one or two feathers for the Miliary Macaw, Thick-billed Parrot, and Blue-and-Gold Macaw.

H. Bullock's model does not mention the inclusion of Scarlet Macaw feathers colored red, yellow, and blue in Pre-Columbian Southwestern artifacts such as circlets, fetishes, and dance aprons. The Lavender Creek Cave, San Juan County, Utah, apron had 2,336 feathers in one apron (Time-Life 1992a:126).

I. Bullock's model also fails to discuss the depictions of Scarlet Macaws in kiva murals and painted pottery. The ivory upper beak of the Scarlet Macaw is a diagnostic which distinguished this species from the Military Macaws, Thick-billed Parrots, and *Amazona* Parrots even on black-and-white painted pottery. The yellow upper wing coverts also serve to distinguish the Scarlet Macaw on Mimbres Polychrome. The red coloration of the Scarlet Macaws is a conspicuous feature of oxidized polychrome pottery and of kiva murals.

J. Bullock's model does not deal with the identical cranial aberrations found in the skeletal remains of macaws at Paquimé and at Point of Pines, which I believe indicate the trade of Scarlet Macaws for Large Indian Domestic Turkeys.

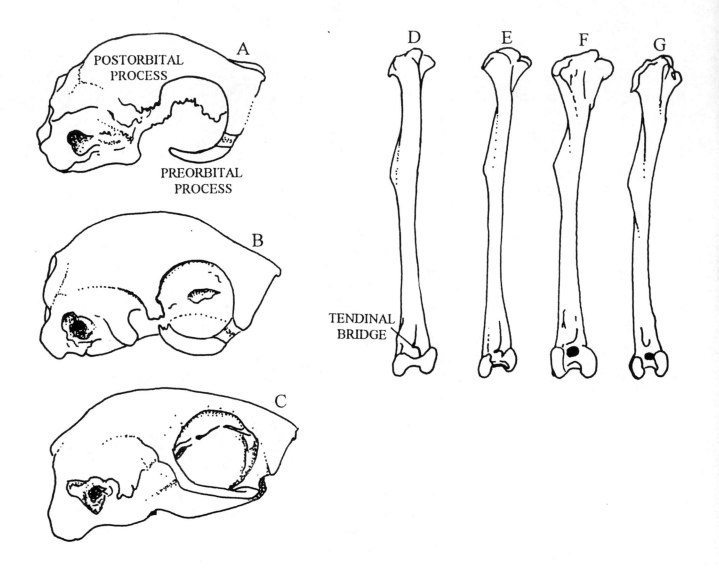

Figure 53. SUMMARY OF SCARLET MACAW AGE STAGE DETERMINATION

A-C, cranium, right lateral view; D-G, tibiotarsus, anterior view. Scale: X 1.

A. CG298, Early Immature, 4+ months, preorbital and postorbital processes beginning to grow.

B. CG246, Late Immature, 8+ months, preorbital and postorbital processes nearly joined.

C. H2107, Newfledged, 11-12 months, orbit complete.

D. CG246, Late Immature, ca. 11 months, tendinal bridge beginning to grow.

E. H2159, Newfledged, 11-12 months tendinal bridge nearly joined.

F. PB2256, Adolescent, 1-3 years, tendinal bridge complete.

G. H2099, Old Adult, 4+ years, tendinal bridge widened.

After McKusick in Hargrave 1970a.

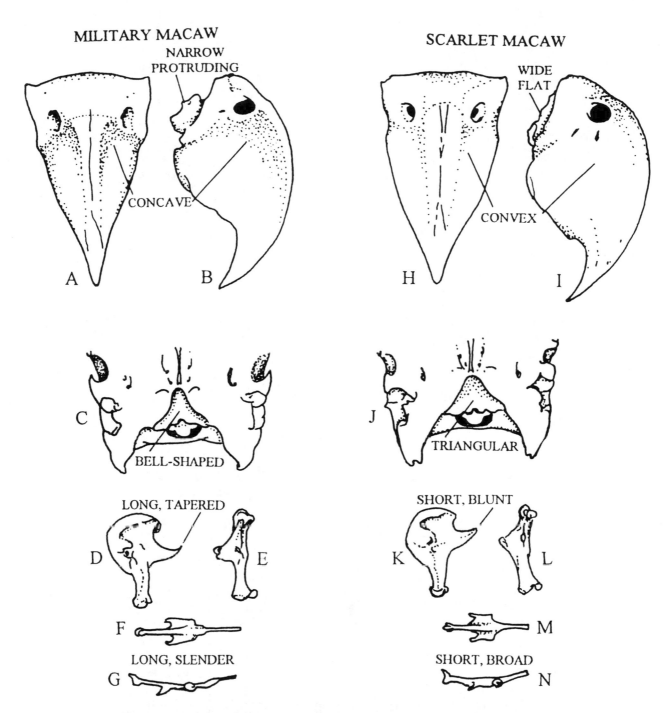

Figure 54. SUMMARY OF SPECIES IDENTIFICATION OF MEXICAN MACAWS
A-G, *Ara militaris*, Military Macaw, UA5386 and Bil351; H-N, *Ara macao*, Scarlet Macaw, H2099
and H2159. Scale: X 1.
A and H, Premaxilla, anterior view.
B and I, Premaxilla, right lateral view.
C and J, Cranium, inferior, posterior surface showing basitemporal plate.
D, E and K, L, Left quadrate, left and anterior views.
F, G and M, N, Basihyal-basibranchial, dorsal and lateral views.
After McKusick in Hargrave 1970a.

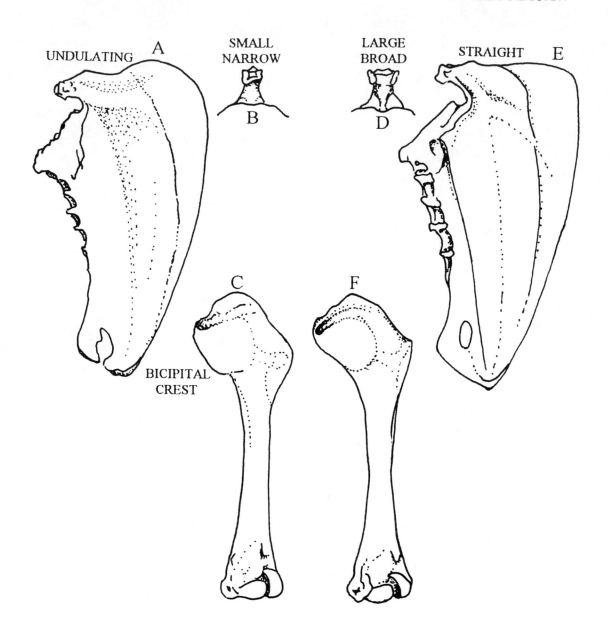

Figure 55. SUMMARY OF SPECIES IDENTIFICATION OF MEXICAN MACAWS
A-C, Military Macaw, *Ara militaris*, H2440 and UA5386; D-F, Scarlet Macaw, *Ara macao*, CG230 and PB22561. Scale: X 1.
A and E, Sternum, right lateral view. The anterior margin (top) of the Military Macaw sternum is curved and ungulates; that of the Scarlet Macaw is more nearly straight.
B and D, Manubrium of sternum, dorsal view. The manubrium of the Military Macaw is small and narrow; the manubrium of the Scarlet Macaw is large and broad.
C and F, Left humerus, palmar view. The bicipital crest of the Military Macaw is bulbous in outline; that of the Scarlet Macaw flows smoothly into the shaft of the humerus.
After McKusick in Hargrave 1970a.

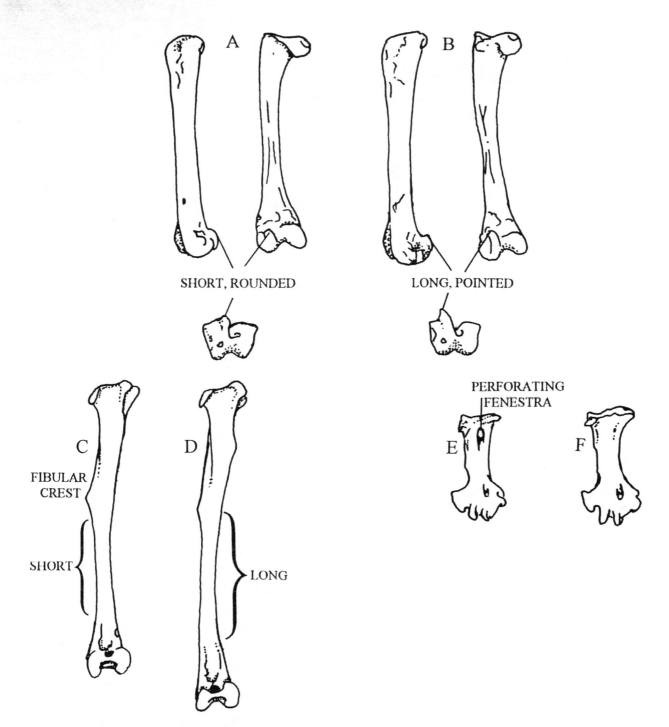

Figure 56 SUMMARY OF SPECIES IDENTIFICATION OF MEXICAN MACAWS
Left femora, lateral, posterior, and distal views; right tibiotarsi, anterior view, left tarsometatarsi, anterior view. Scale: X 1.
A. CG(b)/384, Military Macaw, Adolescent. The lateral condyle is small and rounded.
B. CG(b)/324, Scarlet Macaw, Newfledged. The lateral condyle is large, angular, and prominent.
C. CG292 Military Macaw, Adolescent. The tibiotarsus distal to the fibular crest is short.
D. CG 189, Scarlet Macaw, Newfledged. The tibiotarsus distal to the fibular crest is very long.
E. H2440, Military Macaw. The proximal foramen of the tarsometatarsus is very large fenestra.
F. PB22561, Scarlet Macaw. The proximal foramen of the tarsometatarsus tiny.
After McKusick in Hargrave 1970a and McKusick 1975.

K. Bullock's model does not discuss the associations of macaw remains with Southwestern ceremonial structures such as kivas, great kivas, plazas, dance platforms, and sacred caves. If the commercial acquisition and distribution of colored feathers were the main motive of the inhabitants of the Southwest, that is, if they were suppliers rather than consumers, I doubt if this pattern would be so conspicuous.

L. Bullock's model does not mention historic records of the importance of the Scarlet Macaw trade into the Southwest, the ethnographic record, and modern Pueblo usage.

As early as 1536 Cabeza de Vaca reported that Indians living south of what are now Arizona and New Mexico "...traded parrots' feathers for green stones far to the north." In 1716, Padre Luis Velarde stated that "...at San Xavier del Bac [near Tucson, Arizona] and neighboring rancherias, there are many macaws, which the Pimas raise because of the beautiful feathers of red and of other colors,...which they strip from these birds in the spring, for their adornment" (Hargrave 1970a:1). Reyman (1995) gives other early accounts of the feather trade, and deals with the important concept of value. Even today, Scarlet Macaw feathers are at least as valuable by weight as cocaine, and are more valuable than gold.

M. Bullock's model does not account for the well-documented importance of the Scarlet Macaw in Mesoamerican ceremonialism, not to speak of the important Mesoamerican influences in the Southwest.

I believed that Bullock's model suffers from a lack of acquaintance with the methods of osteological and feather identification, coupled with a lack of familiarity with the literature and basic taxonomic ornithology, which disqualifies its acceptance. The model is not supported by any evidence to invalidate my identifications, or the identifications of Wetmore, Hargrave, Emslie, Lang, Shaffer, the Olsens, or others. Therefore, it is my opinion at this point in time that the Scarlet Macaw identifications published in the archaeological literature of the North American Southwest still stand. The disagreement of Bullock's model with the data is not altogether surprising. It is a common practice among archaeologists to interpret prehistoric avian trade and usage on a basis of comparison with practices of the relatively recent Pueblo Katsina Cult, which is largely concerned with a need for feathers for prayer sticks. In contrast, the trade in live Scarlet Macaws is relevant to the Pan-Southwestern Ceremonial Complex, which preceded the development of the Katsina Cult. It is the live macaw trade which has produced the osteological specimens with which this chapter deals.

CHAPTER 20

COMPARATIVE OSTEOLOGY OF THE
BALD AND GOLDEN EAGLE

The first, inescapable task in the study of faunal remains from any archaeological site is that of identification. In the past much archaeological eagle bone has been relegated to Golden Eagle simply because "they are more numerous." This unfortunate situation is largely attributable to scarcity of modern comparative specimens, a lack which no doubt has also resulted in the long-ago misidentification of fragmentary bones of such disparate forms as geese, cranes, macaws, and jackrabbits (see Figure 71) as those of eagles.

The Bald and Golden Eagles are presented herein according to a plan of study originated by Lyndon L. Hargrave in his osteology of the Mexican Macaws. This method systematically eliminates one variable after the other, such as age changes, sexual dimorphism, and size variation of local populations, until only genus, species, and individual variation remain.

The osteological section of this chapter is arranged with text facing the illustrative figure for easy comparison of identifying characters of the two eagles under consideration. Species having individual bone elements which are commonly confused with those of eagles are noted under the appropriate bone so that they may be checked and eliminated from further consideration.

These illustrations cannot of course take the place of an adequate comparative collection of modern specimens of known age, sex, and place of origin, but are intended as a supplement to bridge the gap between the time the student begins the confusing job of identification and the time years later when generic and specific characters become easily recognizable, and such factors as age, sexual dimorphism, and individual variation are put in proper perspective.

The archaeological section treats only those sites in the Southwest where it was possible to check old identifications. Some published listings of eagles for various sites have been omitted because they are now known to be incorrect, or, where specimens are not available for restudy, are suspect on a basis of samples from subsequent excavations of the site. This of course does not imply any criticism of past investigators. Additional information has changed our picture of prehistoric utilization of Southwest birds so greatly in the past forty years that many familiar concepts have had to be changed. With the flood of faunal remains now being recovered from salvage projects, it is apparent that today's best efforts will soon be modified in the light of more complete data.

SPECIMENS USED IN THIS STUDY

Modern Specimens of the Golden Eagle, *Aquila chrysaëtos*
NPS 289 male, old?, source unknown.
NPS 348 male, source unknown.
NPS 779 male, ca. 2 years, Utah.
NPS 780 male, ca. 2 years, Utah.
NPS 792 male, over 4 years, source unknown.
NPS 890 male, ca. 4 months, too young to measure, Grand Teton National Park.
H1312 male, Canelo Hills, Santa Cruz County, Arizona.
H1324 male, Canelo Hills, Santa Cruz County, Arizona.
H1696 male, near Tucson, Pima County, Arizona.
NPS 394 female, ca. 6 months, too young to measure, source unknown.
NPS 659 female, over 4 years, source unknown.
NPS 859 female, over 4 years, Mesa Verde National Park.
H76 female, ca. 4 months, too young to measure, source unknown.
H167 female, ca. 2 years, Y-Mesa, on Black River, Fort Apache Indian Reservation, Graham County, Arizona.

Modern Specimens of the Bald Eagle, *Haliaeëtus leucocephalus*.
NPS 890 immature male, San Juan Island, Washington.
NPS 930 male, 2 to 3 years, Dinosaur National Monument.
Z8.1789 male, source unknown.
NPS 742 immature female, Amchitka Island, Alaska.
NPS 768 female, 3 to 4 years, Texas.
NPS 911, female, over 4 years, near Point of Pines, San Carlos Apache Reservation, Arizona.
H2170 female, Lake Mary, Coconino County, Arizona.
Z8.1738 female, source unknown.
Z8.1896 female, Vail Lake, Coconino County, Arizona.

Archaeological Golden Eagle Burials
D4780 male, Turkey Creek Pueblo.
D2682 male, Grasshopper Pueblo.
D2218 female, old?, Cedar Creek Site.
D2000 female, AZ Z:1:11.
D2681 female, Grasshopper Pueblo.
D4778a immature female, Turkey Creek Pueblo.
D4778 female, AZ W:10:98.
D9893 female, BM III Pithouse, Yellow Jacket Canyon, Colorado.

Archaeological Bald Eagle Burial
AO849 possible female NA 8042, Houck E, Broadside 1.

GOLDEN EAGLE: *Aquila chrysaëtos*

Description:

    Length - male, 30 to 35 inches; female, 35 to 40 inches.

    Wing - male, 23 to 24.7 inches; female 25 to 27 inches.

    Wingspread - male, 78 to 84 inches; female, 84 to 90 inches.

    Tail - male, 14 to 15 inches; female, 15 to 16 inches.

    Gross weight - 8 to 13 pounds.

    Culmen - male, 1.5 to 1.6 inches; female, 1.7 to 1.8 inches.

    Bill - black.

    Cere - yellow.

    Tarsus - feathered to toes; male, 3.6 to 4.4 inches, female, 3.9 to 4.4 inches.

    Primaries - five feathers cut-out on the inner webs.

    Juvenile Plumage - dark brown, almost black below, basal half to two-thirds of tail plain white.

    Adult Plumage - rich, dark brown, set off with golden brown lanceolate feathers on back of head and neck; attained at about four years.

    Proportions - a short-winged, long-legged eagle, similar in proportions to an out-sized Red-tailed Hawk.

Food: Primarily rodents, some carrion, with various additions ranging from insects to full-grown deer.

Economic Status: Refer to Arnold 1954 and Spofford 1970.

Life History: Refer to Bent 1961.

History Since the Pleistocene: The Golden Eagle is characterized as aggressive, playful, and long-lived. Life spans of 25 to 30 or more years have been reported. As a species, the Golden Eagle has survived since the Pleistocene with relatively little change. The Golden Eagle was the most numerous species recovered from the Rancho La Brea Pleistocene deposits and accounted for 908 of the total of 4728 birds represented in the ten best Pleistocene pits (Howard 1962b:20-24).

A vigorous and adaptable species, *Aquila chrysaëtos* persisted over most of the United States from the Pleistocene until the very recent past. By the early 1900s men had largely exterminated it as a nesting species east of the Mississippi. Protected by law today, the greatest hazard to Golden Eagles remaining in the West appears to be collision with cross-country power lines.

BALD EAGLE: *Haliaeëtus leucocephalus*

Description:
>   Length - male, 30 to 35 inches; female, 34 to 43 inches.
>   Wing - male, 20 to 25.9 inches; female, 23.5 to 28 inches.
>   Wingspread - male, 84 inches; female, 84 to 96 inches.
>   Tail - male, 11 to 15.2 inches; female, 12.5 to 16 inches.
>   Gross weight - male, 8.1 to 14 .1 pounds.
>   Culmen - male, 1.8 to 2.2 inches; female, 1.9 to 2.3 inches.
>   Bill - yellow, massive.
>   Cere - yellow.
>   Tarsus - unfeathered, yellow; male, 2.6 to 3.4 inches; female, 3.2 - 3.7 inches.
>   Primaries - six feathers cut-out in the inner webs.
>   Juvenile Plumage - wholly black, except white bases of feathers, base of tail blotched with whitish, becoming more white with time.
>   Adult Plumage - body brownish-black; head, neck, and tail white; attained at about four years.
>   Proportions - a long-winged, short-legged eagle, similar in proportion to an out-sized Ferruginous Hawk.

Food: Primarily fish, much carrion, some ducks and larger mammals.

Economic Status: Refer to Imler and Kalmbach 1955 and Sprunt 1970.

Life History: Refer to Bent 1961.

History Since the Pleistocene: The Bald Eagle, less aggressive and less predatory than the Golden Eagle, was already rather few in numbers during the Pleistocene. One Bald Eagle lived over 35 years in captivity (Kenyon 1969:13). Although carrion is quite attractive to Bald Eagles, very few were trapped in the asphalt of the La Brea Pelistocene deposits: only 176 out of a total of 4728 birds. Compared with 908 individual Golden Eagles, to whom mired animals were presumably less attractive, this is a very small sample indeed (Howard 1962b:20-24).

Recently the only relatively dense concentrations of Bald Eagles have been in Alaska and in Florida. In 1968, the Florida population was rapidly passing out of existence because of the cumulative effects of pesticides. However, Bald Eagles are increasing in scattered areas over the United States where water is being impounded for irrigation and for generation of electric power. The availability of dead fish, killed by passing through the turbines of electric plants, has been of great benefit to our remaining Bald Eagles (Imler and Kalmbach 1955:4).

MEXICAN EAGLES AND EAGLE-SIZED HAWKS

Most of the Mexican eagles and eagle-sized hawks are forest dwellers found far to the south of the region involved in the study of the Southwest. They are listed here with maximum length measurements and present distribution:

Harpy Eagle, *Harpia harpia*, 34 - 36 inches. Southern Mexico, heavy lowland forests.

Black-and-white Eagle-Hawk, *Spizatur melanoleucus*, 22 - 24 inches. Oaxaca, Chiapas, Veracruz, and Yucatan, heavy lowland forests.

Ornate Eagle-Hawk, *Spizaëtus ornatus vicarius*, 23 - 25 inches. Tamaulipas, Veracruz, Yucatan, Oaxaca, Chiapas, humid lowland forests.

Black Eagle-Hawk, *Spizaëtus tyrannus serus*, 25 - 28 inches. Southeastern and southern Mexico, heavily forested lowlands and foothills (Blake 1953:88-90).

One other southern form merits more detailed consideration. The Solitary Eagle, *Urubitornis solitaria*, 26 - 28 inches, occupies a range starting in the highlands of Mexico, extending across the land bridge between North and South America, and continuing down the Cordillera along the Pacific Coast of South America.

Two subspecies exist in Mexico. The southern race, *U. s. solitaria*, has been recorded only from Oaxaca, Tehuantepec, Jalisco, and Los Hesos. The more northern form, *U. s. sheffleri*, occurs over an isolated range in the mountainous southeastern corner of Sonora adjacent to Chihuahua (Blake 1953:88). This northern race averages larger, has heavier feet and toes, and is darker in color than more southern specimens.

The Solitary Eagle has not yet been identified in collections resulting from archaeological excavations, but the size and proximity of this northern race indicate a possibility of its occurring in future collections from northern Mexican sites.

SIZE VARIATION SINCE THE PLEISTOCENE

In a 1947 study Dr. Hildegarde Howard compared the skulls of more than 20 Golden Eagles from the Rancho La Brea Pleistocene with 18 skulls of the modern bird. Though conspecific with the modern *Aquila chrysaëtos*, the Pleistocene skulls typically were stronger of jaw with broad, heavy beaks, and relatively broad, flat skulls. Some specimens showed definite trends toward the more modern form; because of this intergradation, the La Brea specimens are considered directly ancestral to the modern Golden Eagle (Howard 1947:288).

It is not possible to assign the fossil limb bones to individuals, but the impression persists that the typical Pleistocene form had somewhat shorter legs and longer wings. Although neither structural nor proportional differences are apparent between Pleistocene and Recent long bones (see

Figure 58), fossil tibiotarsi and tarsometatarsi average shorter and humeri and ulnae average longer, up to 10 mm. longer, in maximum length (Howard 1947:287).

Table 8 indicates the position of archaeological eagle bones in relation to developmental trends. Modern specimens combine those measured by Howard with adults examined at the Southwest Archeological Center. Archaeological specimens are eagle burials ranging from 700 to 1300 years old. Early Recent specimens are from Pit 10 at Rancho La Brea, about 9000 years old according to a UCLA - Los Angeles County Museum of Natural History news release from 1969. The Pleistocene specimens, also from Rancho La Brea deposits, are 13,000+ years old (Howard 1962a, personal correspondence 1970). Although minimum and maximum measurements are included in this table, they are to some degree a function of sample size. Therefore, I consider the means as more indicative of osteological trends. In the measurements of the humerus, all archaeological specimens were rated as females, making it impractical to calculate a mean, or even to list a minimum, since the adult minimum usually falls at the lower limit of the male size range.

The extremely large size which has been attributed to archaeological Golden Eagles no longer can be considered valid. By examination of ten eagle burials, which are easily sexed, it has become evident that the large bones made into artifacts, or occurring as isolated or fragmentary specimens, are really derived from a predominantly female group of eagles, rather than from a population significantly larger in size. Hargrave (1965, personal correspondence) suggested that the female may have been easier to capture at the nest.

GEOGRAPHICAL SIZE VARIATION

The Bald Eagle is an often used example of Bergman's Rule that:

> "Within a polytypic warm-blooded species, the body size of a subspecies increases with decreasing mean temperature of its habitat." (Hoebel and Weaver 1979:65).

The northern subspecies, *H. l. alascanus*, is larger than the southern subspecies, *H. l. leucocephalus*, with specimens becoming increasingly larger in higher latitudes and reaching their greatest size in Alaska. Bent (1937:399) also records a gradual increase in average egg size from south to north.

The few specimens of Bald Eagle available for use in this study indicate that although *H. l. alascanus* is a slightly larger population in egg size and gross weight, a more important distinction is the apparent difference in body proportions. *H. l. alascanus* specimens in the National Park Service collection have relatively shorter wing and leg bones in proportion to body size than do specimens of the southern subspecies.
(Text continues on page 146.)

TABLE 8. COMPARISON OF PLEISTOCENE AND MODERN GOLDEN EAGLES

Era	Number of Specimens	Minimum	Mean	Maximum	Difference of Means Pleistocene - Modern
		Maximum Breadth of Cranium			-5.1 mm .
Modern	24	61.0	63.1	66.9	
Archaeological	-	-	-	-	
Early Recent	1	-	-	66.0	
Pleistocene	31	63.7	68.2	71.0	
		Maximum Length of Humerus			-4.0 mm
Modern	33	171.9	188.3	204.5	
Archaeological	4	-	-	200.5	
Early Recent	4	186.0	191.0	198.0	
Pleistocene	146	173.2	192.3	216.6	
		Maximum Length of Ulna			-5.6 mm
Modern	32	201.9	218.3	234.5	
Archaeological	5	208.0	215.3	230.5	
Early Recent	-	-	-	-	
Pleistocene	69	211.5	224.4	244.0	
		Maximum Length of Tibiotarsus			+5.6 mm
Modern	28	153.2	166.6	175.0	
Archaeological	4	165.5	168.4	177.0	
Early Recent	-	-	-	-	
Pleistocene	171	148.0	161.0	172.5	
		Maximum Length of Tarsometatarsus			+3.0 mm
Modern	33	94.3	101.7	110.2	
Archaeological	7	97.7	100.4	106.0	
Early Recent	67	93.0	99.1	107.0	
Pleistocene	660	90.5	98.7	107.8	

AGE STAGES

Figure 57. Age Stages in the Cranium and Sternum of the Bald and Golden Eagles.
Above, right lateral view of crania minus beak; below, dorsal view of sterna. Scale: X 1.
A. NPS 770, *Aquila chrysaëtos*, male, immature plumage, estimated age 1 year.
B. NPS 289, *Aquila chrysaëtos*, male, immature plumage, estimated age 2 years.
C. NPS 659, *Aquila chrysaëtos*, female, adult plumage, estimated age 4+ years.
D. Z8.1738, *Haliaeëtus leucocephalus,*female, estimated age on bone, ca. 1 year.

The youthful Golden Eagle has a fenestra in the interorbital septum (a), which is quite pronounced in the first year, filling in gradually until it disappears. It may well remain open in the female longer than in the male, for NPS 289, a male in immature plumage, has no fenestra remaining in the interorbital septum, whereas NPS 569, a female in adult plumage, has a fenestra in the interorbital septum which is apparently rapidly filling, but is still only half closed. Available specimens indicate that the fenestra in the interorbital septum may close as early as the second or third year in the male and as late as the fourth year in the larger, slower-maturing female.

None of the Bald Eagle specimens examined has shown evidence of a fenestra in the interorbital septum.

The fenestra near the posterior margin of the sternum (b), of some Golden Eagles has in the past been used as an indicator of age. From specimens examined in this study it can be demonstrated that individuals as young as four months may have two large fenestrae, and a few may have only one fenestra. Sex does not appear to affect the presence of these fenestrae, since two of three females, and three of six males in the NPS Collection have one, or more commonly two, fenestrae. Only one Bald Eagle specimen has been secured which has even a small fenestra in the sternum, so this character is unreliable if not completely valueless as a criterion of age.

The posterior margin of the sternum of the Golden Eagle is centrally indented at an age of four to six months; the bone is porous and incompletely ossified. By the end of the first year the posterior margin of the sternum is a relatively smooth curve, but in the adult there is a central convexity (c).

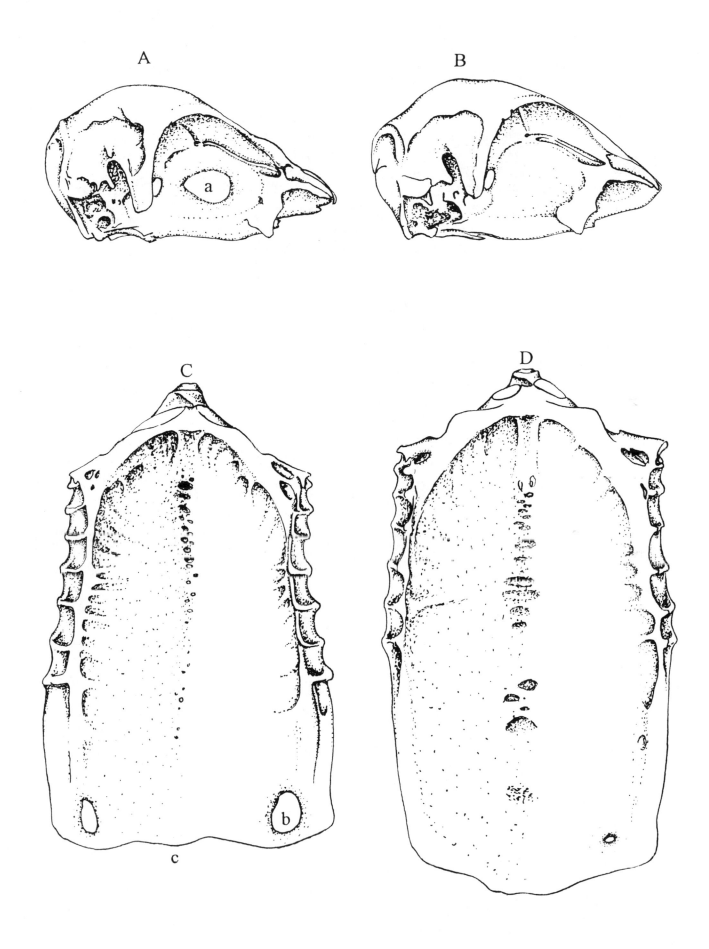

Figure 58. Sexual Dimorphism in Eagle Tarsometatarsi.
Left Tarsometatarsi, posterior view. Scale: X 1.

A. C 9712, *Aquila chrysaëtos,* Golden Eagle, La Brea Pleistocene, rated adult female.
B. NPS 659, *Aquila chrysaëtos,* Golden Eagle, modern, female.
C. D 6554, *Aquila chrysaëtos,* Golden Eagle, La Brea Pleistocene, rated adult male
D. NPS 780, *Aquila chrysaëtos,* Golden Eagle, modern, male.
E. D 2218, *Aquila chrysaëtos,* Golden Eagle, archaeological, rated adult female.
F. NPS 289, *Aquila chrysaëtos,* Golden Eagle, modern, male.
G. NPS 911, *Haliaeëtus leucocephalus leucocephalus,* modern, female.
H. NPS 864, *Haliaeëtus leucocephalus alascanus,* modern, male.

The upper row compares tarsometatarsi of the Golden Eagle from the La Brea Pleistocene with modern specimens. No important differences are noted. Female tarsometatarsi are usually longer than those of males, but even in aberrant individuals such as illustrated in example F where a male exceeds in length example E, the largest female available for comparison, the proportions of the bones are markedly different. Females, Plesistocene, archaeological, or modern, have stocky tarsometatarsi, which are broad of shaft, and particularly broad of proximal articular head (a). Metatarsal facets (b) are large and clearly defined, and the shaft at this point is broad in the female. Metatarsal facets of males tend to be narrower (c), trailing off indistinctly toward the distal foramen (d). Since the shaft of the tarsometatarsus is so narrow in the male, it appears deeply grooved, whereas the broader shaft of the female gives an impression of flatness.

The Bald Eagle tarsometatarsi illustrated in examples G and H follow the same pattern of proportion as do the Golden Eagles. An important point is that the male, which is of the larger northern subspecies, is markedly smaller and less rugose than the female of the smaller southern subspecies.

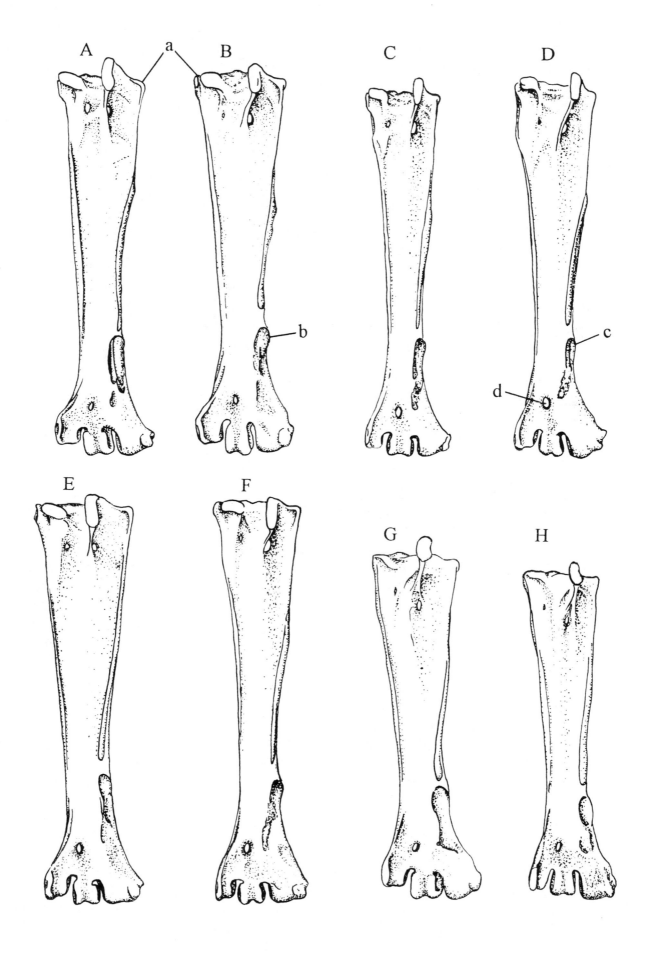

Allen's Rule:

> "In warm-blooded species, the relative size of exposed portions of the body, (limbs, tail, and ears) decrease with decrease of mean temperature." (Hoebel and Weaver 1979:65).

was intended primarily for use with mammalian subspecies, and there has been some question as to its applicability to birds. Much of this no doubt has occurred because ornithologists commonly work only with skins, and the length of primary or tail feathers has little relation to heat loss. However, a positive correlation for large bodies and short wing and leg bones has been found in the bones of the Red-tailed Hawk and the Great Horned Owl from the northern states when compared with specimens of the same species from the Southwest. Particularly conspicuous is the shortness of the tarsometatarsus of the Red-tailed Hawk, which is unfeathered. The northern subspecies of the Bald Eagle is a further example.

Measurements indicate that sexual dimorphism produces a more conspicuous size difference than does subspecies. For this reason, all females and all males of the Bald Eagle are lumped in order to form a more balanced sample. Considering the skew which could occur in a sample in which the sexes are unbalanced, statistics on subspecies of strongly dimorphic avian species must be treated with caution.

Although the Golden Eagle, a holarctic form, has only one subspecies in North America, *Aquila chrysaëtos canadensis,* three specimens from northern Utah have longer body bones and shorter wing and leg bones than do three specimens of similar age and the same sex from southern Arizona. This differentiation has archaeological relevance, since artifacts made from the wing bones of eagles appear to have been trade items. Many archaeological sites produce eagle bone artifacts made from bones larger than those found in refuse bone collections which are presumably derived from local birds killed for their feathers. Evidence indicates that the longest and largest ulnae come from eagles living along the Arizona-Utah and New Mexico-Colorado borders. The north-east periphery of the Southwest is the very area where eagle bones tubes are a commercial specialty.

The smallest Golden Eagles are found in Mexico. Blake gives a maximum length measurement for Golden Eagles from Mexico of only 30-35", slightly smaller than that generally given for specimens from north of the Mexican border.

SEXUAL DIMORPHISM

The most familiar manifestations of sexual dimorphism are the brighter-colored plumage and more elaborate song of the male Passerines, or perching birds. Among members of this order, sexual dimorphism appears to be associated with recognition and pair formation. Eagles do not manifest this difference in plumage; in fact, both Golden and Bald Eagles may pair and breed before their adult plumage has been attained (Bailey 1928:178; Imler and Kalmbach 1955:14).

Among large birds of prey which carry food animals off in their talons, sexual dimorphism is most strikingly expressed by the larger size of the female. In some hawks, the size differential is so great that the male and female actually occupy different ecological niches (Storer 1966:423-436). This suggests that the larger size of the female among raptors may be related to the necessity of providing large quantities of meat for the young. If the parents are able to utilize slightly different resources within their hunting range, their chances of success are increased.

Though smaller, the male eagle is reported to provide most of the food for the incubating female and later for the nestlings. This, the female skins and feeds to the young (Bent 1961:299). Thus, for at least part of the year he is by far the more active of the two, a situation illustrated by the preponderance of males among accidentally killed specimens salvaged for comparative purposes.

Extensive tables of osteological measurements of males and females of both species were prepared in the course of this study, but are not included because of constraints of space. They are available upon request from the author . There is a small overlap in measurements of some skeletal elements between males and females of both species, but this does not present a problem in sexing. Males are small with slender-shafted, gracile bones. The bones of the larger, heavier females, though in some cases no longer than those of the male, are stocky and rugged, with more prominent muscle attachments. The bones of young specimens of both sexes resemble those of males, which display more generalized and earlier-attained characters, while bones of females continue to change over a longer period of time, developing progressively more specialized characters.

If a full skeleton is present, such as in an eagle burial, Golden Eagles may be sexed by examination of the pelvis. In females of all ages the synsacrum fails to fuse with the postacetabular ilium, while in the male it fuses as early as four months (see Figure 67, A, e). The maximum width of the cranium in males of both species tends to exceed that of females; perhaps this is a reflection of their role as provider of food for the incubating female and nestlings, since the point measured is the infraorbital process to which is attached one of the muscles which closes the beak. In both species other measurements of bone length and width of articular ends are usually larger in the female. Two exceptions are the tibiotarsus and tarsometatarsus which are extremely variable in length. Tarsometatarsi are often recovered intact from archaeological sites, and may be sexed by proportion and by the width of the proximal articular head (see Figure 58).

In order to more fully investigate the problem of the apparent very large size of archaeological eagles, a random sample of 100 Pleistocene Golden Eagle tarsometatarsi was borrowed from the La Brea Collections of the Los Angeles County Museum of Natural History in order to determine how long sexual dimorphism has been a factor in eagle osteology. Osteological measurements, proportion of maximum width to maximum length, size of joints, and rugosity of muscle attachments were used to establish the gender of these ancient bones. Of the 100 specimens, 57 were gracile males, 43 were rugged females, and two of these were judged to be immatures. These last are indicated by small "o" on the scatter plot. Archaeological and modern Golden Eagle tarsometatarsi follow the same distribution for adults and immatures as do the Pleistocene specimens. In some bone measurements there is an overlap between the sexes, which is partly a function of age differences; but in general, measurements, especially used in combination to determine the proportions of a bone or of the entire skeleton, are useful in determining sex. The conclusions drawn from examination of the

Pleistocene tarsometatarsi are that there have been no changes in size, proportion, or sexual dimorphism in this bone in over 14,000 years which are of sufficient magnitude that modern specimens would not be usable for comparison with those recovered from archaeological excavations.

TABLE 9. COMPARISON OF GOLDEN EAGLE TARSOMETATARSI FROM LA BREA

WIDTH OF PROXIMAL ARTICULAR HEAD IN MM

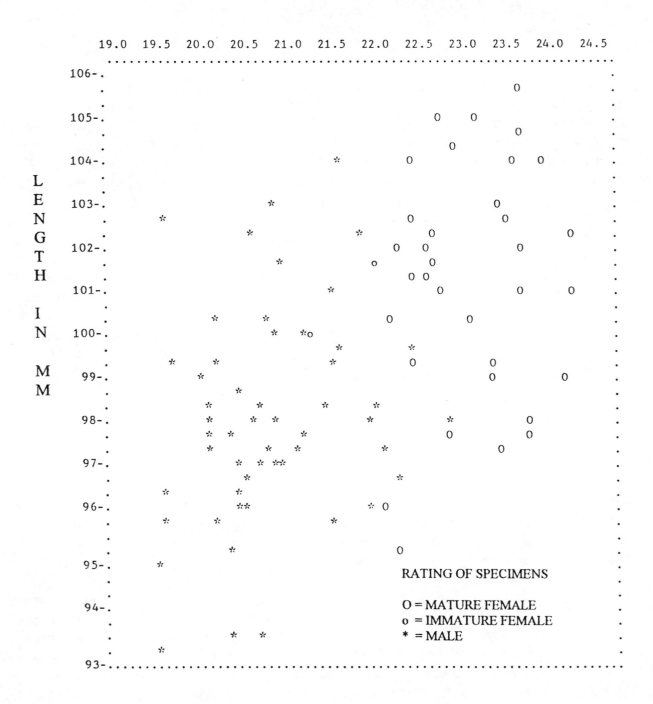

RATING OF SPECIMENS

O = MATURE FEMALE
o = IMMATURE FEMALE
* = MALE

COMPARATIVE OSTEOLOGY:
ARTIFACT IDENTIFICATION

The comparative osteology section was prepared between 1963 and 1968, when eagles first were declared endangered. It was difficult to borrow comparative specimens, and even more difficult to obtain a legal carcass from which to prepare a comparative specimen. The differences identified then have proved useful for almost 40 years. No modifications in the illustrations have been found necessary, although the captions have been expanded and simplified.

Eagle bone artifacts often consist of tubes, claws, and ulnar fipple flutes (Figure 24). An urgent reason for this identification study was the necessity of identifying eagle bone artifacts from Mound 7, Grand Quivira, Salinas National Monument, in central New Mexico.

Even in bird bone tubes which have been polished or worn, or both, the eagle species can usually be identified by placing the artifact on the page with the nutrient foramen (a hole in the shaft of a long bone through which the blood supply flows to the interior of the bone) next to the nutrient foramen in the illustration (see Figure 65). Determine which end of the tube is proximal and which is distal, and orient the tube to correspond with the drawing. In this position it should be possible to determine the species of eagle by comparing the shape of the tube with shape of the shaft, and the distance from the nutrient foramen to the end of the bone. Differences in the papillae to which the secondary flight feathers are attached are very helpful in distinguishing between Bald and Golden Eagles when the artifacts consist of bone tubes which are very short.

Eagle claws are also relatively easy to identify to species. Simply place the claw over the drawing on the page to match the shape and profile (see Figure 70). Bald Eagle claws are much more curved than are those of Golden Eagles.

Figure 59. Differences in the Cranium.
A and B, crania, right lateral view; C and D, crania, dorsal view. Scale: X 1.

A and C, NPS 659, *Aquila chrysaëtos,* Golden Eagle, female.
B and D, Z8.1739, *Haliaeë*tus *leucocephalus*, Bald Eagle, female.

The proportionately larger, thicker beak of the Bald Eagle, with the large nostril situated high up in the lateral surface, is easily distinguishable from that of the Golden Eagle.

The Golden Eagle has a difinite furrow (a) in the interorbital area; whereas the Bald Eagle tends more toward a slight prominence (b).

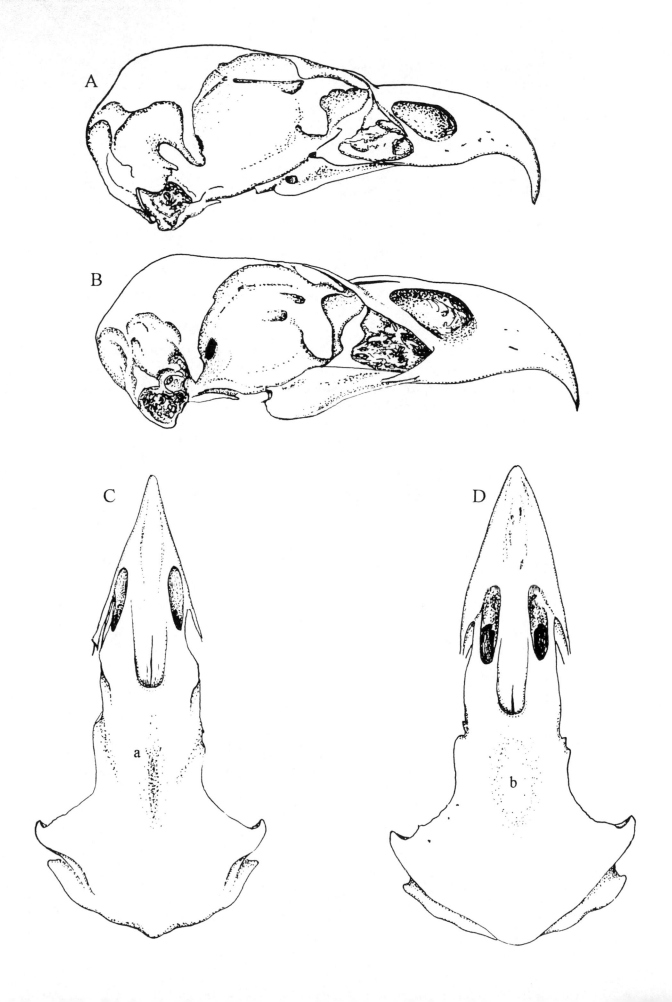

Figure 60. Differences in the Mandible and the Cranium.
A and B, mandible, right lateral view; C and D, mandible, dorsal view; E and F, cranium, ventral view. Scale: X 1.
A, C, and E, NPS 659, *Aquila chrysaëtos*, Golden Eagle, female.
B, D, and F, Z8.1739, *Haliaeëtus leucocephalus*, Bald Eagle, female.

The premaxilla of the Bald Eagle is broader, and the mandible more massive than the slender, tapering mandible of the Golden Eagle.

The maxillo-palatines of Golden Eagles examined have a solid boney surface in the ventral view, those of the Bald Eagles examined exhibit an open lace-work of boney spicules (a).

The basisphenoid of the Golden Eagle has lateral projections (b); that of the Bald Eagle is smoothly tapered.

The occipital area of hawks in general is very difficult to work with. In the youthful hawk or eagle there are channels visible (c) which are later bridged intermittently, and eventually completely covered. The size and shape of the occipital condyle (d) is a reliable criterion for separating partial crania of eagles from those of other large-headed birds such as swans, owls, macaws, or ravens.

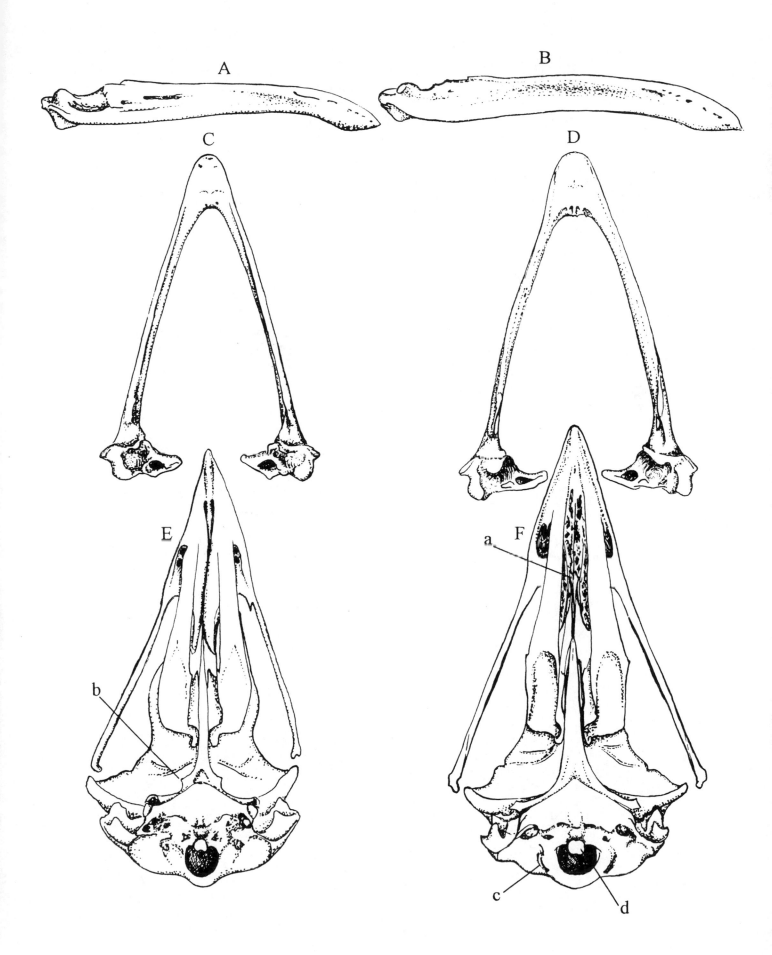

A   B

C   D

E   F

Figure 61. Differences of the Sternum.
A and C, sternum, dorsal view; B and D, sternum, ventral view. Scale: X 1.

A and B, NPS 289, *Aquila chrysaëtos*, Golden Eagle, male.
C and D, Z8.1896, *Haliaëtus leucocephalus*, Bald Eagle, female.

The sternum of the Golden Eagle is most easily identified by the concave outline of the posterior margin. The carina is flat-topped, flowing into a well-defined triangular area (a) of bone at its posterior termination. The costal margin is concave.

The sternum of the Bald Eagle gives an overall impression of roundness. The carinal margin is rounded in outline, the costal margin is slightly convex, and the posterior margin is strongly convex. The posterior termination of the carina is abrupt.

Further distinguishing features are the projections (b) on the anterior margin of the Bald Eagle sternum which rise between the dorsal lip of the coracoidal sulcus and the sterno-coracoidal process. These prominent attachments are represented in the Golden Eagle by narrow ridges on the dorsal edge of the anterior margin (c).

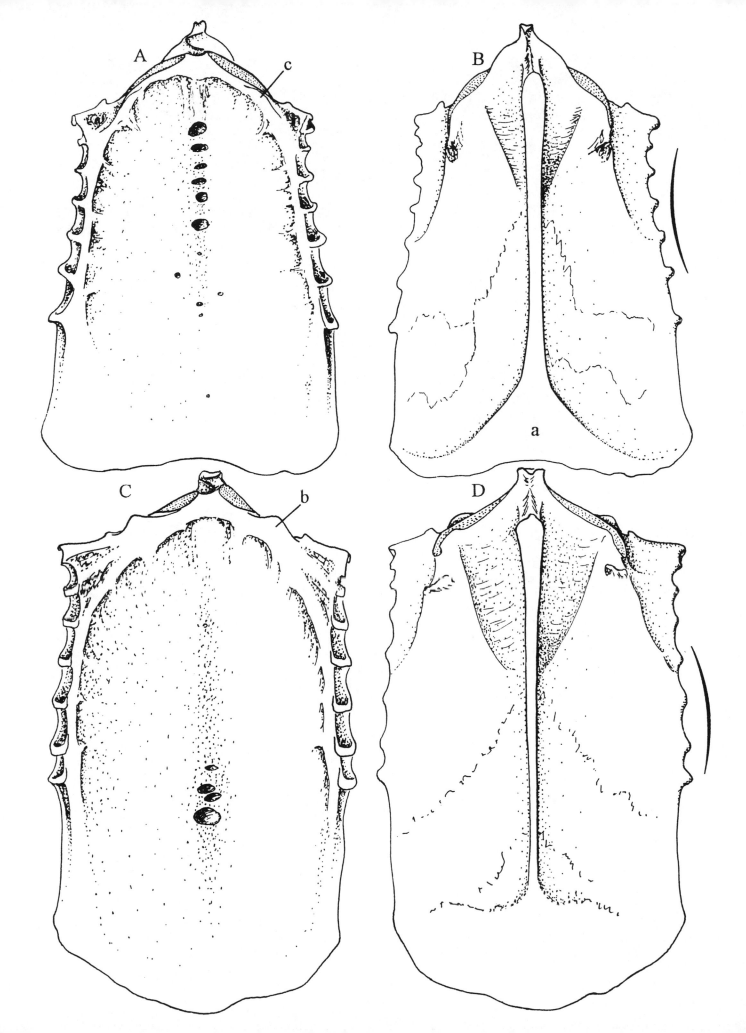

Figure 62. Differences of the Sternum and Coracoid.
A and B, sterna, left lateral view; C and D, left coracoids, ventral view; E and F, left coracoids, dorsal view. Scale: X 1.
A, C, and E, NPS 659, *Aquila chrysaëtos,* Golden Eagle, female.
B, D, and F, Z8.1739, *Haliaeëtus leucocephalus,* Bald Eagle, female

In the lateral view, the sternum of the Golden Eagle is distinguished by the contour of the posterior margin (a), that of the Bald Eagle by the anterior projection of the attachment on the dorsal lip of the anterior margin (b).

The coracoid of the Bald Eagle is much longer and the sterno-coracoidal process (c) broader than that of the Golden Eagle. The coracoidal fenestra is open or enclosed by only a narrow bridge (d) in the Golden Eagle; in the Bald Eagle the bridge tends to be very broad (e). A conspicuous lip (f) distinguishes the sternal facet of the Bald Eagle.

Fragmentary coracoids of eagles are sometimes confused with those of Sandhill Cranes because of the presence of the coracoidal fenestra. Not so likely to be confused, but also displaying this feature, are pelicans and the large owls.

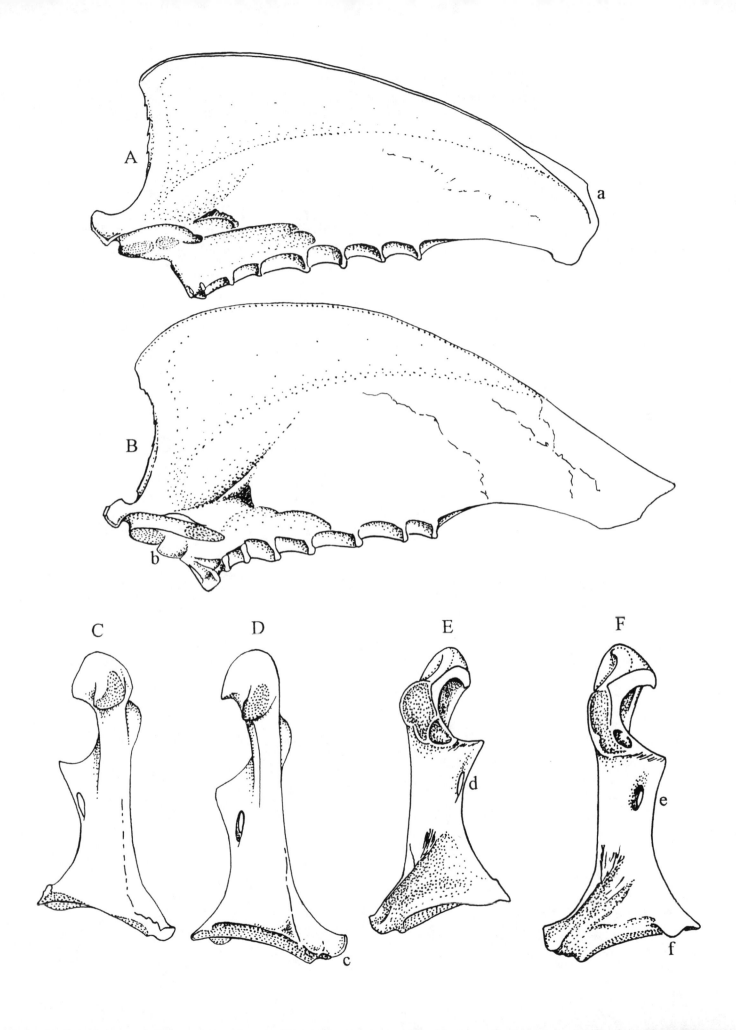

Figure 63. Differences of the Furcula and the Scapula.
A and B, furcula, dorsal view; C and D, furcula, left lateral view; E and F, right scapula, ventral view; G and H, right scapula, articular head; I and J, right scapula, dorsal view. Scale: X 1.

Figures A, C, E, G, and I, NPS 659, *Aquila chrysëtos*, Golden Eagle, female.
Figures B, D, F, H, and J, Z8.1739, *Haliaeëtus leucocephalus*, Bald Eagle, female.

The most apparent difference in the furcula of Golden and Bald Eagles is the scapular tuberosity. That of the Golden Eagle tapers to a point (a), whereas that of the Bald Eagle remains broad and stocky (b).

The articular head of the scapula of the Bald Eagle is almost straight from furcular articulation to glenoid facet (c); that of the the Golden Eagle has a more prominent coracoid articulation (d). The blade of the scapula of the Bald Eagle tapers to a slender apex (e).

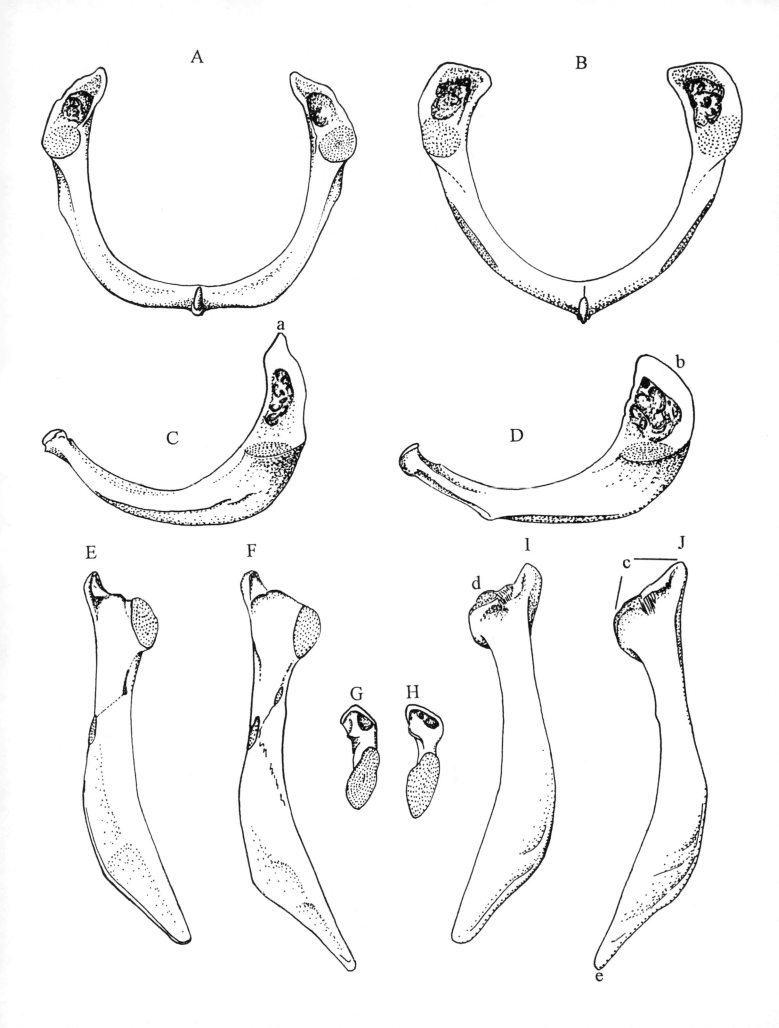

Figure 64. Differences in the Humerus.
A and B, right humerus, palmar view; C and D, right humerus, anconal view. Scale: X 1.

A and C, NPS 659, *Aquila chrysaëtos*, Golden Eagle, female.
B and D, Z8.1739, *Haliaeëtus leucocephalus*, Bald Eagle, female.

In the Golden Eagle, the junction of the bicipital crest with the shaft forms a definite notch, (a). The pneumatic fossa is elongated in the Golden Eagle (b), and abbreviated in the Bald Eagle (c).

The attachment of pronator previs is deep and directed nearly palmad (toward the underside of the extended wing) in the Bald Eagle (e), but is shallow and more lateral in the Golden Eagle (d).

The ectepicondylar prominence (f) is much more well-defined in the Bald Eagle.

Fragmentary humeri of eagles are most often confused with those of swans and cranes.

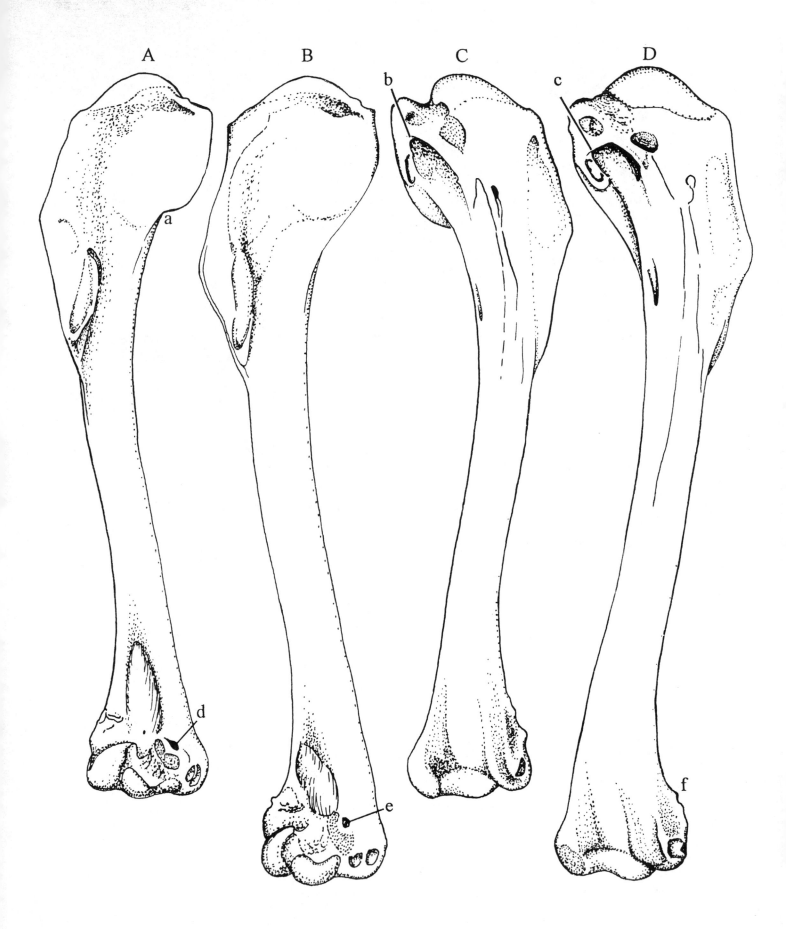

A   B   C   D

Figure 65. Differences of Ulna and Radius.
A and B, left ulna, palmar view; C and D, left ulna, anconal view; E and F, right radius, palmar view.
Scale: X 1.

A, C, and E, NPS 659, *Aquila chrysaëtos*, Golden Eagle, female.
B, D, and F, Z8.1739, *Haliaeëtus leucocephalus*, Bald Eagle, female.

In the Bald Eagle, the palmar margin of the impression of brachialis anticus (a) is a sharp angle; in the Golden Eagle it rounds more smoothly into the shaft.

Each secondary flight feather of the eagles is attached to the ulnae at a raised projection of bone called a papilla. The papillae of the Golden Eagle (b) tend to be separate and directed diagonal to the axis of the shaft. The papillae of the Bald Eagle (c) run longitudinally and are joined by a continuous ridge. This ridge is especially helpful in the identification of bone tubes and beads. In general, papillae are among the most dependable of identification characters. Their size, shape, spacing, and orientation are used in the identification of many artifacts worked from the ulna.

The external crest of the distal trochlea of the ulna extends farther up the shaft in the Golden Eagle (e) than it does in the Bald Eagle (f).

The ulnae of the eagles are most commonly confused with those of the Great Blue Heron, Whistling Swan, and Sandhill Crane.

The radius of the Bald Eagle is distinguished by a more prominent bicipital tuberosity (d), and by an elongated, less rounded distal articular end. The shaft of the Golden Eagle is short, straight, and stocky in comparison to that of the Bald Eagle, which is relatively long, curved, and slender.

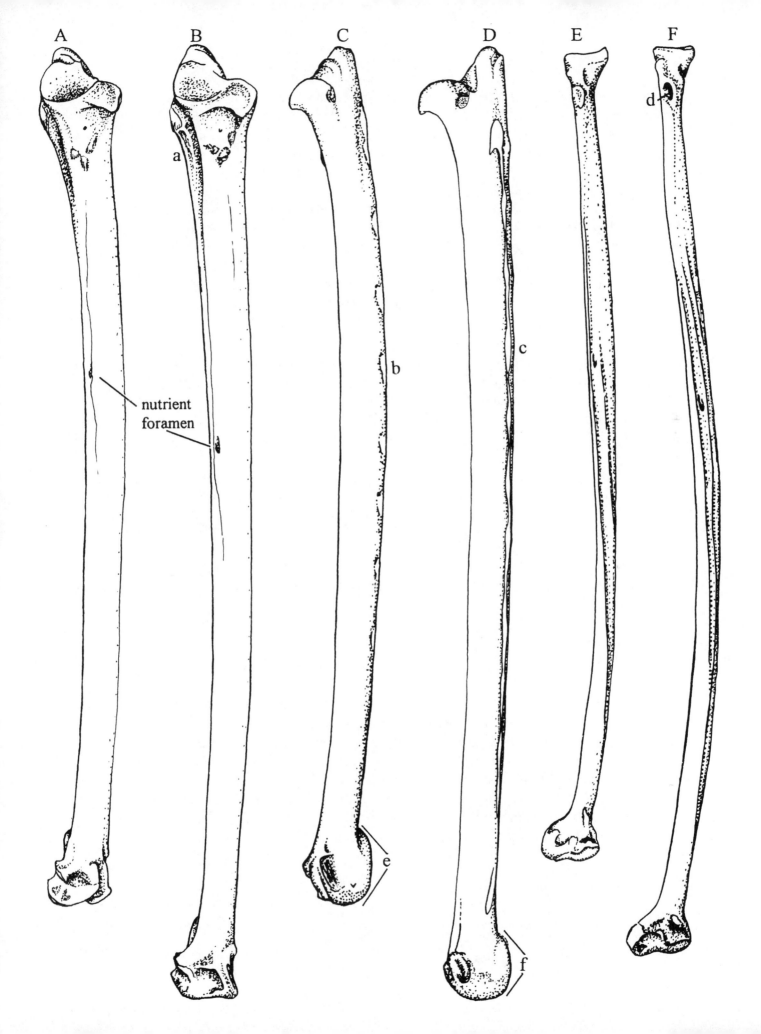

A   B   C   D   E   F

a

nutrient foramen

b

c

d

e

f

Figure 66. Differences of Radius, Carpometacarpus, and Manus.
A and B, right radius, anconal view; C and D, right carpometacarpus internal view; E and F, right carpometacarpus, external view; left manus, external view: G and H, "pollex"; I and J, "digit II, phalanx 1"; K and L, "digit II, phalanx 1"; M and N, "digit III".
Scale: X 1.

A, C, E, G, I, K, and M, *Aquila chrysaëtos*, NPS 659, Golden Eagle, female.
B, D, and F, *Haliaeëtus leucocephalus*, Z8.1739, Bald Eagle, female.
H, J, L, and N, *Haliaeëtus leucocephalus*, NPS 864, Bald Eagle, immature male.

In the anconal view of the radius and the entire manus, the general proportions of the two birds are reflected: short wings and long shanks in the Golden Eagle, long wings and short shanks in the Bald Eagle.

There is a dispute of long-standing as to the correct numbering of the digits of the avian manus. Howard (1929: Figs. 28-33), Hyman (1947:46), and Van Tyne and Berger (1959:84) use the designation I, II, and III, apparently on a basis of vertebrate palaeontology. Shufelt (1883: Plate VII) and Harvey, Kaiser, and Rosenberg (1968: Plate 85) use the designations II, III, and IV, apparently on a basis of embryology. Libbie Henrietta Hyman (1947:147) sums up the problem:

The wrist is greatly altered, consisting of but two separate bones, the homologies of which are unclear. The remaining wrist bones are fused to the metacarpals to form the *carpometacarpus*, which includes three metacarpals - two long ones and a short hump on the radial side of these. These three metacarpals...bear the corresponding digits.

To conform to previously published works, the metacarpals and corresponding digits will be referred to herein as I, II, and III. The "pollex" or Digit I supports the alula or "spurious wing." Digit II, phalanx 2 is very firmly attached to the outermost primary. Care must be taken in preparing comparative skeletons that this bone is not detached and lost when the wing feathers are removed. Digit III is more firmly attached to the carpometacarpus.

The pollex of the Bald Eagle is more slender than that of the Golden Eagle, tapering distally to a narrow apex (a). Digit II, phalanx 1 is short in the Golden Eagle (I) with the thinner, lateral margin curved. In the Bald Eagle (J), this bone is longer, even in the smaller male, shown, with margins more nearly parallel. Digit II, phalanx 2 is short in the Golden Eagle (K), tapering smoothly from the articular end to the distal apex. In the Bald Eagle (L), the articular head forms a right angle with the shaft (b), which is long and substantial, even in the smaller male. Digit III of the Golden Eagle (M), broadens below the articular head to a wedge shape; that of the Bald Eagle (N), is notched below the articular head, reaching its maximim width midway along the length of the bone (c).

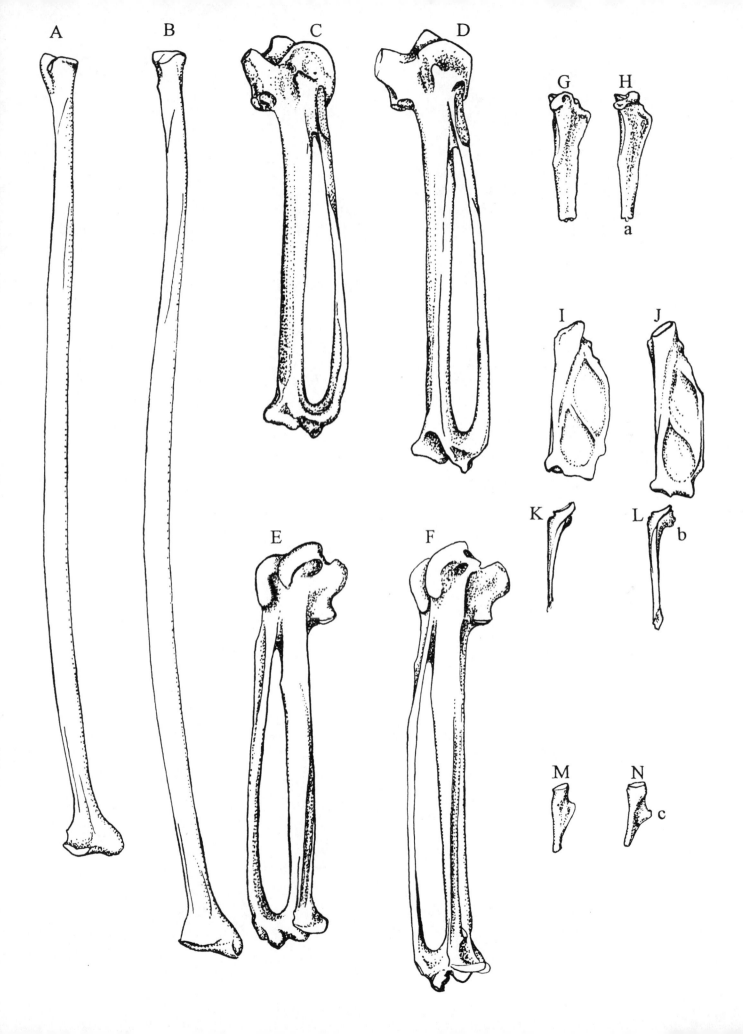

Figure 67. Differences of the Pelvis.
A and B, pelvis, dorsal view; C and D, pelvis, left lateral view. Scale: X 1.

A and C, NPS 659, *Aquila chrysaëtos,* Golden Eagle, female.
B and D, Z8.1739, *Haliaeëtus leucocephalus,* Bald Eagle, female.

The median dorsal ridge of the Bald Eagle (b) tends to be broader and flatter than that of the Golden Eagle (a). The preacetabular ilia of the Golden Eagle tend to flare somewhat, giving an hour-glass profile.

In the lateral view, the most striking contrast is the long, tapering ischial angle (c) of the Bald Eagle.

The synsacra of all Bald Eagles examined are separate from the postacetabular ilia (d) regardless of age or sex. Among Golden Eagles, all females examined maintain a separation between the synsacrum and the postacetabular ilium (e) even when fully adult, and all males examined had the synsacrum fused to the postacetabular ilium, even as early as age ca. four months.

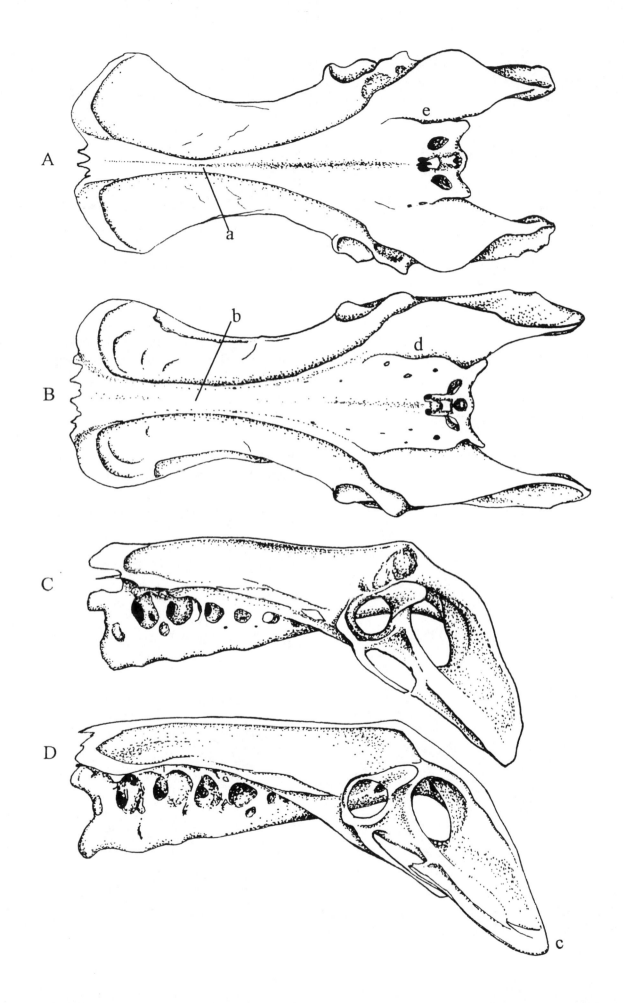

Figure 68. Differences of Femur and Tibiotarsus.
A and B, right femur, anterior view; C and D, right femur, posterior view; right tibiotarsus, anterior view. Scale: X 1.

A, C, and E, NPS 659, *Aquila chrysaëtos,* Golden Eagle, female.
B, D, and F, Z8.1739, *Haliaeétus leucocephalus,* Bald Eagle, female.

The trochanteric ridge of the Golden Eagle femur flows smoothly into the shaft, whereas that of the Bald Eagle is notched (a and b). The attachment proximal to the internal condyle is directed axially in the Golden Eagle (c), but more laterally in the Bald Eagle (d). The pattern of the intermuscular lines surrounding the nutrient foramen (e) is especially helpful in the identification of bone tubes.

The popliteal area is deeper (f) in the Bald Eagle, and the adjacent attachments are oriented differently (g). The attachment proximal to the fibular condyle is more prominent in the Golden Eagle (h). The eagle femur is most often confused with that of the male turkey or the Sandhill Crane.

If whole elements are present, the relative shortness of the femur and tibiotarsus of the Bald Eagle is immediately apparent.

In the anterior view of the tibiotarsus, the relative flatness of the proximal articular head (i) of the Bald Eagle and the deep notch at the proximal termination of the fibular crest (j) are easily discernible. Distally, the shape of the tendinal groove (k) and the location of the attachment of the facia sling (l) are diagnostic. The distal articular end of the Bald Eagle tibiotarsus is relatively broader with a shallow intercondylar profile (m).

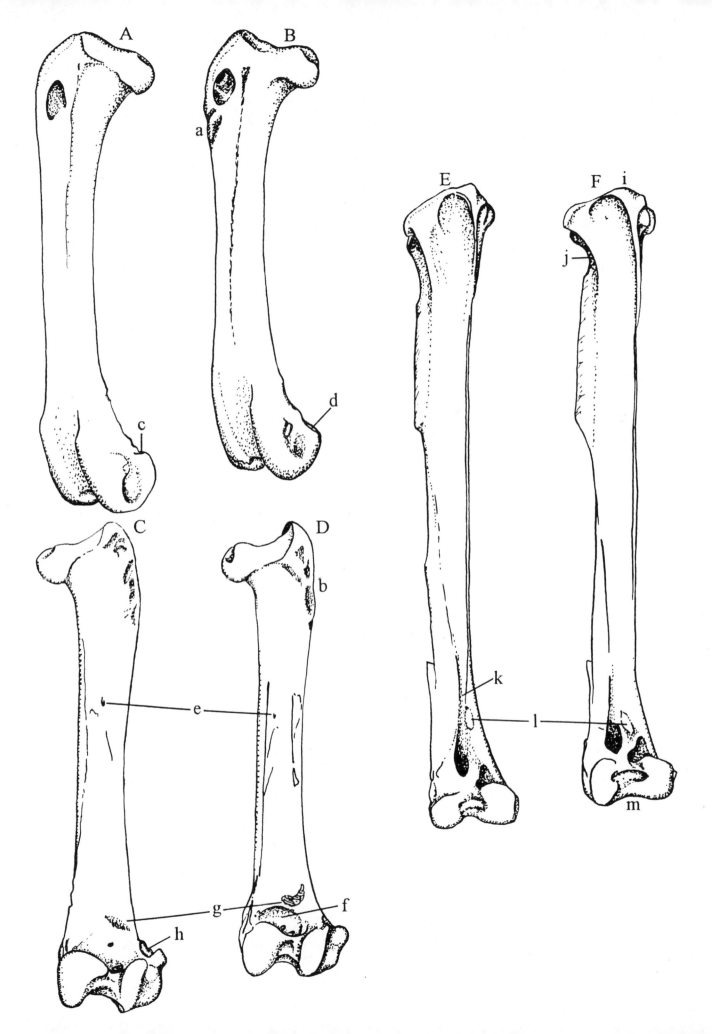

Figure 69. Differences of Tibiotarsus, Tarsometatarsus.
A and B, right tibiotarsus, posterior view; C and D, left tarsometatarsus, anterior view; E and F, left tarsometatarsus, posterior view; G and H, left tarsometatarsus, proximal articular surface. Scale:X 1.
A, C, E, and G, NPS 658, *Aquila chrysaëtos,* Golden Eagle, female.
B, D, F, and H, Z8.1739, *Haliaeëtus leucocephalus,* Bald Eagle, female.

In the posterior view, the tibiotarsus of the Bald Eagle (B) gives the impression of being flat and featureless; there is not the definite separation of the fibular crest observable in the Golden Eagle (A).

The tarsometatarsus of the Golden Eagle is longer, with prominent metatarsal facet (a). The profile of the trochleae is rounded in the Golden Eagle (E), but is diagonal to the axis of the shaft in the Bald Eagle (F). The external calcaneal ridge of the hypotarsus is not separated from the shaft in the Bald Eagle (b).

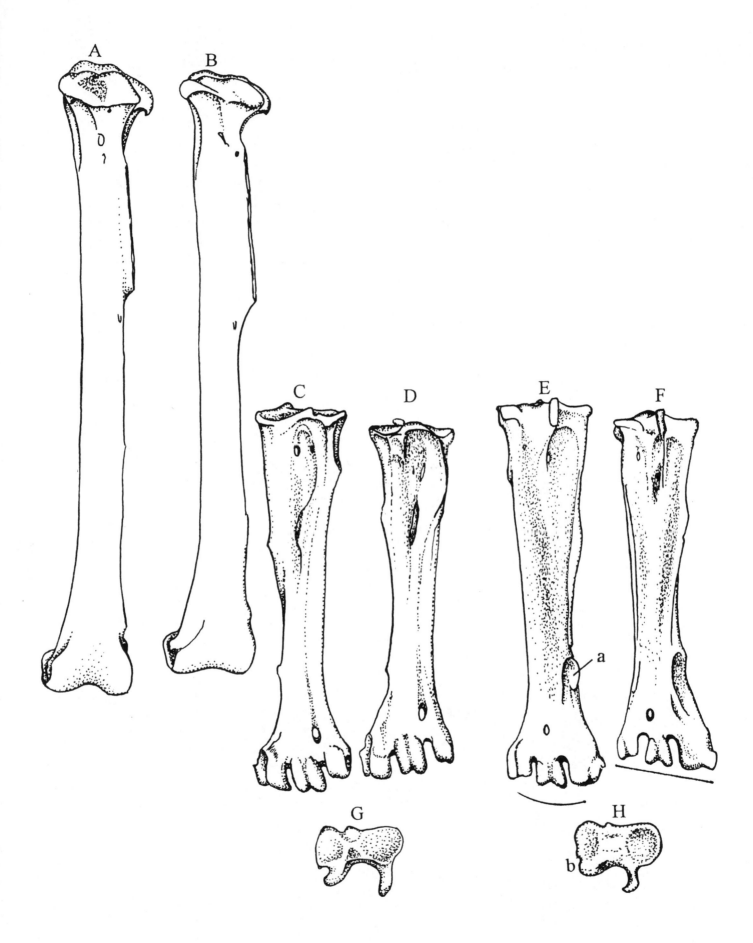

Figure 70. Differences of Pes.
A and B, right pes, bottom to top: metatarsal I and digit I, phalanges 1 and 2; digit II, phalanges 1, 2, and 3; digit III, phalanges 1, 2, 3, and 4; and digit IV, phalanges 1, 2, 3, 4, and 5.
Scale: X 1.
A, NPS 658, *Aquila chrysaëtos,* Golden Eagle, female.
B, Z8.1739, *Haliaeëtus leucocephalus*, Bald Eagle, female.

Metatarsal I is more deeply grooved (a) and more angular in outline in the Bald Eagle. Digit I, phalanx 1 (b) and digit II, phalanx 2 (c) are proportionately longer in the Golden Eagle. In addition, phalanges 1 and 2 of digit II are fused (d) in all Bald Eagles examined. No phalanges were fused in any Golden Eagles examined. Phalanges 1 and 2 (e and f) of digit IV are extremely broad in Bald Eagles. The unguals of the Golden Eagle are less curved than those of the Bald Eagle, and have a projection at the dorsal margin of the articular surface (g).

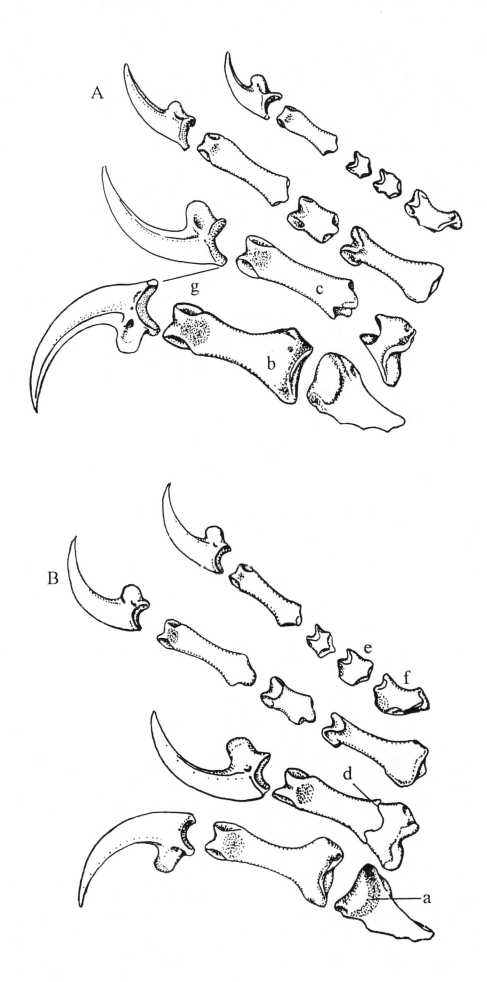

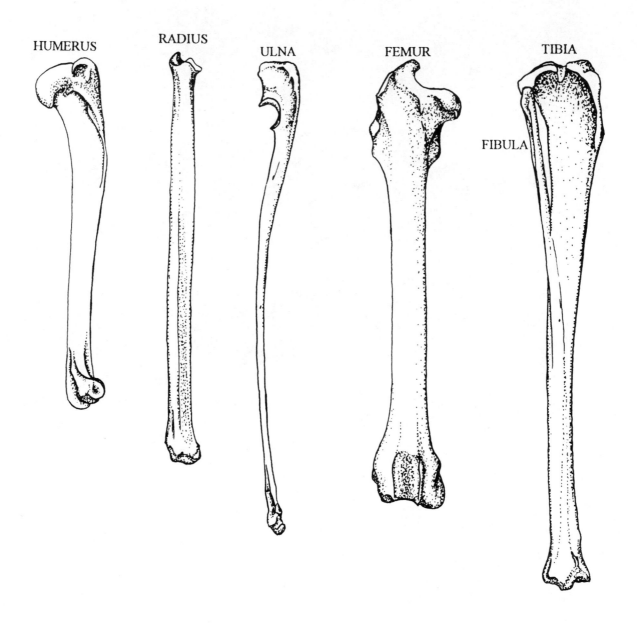

HUMERUS RADIUS ULNA FEMUR TIBIA

FIBULA

Figure 71. Major Skeletal Elements of the Blacktailed Jackrabbit.

Lepus californicus, large, fully adult female from Gila County, Arizona.
 Scale: X 1.

Eagle bones, turkey bones, and the bones of other large birds are commonly confused with those of jackrabbits.

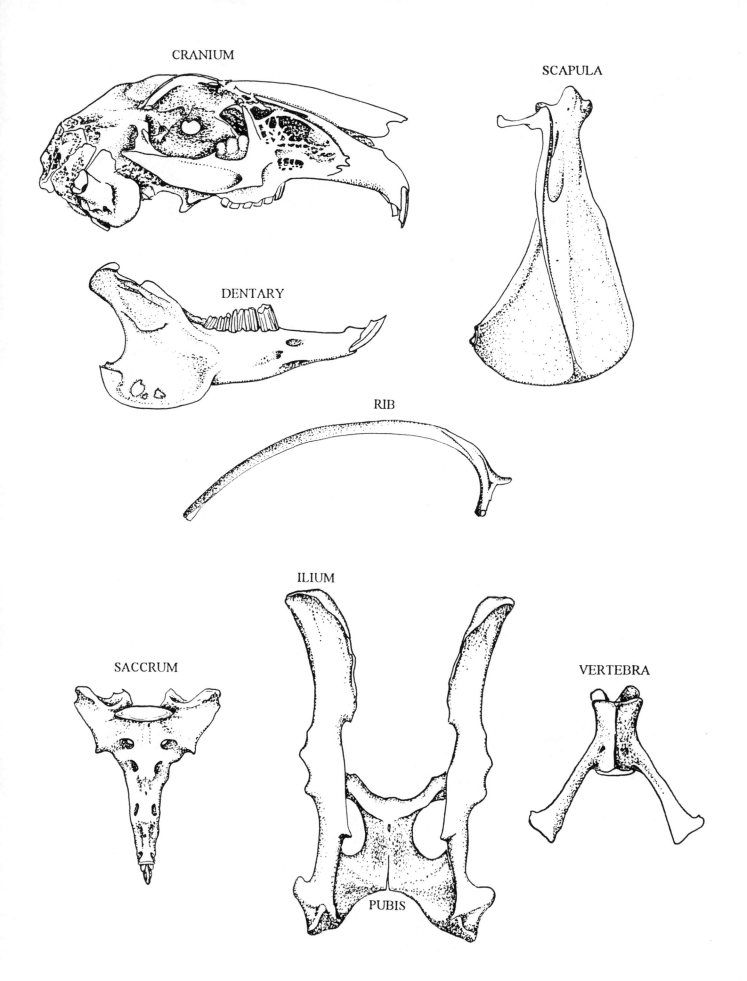

CRANIUM

SCAPULA

DENTARY

RIB

ILIUM

SACCRUM

VERTEBRA

PUBIS

TABLE 10. ARCHAEOLOGICAL OCCURRENCES OF EAGLES

The following table summarizes the archaeological eagle specimens which I have personally examined by type of occurrence and by species. One other specimen deserves consideration. Ann Axtell Morris (1941:200) clearly describes a dessicated eagle burial from Basketmaker III levels at Tseahatso Cave in Canyon del Muerto. The feathered carcass had a string of beads around its neck, and was provided with a deposit of mice and gophers, presumably a food offering. The burial was covered with shreaded cedar bark, and topped with a large, inverted tray basket. Since it was feathered, it certainly was correctly identified as eagle, but species was not given. Presumably, it was a Golden Eagle. Dessicated feathered carcasses of 300 domestic turkeys were recovered from the same cave.

SITE	DATES*	NUMBER OF EAGLES	% OF TOTAL BIRDS
GOLDEN EAGLE BURIALS			
Yellow Jacket Canyon	ca. 600	1	100.00
NA 7523 Sand Dune Cave	ca. 700	1	100.00
AZ W:9:123 Turkey Creek	1225-1286	3	1.23
Cedar Creek	1250-1450	1	100.00
AZ P:16:1 Grasshopper Pueblo	1275-1400	2	0.33
AZ Z:1:11 Tohono O'Odham Reservation	-	1	100.00
Wind Mountain	-	2	-
NAN Ruin	1010-1150	1	-

SITE	DATES*	NUMBER OF EAGLES	% OF TOTAL BIRDS
BALD EAGLE BURIAL			
NA 8042, Houck E	-	1	100.00
GOLDEN EAGLE SKINS			
LA 4470 A Red Willow Site	1100-1200	1	12.50
Mound 7, Gran Quivira	1275-1672	3	0.13
RANDOM GOLDEN EAGLE BONES			
Tse-Ta'a	BM III - P III	1	2.94
NA 8440, Houck K	pre-1100 - ca. 1250	1	11.11
NA 8039, Houck B	-	1	7.14
Hawiku	P IV	1	50.00
Atsinna	1200-1400	2	1.32
Bc 24, Una Vida	P II, early P III	5	6.85
Bc 26, Leyit Kin	800-900; 1040-1125	6	12.50
Bc 50, Tseh So	TR 922+	1	5.88
Bc 51, Chaco Canyon	TR 1043 and 1077	2	6.06
Bc 53, Chaco Canyon	P II, early P III	1	7.14
Bc 362, Chaco Canyon	Late 1000s, early 1100s	3	6.12
Chetro Ketl	945-1116	2	5.88
Kin Kletso	1059-1176	2	5.71

SITE	DATES*	NUMBER OF EAGLES	% OF TOTAL BIRDS
Talus Unit	1040-1082+	1	3.23
Aztec West Ruin	P III	1	3.13
Aztec East Ruin	1200s	1	33.33
Site #1200, Long House	ca. 650; 1200-1278	3	0.02
AZ P:16:1, Grasshopper	1275-1400	4	0.66
AZ W:10:50 Point of Pines	1200-1400	23	2.83
AZ W:9:123 Turkey Creek	1225-1286	11	4.53
Besh-Ba-Gowah	shortly pre-1440	1	**
Geronimo Ruin, AZ	1250-1400	1	100.00
University Indian Ruin	1200-1400 or later	1	2.78
Paquimé	1200-1400+	1	0.11
Cuyamungue	P IV, 1300-1600	1	0.83
Los Aguajes	P IV, 1300-1500	3	1.88
Pottery Mound	P IV	1	0.74
Puaray	1400-1540	2	2.40
Las Humanas, Mound 7	1275-1672	193	8.49
Las Humanas, House A	1540-1672	2	7.70
San Buenaventura de Las Humanas	1540-1672	15	10.56
Pueblo Pardo	1400-1672	7	10.44

SITE	DATES*	NUMBER OF EAGLES	% OF TOTAL BIRDS
Pecos Convento	1620-1680, 1696-1778	3	12.00
Picuris	1150-present	629	29.31
Red Willow Site, NM	1100-1200	5	62.50
Cedro Canyon	-	1	6.67
Bg 20, Rattlesnake Point	1085-1225	1	20.00
LA 183, Pueblo Largo	1300s	11	2.06
Citadel Pueblo	1125-1200	1	50.00

RANDOM BALD EAGLE BONES

NA 8039, Houck B	-	1	7.14
Las Humanas, Mound 7	1275-1672	8	0.35
Picuris	1150 - present	15	0.70

GOLDEN EAGLE BONE ARTIFACTS

SITE	DATES*	NUMBER OF ARTIFACTS	% OF WORKED BIRD BONE
Bc 51, Chaco Canyon	TR 1043 and 1077	9	52.94
Chetro Ketl	945-1116	2	100.00
Kin Kletso	1059-1176	2	8.00
#1200, Long House	650; 1200-1300	2	0.77
#1229, Mug House	1050-1300	7	0.58

SITE	DATES*	NUMBER OF ARTIFACTS	% OF WORKED BIRD BONE
#1452, Badger House	800-1250	1	12.50
#1595, Big Juniper House	900-1150	1	3.33
LA 2690, Ft. Wingate	Kivas 1150-1200	1	100.00
AZ P:14:1, Grasshopper	1275-1400	9	11.39
Paquimé	1200-1400+	9	27.27
Las Humanas, Mound 7	1275-1672	77	36.19
San Buenaventura de Las Humanas	1540-1672	1	25.00
Pecos Convento	1620-1680, 1696-1788	12	100.00
Picuris	1150-present	14	43.75
Bg 52, Largo-Gallina	pre-1300	1	100.00
LA 25, Las Madres	1200s, early 1300s	5	8.20
LA 183, Pueblo Largo	1300s	5	2.06
NA 405, Wupatki	1073-1230	1	100.00

BALD EAGLE BONE ARTIFACTS

Las Humanas, Mound 7	1275-1672	4	1.88

RANDOM GOLDEN EAGLE FEATHERS

SITE	DATES	NUMBER OF EAGLE FEATHERS	% OF TOTAL FEATHERS
NA 7523 Sand Dune Cave	ca. 700	24	-
Chetro Ketl	945-1116	1	16.67
Antelope House	ca. 600-1270	3	0.07
Gila Cliff Dwellings	1275-1300	1	-

RANDOM BALD EAGLE FEATHERS

SITE	DATES	NUMBER OF EAGLE FEATHERS	% OF TOTAL FEATHERS
Antelope House	ca. 600-1270	1	0.02

WORKED GOLDEN EAGLE FEATHERS

SITE	DATES	NUMBER OF EAGLE FEATHERS	% OF TOTAL FEATHERS
Antelope House	ca. 600-1270	1	0.06
Bc 288, Chaco Canyon	P III	1	-

*   Table 10 dates are derived from U. S. National Park Service Avian Files, Southwest Bird Laboratory Avian Files, Bannister (1964), Colton (1946), Griffin (1967:37-53), Green (1956:188-193), Hayden (1957), Hayes (1964), Lincoln (1962), Lindsay, Ambler, Stein, and Hobler (1968), Morris (1986), O'Bryan (1950), Peckham (1963), Rickert (1964), Rhon (1971), Shaffer (1991:8, 164), and Swannack (1969). TR indicates tree-ring dates. All dates are A.D.

**   Analysis of the faunal materials from Besh-Ba-Gowah is ongoing by the author.

REFERENCES CITED

Adams, E. Charles
1991   *The Origin and Development of the Pueblo Katsina Cult.* University of Arizona Press, Tucson.

Anderson, Keith M., Gloria J. Fenner, Don P. Morris, George A. Teague, and Charmion McKusick
1986   *The Archeology of Gila Cliff Dwellings.* Publications in Anthropology 36, Western Archeological and Conservation Center, National Park Service, Tucson.

Arnold, Lee W.
1954   *The Golden Eagle and its Economic Status.* Circular 27, Fish and Wildlife Service, U. S. Department of the Interior, Washington, D.C.

Bailey, Florence Merriam
1928   *Birds of New Mexico.* New Mexico Department of Game and Fish in cooperation with the State Game Protective Association and the Bureau of Biological Survey.

Bancroft, Anne
1987   *Origins of the Sacred.* Arkana Paperbacks, New York.

Bannister, Bryant
1964   *Tree-ring Dating of the Archeological Sites in the Chaco Canyon Region, New Mexico.* Southwestern Monuments Association Technical Series 6, Part 2. Globe, Arizona.

Bent, Arthur Cleveland
1961   *Life Histories of North American Birds of Prey, Part One.* Dover Books, New York.

Berlant, Tony
1983   Mimbres Painting: An Artist's Perspective. In *Mimbres Pottery: Ancient Art of the American Southwest,* by J. J. Brody, Catherine J. Scott, Steven A. LeBlanc, and Tony Berlant, pp. 12-22. Hudson Hills Press, New York.

Bernal, Ignacio (translated by Willis Barnstone)
1975   *Mexico Before Cortez.* Anchor Press/Doubleday, Garden City.

Blake, Emmet Reid
1953   *Birds of Mexico.* University of Chicago Press.

Bradfield, Wesley
1931   *Cameron Creek Village: A Site in the Mimbres Area in Grant County, New Mexico.* Monographs of the School of American Research 1, Santa Fe.

Breitburg, Emanuel
1988   *Prehistoric New World Turkey Domestication: Origins, Developments, and Consequences.* Ph.D. dissertation, Southern Illinois University, Carbondale.

Brody, J. J.
1977   *Mimbres Painted Pottery.* School of American Research, Santa Fe, and University of New Mexico Press, Albuquerque.

Brody, J. J., Catherine J. Scott, Steven A. LeBlanc, and Tony Berlant
1983   *Mimbres Pottery: Ancient Art of the American Southwest.* Hudson Hills Press, New York.

Brundage, Burr Cartwright
1979   *The Fifth Sun, Aztec Gods, Aztec World.* University of Texas Press, Austin.

1982   *The Phoenix of the Western World, Quetzalcoatl and the Sky Religion.* University of Oklahoma Press, Norman.

Bullock, Peter Y.
1991   *Macaws at Casas Grandes and in the American Southwest.* Manuscript on file, Office of Archaeological Studies, Museum of New Mexico, Santa Fe.

Burland, Cottie, and Werner Forman
1975   *Feathered Serpent and Smoking Mirror.* Orbis Publishing, London.

Carter, George F.
1945   *Plant Geography and Culture History in the American Southwest.* Viking Fund Publication in Anthropology 5.

Cochran, Doris M.
1930   Caecilians and Salamanders. In *Cold Blooded Vertebrates* by Samuel F. Hildebrand, Charles W. Gilmore, and Doris M. Cochran, pp. 177-192. Smithsonian Scientific Series, Vol. 8, Smithsonian Institution, Washington, D.C.

Codex Mendoza
1978   Commentaries by Kurt Ross. Productions Liber S. A., Fribourg.

Coe, Michael D.
1975   Native Astronomy in Mesoamerica. In *Archaeoastronomy in Pre-Columbian America*, edited by Anthony F. Aveni, pp. 3-31. University of Texas Press, Austin.

Colton, Harold S.
1946   *The Sinagua: A Summary of the Archaeology of the Region of Flagstaff, Arizona.* Museum of Northern Arizona Bulletin 22. Flagstaff.

Cordell, Linda S.

    1984   *Prehistory of the Southwest.* Academic Press, Inc., San Diego.

    1997   *Archaeology of the Southwest.* Academic Press, Inc., San Diego.

Cosgrove, H. S., and C. B. Cosgrove

    1932   *The Swarts Ruin: A Typical Mimbres Site in Southwestern New Mexico: Report of the Mimbres Valley Expedition Seasons of 1924-1927.* Papers of the Peabody Museum of American Archaeology and Ethnology 15(1). Harvard University, Cambridge.

Creel, Darrell, and Charmion McKusick

    1994   Prehistoric Macaws and Parrots in the Mimbres Area, New Mexico. *American Antiquity* 59(3):510-524.

Crosswhite, Frank S.

    1985   "*Xólotl* and *Quetzalcóatl* in Relation to Monstrosities of *Maguey* (Agave) and *Teocentli* (Zea), with Notes on the Pre-Columbian Religion of Mexico", pp. 114-115, and "Agave and the Pre-Cortés Religion", pp. 50, 115, 116, *Desert Plants* 7(2). University of Arizona at the Boyce Thompson Southwestern Arboretum, Superior, Arizona.

Cunkle, James R.

    1993   *Talking Pots: Prehistoric Pottery Icons of the White Mountains of Arizona.* Golden West Publishers, Phoenix.

Davis, Edward H.

    1920   *The Papago Ceremony of Víkita.* Indian Notes and Monographs 3(4). Museum of the American Indian, Heye Foundation, New York.

de la Haba, Louis

    1976   *Clues to America's Past.* The National Geographic Society, Washington, D.C.

Dean, Jeffrey S.

    1991   Thoughts on Hohokam Chronology. In *Exploring the Hohokam: Prehistoric Desert Peoples of the American Southwest*, edited by George J. Gumerman, pp. 61-149. Amerind Foundation New World Studies Series 1. Amerind Foundation, Dragoon, Arizona, and University of New Mexico Press, Albuquerque.

Dibble, C. E., and A. J. O. Anderson

    1963   *Fray Bernardino de Sahagun: General history of the things of New Spain, Book 11: Earthly Things, Florentine Codex.* Monographs of the School of American Research and the Museum of New Mexico, Santa Fe.

Di Peso, Charles C.

    1972   Casas Grandes and the Gran Chichimeca. *El Palacio* 75(4):45-61.

Di Peso, Charles C., John B. Rinaldo, Gloria J. Fenner
    1974   *Casas Grandes: A Fallen Trading Center of the Gran Chichimeca,* Volumes 2, 3, and 8. Amerind Foundation Series 9, Amerind Foundation, Dragoon, and Northland Press, Flagstaff, Arizona.

Dutton, Bertha P.
    1963   *Sun Father's Way: the Kiva Murals of Kuaua.* The University of New Mexico Press, the School of American Research, and the Museum of New Mexico Press.

Ellis, Florence Hawley
    1975   A Thousand Years of the Pueblo Sun-Moon-Star Calendar. *Archaeoastronomy in Pre-Columbian America,* edited by Anthony F. Aveni, pp. 59-87. University of Texas Press, Austin.

Ellis, Florence Hawley, and Laurens Hammack
    1968   The Inner Sanctum of Feather Cave, a Mogollon Sun and Earth Shrine Linking Mexico and the Southwest. *American Antiquity* 33(1):25-44.

Feher-Elston, Catherine
    1991   *Raven Song, A Natural and Fabulous History of Ravens and Crows.* Northland Press, Flagstaff.

Fenner, Gloria J.
    1986   Feather Artifacts. In *The Archeology of Gila Cliff Dwellings*, by Keith M. Anderson, Gloria J. Fenner, Don P. Morris, George A. Teague, and Charmion McKusick, pp. 235-243. Publications in Anthropology 36, Western Archeological and Conservation Center, National Park Service, Tucson.

Ferg, Alan
    1982   14th Century Kachina Depictions on Ceramics. In *Collected Papers in Honor of John W. Runyan*, edited by Gerald X. Fitzgerald, pp. 13-29. Papers of the Archaeological Society of New Mexico 7.

    1985   Avifauna of the University Indian Ruin. *The Kiva* 50(2-3):111-128.

Fish, Paul R., Peter J. Pilles, Jr., and Suzanne K. Fish
    1980   Colonies, Traders and Traits: The Hohokam in the North. In *Current Issues in Hohokam Prehistory,* edited by David Doyel and Fred Plog, pp. 151-175. Arizona State University, Anthropological Research Papers 23. Tempe.

Ford, Richard I.
    1981   Gardening and Farming Before A.D. 1000: Patterns of Prehistoric Cultivation North of Mexico. *Journal of Ethnobiology* 1(1):6-27.

Foster, Michael S.
  1986   The Mesoamerican Connection: A View from the South. In *Ripples in the Chichimec Sea*, edited by Frances Joan Mathien and Randall H. McGuire, pp. 55-69. Southern Illinois University Press, Carbondale.

Franciscan Fathers, St. Michaels, Arizona
  1929   *An Ethnographic Dictionary of the Navajo Language.* Max Breslauer, Graphische Kunstranslalten, Leipzig.

Gilbert, B. Miles, Larry D. Martin, and Howard G. Savage
  1985   *Avian Osteology.* B. Miles Gilbert, Publisher, Flagstaff.

Gilmore, Frances
  1949   *Flute of the Smoking Mirror.* University of Arizona Press, Tucson.

Gilpin, Laura
  1968   *The Enduring Navajo.* University of Texas Press, Austin.

Green, Roger C.
  1956   A Pit House of the Gallina Phase. *American Antiquity* 22(2):188-193.

Griffin, Bion
  1967   A High Status Burial from Grasshopper Ruin, Arizona. *The Kiva* 33(2):37-53.

Hargrave, Lyndon L.
  1970a   *Mexican Macaws: Comparative Osteology and Survey of Remains From the Southwest.* Anthropological Papers of the University of Arizona 20. University of Arizona Press, Tucson.

  1970b   *Feathers from Sand Dune Cave: A Basketmaker Cave Near Navajo Mountain, Utah.* Museum of Northern Arizona Technical Series 9. Flagstaff.

Hargrave, L. L., and S. D. Emslie
  1979   Osteological Identification of Sandhill Crane Versus Turkey. *American Antiquity* 44(2):295-299.

Harner, Michael
  1982   *The Way of the Shaman.* Bantam Books, New York.

Harvey, E. B., H. E. Kaiser, and L. E. Rosenberg
  1968   *An Atlas of the Domestic Turkey.* United States Atomic Energy Commission, Division of Biology and Medicine. Washington, D.C.

Haury, Emil W.
　　1958　Evidence at Point of Pines for a Prehistoric Migration From Northern Arizona. *Migrations in New World Culture History*, edited by Raymond H. Thompson, pp. 1-6. University of Arizona Bulletin 29(2), Social Science Bulletin 27.

　　1975　*The Stratigraphy and Archaeology of Ventana Cave*. New Edition. University of Arizona Press, Tucson.

　　1976　*The Hohokam: Desert Farmers & Craftsmen. Excavations at Snaketown, 1964-1965*. University of Arizona Press, Tucson.

Hayden, Julian D.
　　1957　*Excavations, 1940, at the University Indian Ruin, Tucson, Arizona*. Southwestern Monuments Association Technical Series 5. Globe, Arizona.

Hayes, Alden C.
　　1964　*The Archeological Survey of Wetherill Mesa*. Archeological Research Series 7A. National Park Service, Washington, D.C.

Hayes, Alden C. (editor)
　　1981　*Contributions to Gran Quivira Archaeology, Gran Quivira National Monument, New Mexico*. Archeological Research Series 17. National Park Service, Washington, D.C.

Hayes, Alden C., Jon Nathan Young, and A. H. Warren
　　1981　*Excavation of Mound 7, Gran Quivira National Monument, New Mexico*. Archeological Research Series 16. National Park Service, Washington, D.C.

Helfritz, Hans
　　1968　*Mexican Cities of the Gods*. Praeger Publishers, Inc., New York.

Herzberg, Max J.
　　1945　*Myths and Their Meanings*. Allyn and Bacon, Boston.

Hester, James J.
　　1962　*Early Navajo Migrations and Acculturation in the Southwest*. Museum of New Mexico Papers in Anthropology 6. Santa Fe.

Hibben, Frank C.
　　1975　*Kiva Art of the Anasazi at Pottery Mound*. KC Publishing, Las Vegas.

Hoebel, E. Adamson, and Thomas Weaver
　　1979　*Anthropology and the Human Experience*. McGraw-Hill Book Company, Fourth Edition, New York.

Holien, Thomas
    1975   Pseudo-Cloisonné in the Southwest. In *Collected Papers in Honor of Florence Hawley Ellis,* edited by Theodore R. Frisbie, pp. 157-177. Papers of the Archaeological Society of New Mexico 2.

Howard, Hildegarde
    1929   The Avifauna of the Emeryville Shellmound. *University of California Publications in Zoology* 32:301-394.

    1947   A Preliminary Survey of Trends in Avian Evolution from Pleistocene to Recent Time. *The Condor* 49(1):10-13.

    1962a   Significance of Carbon-14 Dates for Rancho La Brea. *Science* 131(3402):712-714. March 11.

    1962b   A Comparison of Prehistoric Avian Assemblages from Individual Pits at Rancho La Brea, California. *Contributions in Science* 58:1-24. Natural History Museum of Los Angeles County.

Howard, Richard M.
    1981   An Adobe-lined Pit at Gran Quivira. In *Contributions to Gran Quivira Archaeology, Gran Quivira National Monument, New Mexico*, edited by Alden C. Hayes, pp. 12-14. National Park Service, Archeological Research Series 17. Washington, D.C.

Hultkrantz, Åke (translated by Monica Setterwall)
    1979   *The Religions of the American Indians*. University of California Press, Berkeley.

Hyman, Libbie Henrietta
    1947   *Comparative Vertebrate Anatomy*. University of Chicago Press.

Imler, Ralph H., and Edwin R. Kalmbach
    1955   *The Bald Eagle and its Economic Status*. Circular 30, Fish and Wildlife Service, U.S. Department of the Interior, Washington, D.C.

Johnson, Ann S.
    1971   Finger-Loops and Cruciform Objects. *American Antiquity* 36(2):188-194.

Judd, Neil M.
    1954   *The Material Culture of Pueblo Bonito*. Smithsonian Miscellaneous Collections 124.

Jung, Carl G.
    1968   *Man and His Symbols*. Dell Publishing Co., Inc., New York.

Kelley, J. Charles
1986   The Mobile Merchants of Molino. In *Ripples in the Chichimec Sea,* edited by Frances Joan Mathien and Randall H. McGuire, pp. 81-104. Southern Illinois University Press, Carbondale.

Kennamer, James Earl, Mary Kennamer, and Ron Brenneman
1992   History. In *The Wild Turkey, Biology and Management,* edited by James G. Dickson, pp. 6-17. Southern Forest Experiment Station, A National Wild Turkey Federation and USDA Forest Service Book, Stackpole Books, Harrisburg.

Kenyon, Karl W.
1969   The American Bald Eagle. *ZooNooz,* July, p. 13. Zoological Society of San Diego.

Keys, David
1999   *Catastrophe: An Investigation into the Origins of the Modern World.* Ballantine Books, New York.

Kidder, Alfred Vincent
1932   *The Artifacts of Pecos.* Papers of the Southwestern Expedition No. 6. Published for Phillips Academy by the Yale University Press, New Haven.

King, Dale S.
1949   *Nalakihu: Excavations at a Pueblo III Site on Wupatki National Monument, Arizona.* Museum of Northern Arizona Bulletin 23. Flagstaff.

Krupp, E. C.
1983   *Echoes of the Ancient Skies.* Harper and Row, New York.

Ladd, Edmund J.
1963   *Zuni Ethno-Ornithology.* Master of Science Thesis, University of New Mexico, Albuquerque.

La Fay, Howard
1975   The Maya, Children of Time. *National Geographic* 148(6):728-767. December.

Lang, Richard W., and Arthur H. Harris
1984   *The Faunal Remains from Arroyo Hondo Pueblo, New Mexico: A Study in Short-term Subsistence Change.* Arroyo Hondo Archaeological Series 5, School of American Research Press, Santa Fe.

Lange, Richard C.
1992   Pots, People, Politics, and Precipitation: Just Who or What Are the Salado Anyway? In *Proceedings of the Second Salado Conference, Globe, AZ 1992,* edited by Richard C. Lange and Stephen Germick, pp. 325-333. Arizona Archaeological Society Occasional Paper, Phoenix.

LeBlanc, Steven A.
1999   *Prehistoric Warfare in the American Southwest*. University of Utah Press, Salt Lake City.

Lebo, Cathy J., and Miranda Warburton
1982   Arizona D:7:239. In *Excavations on Black Mesa, 1980: A Descriptive Report*, edited by Peter P. Andrews, Robert Layhe, Deborah Nichols, and Shirley Powell, pp. 71-85. Center for Archaeological Investigations Research Paper 24. Southern Illinois University, Carbondale.

Lekson, Stephen H.
1999   *The Chaco Meridian: Centers of Political Power in the Ancient Southwest*. AltaMira Press, Walnut Creek.

Leopold, A. Starker
1959   *Wildlife of Mexico*. University of California Press, Berkeley.

Leonard, Robert D.
1989   *Anasazi Faunal Exploitation: Prehistoric Subsistence on Northern Black Mesa, Arizona*. Occasional Paper 13. Center for Archaeological Investigations, Southern Illinois University, Carbondale.

Leonard, Robert D., Janet E. Belser, David A. Jessup, and James Carucci
1984   Arizona D:11:3133. In *Excavations on Black Mesa, 1982: A Descriptive Report*, edited by Deborah L. Nichols and F. E. Smiley, pp. 370-394. Center for Archaeological Investigations Research Paper 39. Southern Illinois University, Carbondale.

Ligon, J. S.
1946   *History and Management of Merriam's Wild Turkey*. University of New Mexico Publications in Biology 1, Albuquerque.

Lincoln, Edward P.
1962   Mammalian Fauna From Wupatki Ruin. *Plateau* 34(4):129-134.

Lindsay, Alexander J., Jr., J. Richard Ambler, Mary Anne Stein, and Philip M. Hobler
1968   *Survey and Excavations North and East of Navajo Mountain, Utah, 1959-1962*. Museum of Northern Arizona Bulletin 45, Glen Canyon Series 8, Flagstaff.

Luckert, Karl W.
1975   *The Navajo Hunter Tradition*. University of Arizona Press, Tucson.

Matthews, Caitlin
1987   *Mabon and the Mysteries of Britain*. Arkana, New York.

McGahan, Jerry
    1971   The Condor, Soaring Spirit of the Andes. *National Geographic* 139(5):684-709. May.

McGuire, Randall H.
    1986   Economies and Modes of Production in the Prehistoric Southwestern Periphery. In *Ripples in the Chichimec Sea,* edited by Frances Joan Mathien and Randall H. McGuire, pp. 243-269. Southern Illinois University Press, Carbondale.

McKusick, Charmion R.
    1974   The Casas Grandes Avian Report. In *Casas Grandes, A Fallen Trading Center of the Gran Chichimeca*, Volume 8, by Charles C. Di Peso, John B. Rinaldo, and Gloria J. Fenner, pp. 273-284. Amerind Foundation, Dragoon, Arizona.

    1976   Avifauna. In *The Hohokam: Desert Farmers & Craftsmen. Excavations at Snaketown, 1964-1965*, by Emil W. Haury, pp. 374-377. University of Arizona Press, Tucson.

    1980   Three Groups of Turkeys from Southwestern Archaeological Sites. In *Papers in Avian Paleontology Honoring Hildegarde Howard,* edited by Kenneth E. Campbell, Jr., pp. 225-235. Contributions in Science 330. Natural History Museum of Los Angeles County.

    1981   The Faunal Remains of Las Humanas. In *Contributions to Gran Quivira Archaeology, Gran Quivira National Monument, New Mexico*, edited by Alden C. Hayes, pp. 39-65. National Park Service, Archeological Research Series 17. Washington, D.C.

    1982   Avifauna from Grasshopper Pueblo. In *Multidisciplinary Research at Grasshopper Pueblo, Arizona,* edited by William A. Longacre, Sally J. Holbrook, and Michael W. Graves, pp. 87-96. Anthropological Papers of the University of Arizona 40. University of Arizona Press, Tucson.

    1986a   The Avian Remains. In *Archeological Investigations at Antelope House,* edited by Don P. Morris, pp. 142-158. National Park Service, Archeological Research Series 19. Washington, D.C.

    1986b   Faunal Remains. In *The Archeology of Gila Cliff Dwellings,* by Keith M. Anderson, Gloria J. Fenner, Don P. Morris, George A. Teague, and Charmion McKusick, pp. 245-272. Publications in Anthropology 36, Western Archeological and Conservation Center, National Park Service, Tucson.

    1986c   *Southwest Indian Turkeys: Prehistory and Comparative Osteology.* Southwest Bird Laboratory, Globe, Arizona.

1992 Evidences of Hereditary High Status at Gila Pueblo. In *Proceedings of the Second Salado Conference,* edited by Richard C. Lange and Stephen Germick, pp. 86-91. Arizona Archaeological Society Occasional Paper, Phoenix.

1997 Ancho Canyon Mine Project Turkeys. In *Cultural Definition on the Southern Park Plateau of Northeast New Mexico: The Ancho Canyon Archaeological Project, Volume II,* edited by Jan V. Biella and Wetherbee B. Dorshow, pp. 903-904. Southwest Archaeological Consultants, Santa Fe.

McKusick, Charmion R., and Jon Nathan Young
1997 *The Gila Pueblo Salado.* Salado Chapter, Arizona Archaeological Society, Globe, Arizona.

Miller, Mary, and Karl Taube
1993 *An Illustrated Dictionary of The Gods and Symbols of Ancient Mexico and the Maya.* Thames and Hudson, New York.

Mock, Karen E., Tad C. Theimer, David L Greenberg, and Paul Keim
1999 *Conservation of Genetic Diversity Within and Among Subspecies of Wild Turkey.* Paper submitted to National Wild Life Symposium 2000. On file, Southwest Bird Laboratory, Globe, Arizona.

Morris, Ann Axtell
1941 *Digging in the Southwest.* Doubleday, Doran & Co., Inc., Garden City.

Morris, Don P.
1986 *Archeological Investigations at Antelope House.* National Park Service, Archeological Research Series 19. Washington, D.C.

Nabhan, Gary Paul
1989 *Enduring Seeds.* North Point Press, San Francisco.

Nelson, Richard S.
1986 Pochtecas and Prestige: Mesoamerican Artifacts in Hohokam Sites. In *Ripples in the Chichimec Sea,* edited by Frances Joan Mathien and Randall H. McGuire, pp. 155-182. Southern Illinois Press, Carbondale.

O'Bryan, Deric
1950 *Excavations in Mesa Verde National Park 1947-1948.* Medallion Papers 39, Gila Pueblo Archaeological Foundation, Globe, Arizona.

Olsen, Stanley J.

    1968   *Fish, Amphibian and Reptile Remains from Archaeological Sites, Part I, Southeastern and Southwestern United States. Appendix: The Osteology of the Wild Turkey.* Papers of the Peabody Museum of Archaeology and Ethnology 56(2). Harvard University, Cambridge.

Olsen, Stanley J., and John W. Olsen

    1974   The Macaws of Grasshopper Ruin. *The Kiva* 40(1-2):67-70.

Parsons, Elsie Clews (editor)

    1936   *Hopi Journal of Alexander M. Stephen.* Columbia University Contributions to Anthropology, Vol. 23. New York.

Peckham, Stewart (assembler)

    1963   *Highway Salvage Archaeology Volume 4.* The New Mexico State Highway Department and the Museum of New Mexico, Santa Fe.

Pilles, Peter J., and Edward B. Danson

    1974   The Prehistoric Pottery of Arizona. *Arizona Highways* 50(2):2-5, 10-32. February.

Prideaux, Tom, and the Editors of Time-Life

    1973   *Cro-Magnon Man.* Time-Life Books, New York.

Purce, Jill

    1974   *The Mystic Spiral, Journey of the Soul.* Thames and Hudson, New York.

Pyle, Peter, Steven N. G. Howell, Robert P. Yunick, and David F. De Sosta

    1987   *Identification Guide to North American Passerines.* Slate Creek Press, Bolinas, California.

Rea, Amadeo M.

    1980   Late Pleistocene and Holocene Turkeys in the Southwest. In *Papers in Avian Paleontology Honoring Hildegarde Howard,* edited by Kenneth E. Campbell, Jr., pp. 209-224. Contributions in Science 330. Natural History Museum of Los Angeles County.

    1983   *Once a River: Bird Life and Habitat Changes on the Middle Gila.* University of Arizona Press, Tucson.

Reid, Jefferson, and Stephanie Whittlesey

    1997   *The Archaeology of Ancient Arizona.* University of Arizona Press, Tucson.

    1999   *Grasshopper Pueblo: A Story of Archaeology and Ancient Life.* University of Arizona Press, Tucson.

Reyman, Jonathan E.

1971 *Mexican Influence on Southwestern Ceremonialism.* Ph.D. dissertation, Southern Illinois University, Carbondale. University Microfilms, Ann Arbor.

1990 The Macaw Feather Project. In *Cultural Survival Quarterly* 14(4):77-79.

1995 Value in Mesoamerican-Southwestern Trade. In *The Gran Chichimeca: Essays on the Archaeology and Ethnohistory of Northern Mesoamerica,* edited by Jonathan E. Reyman, pp. 271-280. Avebury, Brookfield, Vermont.

1996 4,000,000 Gifts for the Gods, The Feather Distribution Project. *The Living Museum* 58(2-3):32-35. Illinois State Museum.

Richert, Roland

1964 *Excavation of a Portion of the East Ruin, Aztec Ruins National Monument, New Mexico.* Southwestern Monuments Association Technical Series 4. Globe, Arizona.

Rohn, Arthur H.

1971 *Mug House, Mesa Verde National Park, Colorado.* National Park Service, Archeological Research Series 7D. Washington, D.C.

Russell, Frank

1908 *The Pima Indians.* Twenty-Sixth Annual Report of the Bureau of American Ethnology, 1904-1905. Smithsonian Institution, Washington, D.C.

Schaafsma, Polly

1999 Tlalocs, Kachinas, Sacred Bundles, and Related Symbolism in the Southwest and Mesoamerica. In *The Casas Grandes World,* edited by Curtis F. Schaafsma and Carroll L. Riley, pp. 164-192. University of Utah Press, Salt Lake City.

Schorger, A. W.

1961 An Ancient Pueblo Turkey. *The Auk* 78(2):138-144.

1966 *The Wild Turkey: Its History and Domestication.* University of Oklahoma Press, Norman.

1970 A New Subspecies of Meleagris gallopavo. *The Auk* 87(1):168-170.

Schroeder, Albert H.

1968 Birds and Feathers in Documents Relating to Indians of the Southwest. In *Collected Papers in Honor of Lyndon Lane Hargrave,* edited by Albert H. Schroeder, pp. 95-114. Papers of the Archaeological Society of New Mexico 1.

1977 *Of Men and Volcanos: The Sinagua of Northern Arizona.* Southwest Parks and Monuments Association, Globe, Arizona.

Shafer, Harry J.
1990   Life Among the Mimbres: Excavating the NAN Ruin. *Archaeology* 43(6):48-51. November-December.

Shaffer, Brian
1991   *The Economic Importance of Vertebrate Faunal Remains from the NAN Ruin (LA15049), A Classic Mimbres Site, Grant County, New Mexico.* Master of Arts Thesis, Texas A & M University, College Station.

Shaw, Harley G.
1995   *Merriam Turkey Prehistory - A Biologist's Perspective.* Paper submitted to the Robert Euler Festschrift, 2000. On file at Southwest Bird Laboratory, Globe, Arizona.

Shufelt, R. W.
1883   Osteology of the North American Tetraonidae. *Twelfth Annual Report of the Geological and Geographical Survey of the Territories: A Report of the Progress of the Exploration in Wyoming and Idaho for the Year 1878, in Two Parts, Part 1*, pp. 653-718. Government Printing Office, Washington, D.C.

Smith, Watson
1952   *Kiva Mural Decorations at Awatovi and Kawaika-a, With a Survey of Other Wall Paintings in the Pueblo Southwest.* Papers of the Peabody Museum of American Archaeology and Ethnology 37. Harvard University, Cambridge.

Smith, Watson, Richard B. Woodbury, and Nathalie F.S. Woodbury
1966   *The Excavation of Hawikuh by Frederick Webb Hodge; Report of the Hendricks-Hodge Expedition, 1917-1923.* Contributions From the Museum of the American Indian, Heye Foundation 20. Museum of the American Indian, Heye Foundation, New York.

Snodgrass, O. T.
1975   *Realistic Art and Times of the Mimbres Indians.* Privately Printed, El Paso.

Sorensen, Ella D., and Charles E. Dibble
1993   An Aztec Bestiary. *Audubon* 95(1):50-54. January-February.

Spofford, Walter R.
1969   Problems of the Golden Eagle in North America. In *Peregrine Falcon Populations, Their Biology and Decline,* edited by Joseph J. Hickey, pp. 345-347. University of Wisconsin Press, Madison.

Storer, Robert W.
1966   Sexual Dimorphism and Food Habits in Three North American Accipiters. *The Auk* 83(3):423-436.

Storer, Tracy I.
  1943   *General Zoology*. McGraw-Hill Book Company, Inc., New York.

Stuart, Gene S.
  1988   *America's Ancient Cities*. National Geographic Society, Washington, D.C.

Stuart, George E.
  1989   Copán, City of Kings and Commoners. *National Geographic* 176(4):488-505.
          October.

Swannack, Jervis D., Jr.
  1969   *Big Juniper House, Mesa Verde National Park, Colorado*. Archeological Research
          Series 7C. National Park Service, Washington.

Time-Life Books
  1992a   *Aztecs: Reign of Blood and Splendor*. Time-Life Books, Alexandria.

  1992b   *Mound Builders and Cliff Dwellers*. Time-Life Books, Alexandria.

Torbrügge, Walter (translated by Norbert Guterman)
  1968   *Prehistoric European Art*. Harry N. Abrams, New York.

Turner, Christy G. II, and Jacqueline A. Turner
  1999   *Man Corn: Cannibalism and Violence in the Prehistoric American Southwest*.
          University of Utah Press, Salt Lake City.

van Renterghem, Tony
  1995   *When Santa Was a Shaman*. Llewellyn Publications, St. Paul.

Van Tyne, Josselyn, and Andrew J. Berger
  1959   *Fundamentals of Ornithology*. Chapman & Hall, New York.

Vaillant, George C.
  1950   *Aztecs of Mexico*. Doubleday and Company, Garden City.

Warren, Bruce W., and Thomas Stuart Ferguson
  1987   *The Messiah in Ancient America*. Book of Mormon Research Foundation, Provo.

Wasley, William W.
  1960   A Hohokam Platform Mound at the Gatlin Site, Gila Bend, Arizona. *American
          Antiquity* 26(2):244-262.

  1962   A Ceremonial Cave on Bonita Creek, Arizona. *American Antiquity* 27(3):380-394.

Wernet, Susan J.
    1982   *North American Wildlife.* The Reader's Digest Association, Inc., Pleasantville.

White, Tim D.
    1992   *Prehistoric Cannibalism at Mancos 5MTUMR-2346.* Princeton University Press, Princeton.

Whitecotton, Stephen R., and Cathy J. Lebo
    1980   Arizona D:7:236. In *Excavation on Black Mesa, 1979: A Descriptive Report,* edited by Shirley Powell, Robert Layhe, and Anthony L. Klesert, pp. 129-168. Center for Archaeological Investigations Research Paper 18. Southern Illinois University, Carbondale.

Whittlesey, Stephanie M.
    1995   Mogollon, Hohokam, and O'Otam: Rethinking the Early Formative Period in Southern Arizona. *Kiva* 60(4):465-480.

Willey, Gordon R.
    1966   *An Introduction to American Archaeology. Volume One: North and Middle America.* Prentice-Hall, Inc., Englewood Cliffs, New Jersey.

Zim, Herbert S. (editor)
    1961   *Birds of the World.* Golden Press, New York.

ARIZONA ARCHAEOLOGICAL SOCIETY PUBLICATIONS

THE ARIZONA ARCHAEOLOGIST

$ 5   1.   *COMMENTS ON "SALVAGE ARCHAEOLOGY IN THE PAINTED ROCKS RESERVOIR, WESTERN ARIZONA"* by Albert H. Schroeder. *THE IMPORTANCE OF ARCHAEOLOGICAL FIELD RECORDS* by Robert G. Chenhall. *A SITE ON THE VERDE* by E.M. Valehrach. *SOME ARCHAEOLOGICAL DISCOVERIES* by Sam and Edith Turner. 1967.

$ 5   2.   *THE SILO SITE: 1967* by Robert G. Chenhall. 1967.

$ 5   3.   *MINERALS AND ROCKS AT ARCHAEOLOGICAL SITES: SOME INTERPRETATIONS FROM CENTRAL WESTERN NEW MEXICO* by Alfred E. Dittert, Jr. *FOURTEEN PREHISTORIC SITES IN NANKOWEAP CANYON, GRAND CANYON NATIONAL PARK* by Roger E. Kelly. 1968.

$ 5   4.   *THE CASA GRANDE CALENDAR HOLES: FACT OR FABLE?* by Roy W. Reaves, III. *PIMA BASKETRY* by Clark Field. *A GLANCE AT THE HISTORY AND ARCHAEOLOGY OF THE LOWER VERDE RIVER* by Brett Hagenstad. 1969.

$ 5   5.   *A SITE SURVEY ALONG THE LOWER AGUA FRIA RIVER, ARIZONA* by Donald E. Dove. *OBSIDIAN DEBITAGE FROM ELDEN PUEBLO, NORTH CENTRAL ARIZONA: A TRIAL STUDY* by Roger E. Kelly. *PREHISTORIC WARFARE IN THE PRESCOTT AREA* by Robert G. Page, Jr. 1970.

$ 5   6.   *EXCAVATIONS AT BRAZALETES PUEBLO* by Emil M. Valehrach and Bruce S. Valehrach. 1971.

o.p.   7.   *EXCAVATIONS AT VALSHNI VILLAGE, ARIZONA* by Arnold M. Withers (edited by Walter Thomas Duering). 1973.

o.p.   8.   *PREHISTORIC LAND USE IN THE PERKINSVILLE VALLEY* by Paul R. Fish. *PREHISTORIC RUINS AND IRRIGATION IN THE EASTERN BUCKEYE VALLEY* by Frank Midvale. 1974.

o.p.   9.   *INVESTIGATIONS CONCERNING THE HOHOKAM CLASSIC PERIOD IN THE LOWER SALT RIVER VALLEY, ARIZONA* by Donald E. Weaver, Jr. 1977.

o.p.   10.   *PROCEDURAL MANUAL FOR ARCHAEOLOGICAL FIELD RESEARCH PROJECTS OF THE MUSEUM OF NEW MEXICO* by Alfred E. Dittert, Jr. and Fred Wendorf. 1977. (Reprint of Museum of New Mexico Papers in Anthropology Number 12, 1963.)

o.p.   11.   *ARCHAEOLOGICAL AND PALEOENVIRONMENTAL INVESTIGATIONS IN THE CAVE BUTTES AREA NORTH OF PHOENIX, ARIZONA* by Landon Douglas Smith. 1977.

o.p.   12.   *WHITE GOAT HOUSE: A PREHISTORIC ANASAZI COMMUNITY IN NORTHEASTERN ARIZONA* by Dee Travis Hudson. 1980.

o.p.   13.   *ST. MICHAELS PUEBLO: PUEBLO III SUBSISTENCE AND ADAPTATION IN BLACK CREEK VALLEY, ARIZONA* by Michael John Andrews. 1980.

o.p.   14.   *HOHOKAM SOCIAL ORGANIZATION: A RECONSTRUCTION* by Martin Edward McAllister. 1980.

$ 18   15.   *SOUTHWESTERN CERAMICS: A COMPARATIVE REVIEW* edited by Albert H. Schroeder. 1982. {photocopy}

$ 6   16.   *ALICIA: THE HISTORY OF A PIMAN HOMESTEAD* edited by Glen Rice, Steadman Upham and Linda Nicholas. 1983. (Arizona State University Anthropological Field Studies Number 4.)

$ 6   17.   *SINAGUA SOCIAL DIFFERENTIATION: INFERENCES BASED ON PREHISTORIC MORTUARY PRACTICES* by John W. Hohmann. 1983.

$ 6   18.   *THE STORM SITE, NA13407, EXCAVATION OF TWO SMALL PRESCOTT CULTURE RUINS* by Joanne and Earl Cline. 1983.

$ 6   19.   *GRAY MOUNTAIN, A PREHISTORIC CHERT SOURCE SITE IN COCONINO COUNTY, ARIZONA* by Donald R. Keller. 1984.

$ 15   20.   *EARTH FIGURES OF THE LOWER COLORADO AND GILA RIVER DESERTS: A FUNCTIONAL ANALYSIS* by Boma Johnson. 1986. {photocopy}

$ 15   21.   *CHECKLIST OF POTTERY TYPES FOR THE TONTO NATIONAL FOREST: AN INTRODUCTION TO THE ARCHAEOLOGICAL CERAMICS OF CENTRAL ARIZONA* by J. Scott Wood. 1987. {photocopy}

$ 8   22.   *HISTORICAL ARCHAEOLOGY AT JOSEPH CITY, ARIZONA* by Alan Ferg, William H. Liesenbein, Peter J. Pilles, Jr. and Pamela Haas. 1988.

o.p.   23.   *WALNUT CANYON SETTLEMENT AND LAND USE* by J. Michael Bremer. 1989.

$ 15   24.   *ARCHAEOLOGICAL INVESTIGATIONS AT LA CIUDAD DE LOS HORNOS: LASSEN SUBSTATION PARCEL* compiled by Richard W. Effland, Jr. 1990.

$ 15   25.   *KATSINA ICONOGRAPHY IN HOMOL'OVI ROCK ART, CENTRAL LITTLE COLORADO RIVER VALLEY, ARIZONA* by Sally J. Cole. 1992.

$ 12   26.   *RED CAVE - A PREHISTORIC CAVE SHRINE IN SOUTHEASTERN ARIZONA* by Alan Ferg and Jim I. Mead. 1993.

$ 15   27.   *MIDDLE LITTLE COLORADO RIVER ARCHAEOLOGY: FROM THE PARKS TO THE PEOPLE* edited by Anne Trinkle Jones and Martyn D. Tagg. 1994.

$ 15 28. *PREHISTORY OF PERRY MESA: THE SHORT-LIVED SETTLEMENT OF A MESA-CANYON COMPLEX IN CENTRAL ARIZONA, CA. A.D. 1200-1450* by Richard V.N. Ahlstrom and Heidi Roberts. 1995.

$ 12 29. *APACHEANS BEARING GIFTS: PREHISPANIC INFLUENCE ON THE PUEBLO INDIANS* by Stuart J. Baldwin. 1997.

$ 20 30. *THE SUNDOWN SITE, NA 16385, A PRESCOTT AREA COMMUNITY* by the Yavapai Chapter, AAS. 1999.

$ 15 31. *SOUTHWEST BIRDS OF SACRIFICE* by Charmion R. McKusick. 2001.

OCCASIONAL PAPERS

$ 5   *EXPLORATION AND EXCAVATIONS AT SITIO con DIOS RANCH RUINS (SITE:AZ:ScD:1), A PHASE OF THE HOHOKAM INDIANS OF THE UPPER CAVE CREEK BASIN, ARIZONA* by Marjorie T. Van Dyke. 1981. Occasional Paper No. 1 of the Desert Foothills Chapter.

o.p. *NEW RIVER: A LITHIC INDUSTRY IN MARICOPA COUNTY, ARIZONA* by Donald V. Peru. 1984. Occasional Paper No. 1 of the Phoenix Chapter.

o.p. *PROCEEDINGS OF THE 1983 HOHOKAM SYMPOSIUM* edited by Alfred E. Dittert, Jr. and Donald E. Dove (2 volumes). 1985. Occasional Paper No. 2 of the Phoenix Chapter.

o.p. *CASA DE PIEDRAS SITE REPORT: ARCHAEOLOGICAL INVESTIGATIONS IN THE AGUA FRIA RIVER VALLEY OF ARIZONA* by Rueben H. Nelson. 1993. Occasional Paper No. 3 of the Phoenix Chapter.

o.p. *PROCEEDINGS OF THE SECOND SALADO CONFERENCE, GLOBE AZ 1992* edited by Richard C. Lange and Stephen Germick. 1992.

Distributed for the SOUTHWEST BIRD LABORATORY

$ 10 *SOUTHWEST INDIAN TURKEYS: PREHISTORY AND COMPARATIVE OSTEOLOGY* by Charmion R. McKusick. 1986.

ORDER FROM: Alan Ferg, Editor
Arizona Archaeologist
Arizona State Museum
University of Arizona
Tucson   AZ   85721-0026

Add $ 3.00 for postage and handling. No postage charge for orders of $50.00 or more.

ferg@email.arizona.edu

ARIZONA ARCHAEOLOGICAL SOCIETY

INSTRUCTIONS TO AUTHORS

The Arizona Archaeologist is published on an annual basis by the Arizona Archaeological Society. The Society welcomes unsolicited, original papers relating to the prehistoric and historic archaeology, ethnology, history, and ethnohistory of the southwestern United States and northwestern Mexico.

CORRESPONDENCE: Correspondence should be addressed to: Alan Ferg, Editor, The Arizona Archaeologist, Arizona State Museum, University of Arizona, Tucson, Arizona 85721.

MANUSCRIPTS: Manuscripts for review must be typed, single-spaced, on 8½ by 11 inch paper in *American Antiquity* format. Submit two copies, complete with mocked-up photocopies of all illustrations. Content of the manuscript should be indicated by appropriate headings and subheadings. An Abstract no longer than half a page should be included. The References should include only those cited in the manuscript.

FIGURES, AND TABLES: *The Arizona Archaeologist* printed page is 8½ by 11 inches with 1-inch margins. Authors should size all photographs, line art, tables and charts to these dimensions. Drawings should be in black ink. All figures and tables must be cited in the text, be numbered consecutively, and have descriptive titles. Do NOT submit original illustrations until the manuscript has been accepted for publication.

PAGE LENGTH: Manuscripts should not exceed 130 single-spaced pages in length. This means 65 sheets of paper printed on both sides. This includes all photographs, line art, tables, charts, and references. Font size for the text will be 12 point; font size for headings, subheadings, tables and captions may vary.

REVIEW PROCESS: All manuscripts submitted are reviewed by the Manuscript Review Committee of AAS, with the option of additional outside peer review by scholars familiar with the specific subject matter of the manuscript. The Editor will then return the manuscript to the author either (1) accepting it for publication as is, (2) tentatively accepting it for publication if the author makes recommended revisions, or (3) declining the manuscript.

If a manuscript is accepted, the author is responsible for preparing a camera-ready version for printing. After acceptance of a manuscript, specifics of headings, style, font, preparation of a Spanish translation of the Abstract, etc., will be coordinated with the Editor. Each author will receive 2 copies of the published report, and may purchase additional copies at a reduced price. The manuscript will be published and distributed by the Arizona Archaeological Society. Published manuscripts become the copyright of the Arizona Archaeological Society.